W\

IVY LEAGUE ATHLETES

SAL MAIORANA

Foreword by Ryan Fitzpatrick

IVY LEAGUE

ATHLETES

PROFILES IN EXCELLENCE

AT AMERICA'S MOST

COMPETITIVE SCHOOLS

Northeastern University Press | Boston

Northeastern University Press
An imprint of
University Press of New England
www.upne.com
© 2014 Sal Maiorana
All rights reserved
Manufactured in the United States of
America
Designed by Mindy Basinger Hill
Typeset in Minion Pro

University Press of New England is
a member of the Green Press Initiative.
The paper used in this book meets
their minimum requirement for
recycled paper.

For permission to reproduce any
of the material in this book, contact
Permissions, University Press of
New England, One Court Street,
Suite 250, Lebanon NH 03766; or
visit www.upne.com

Library of Congress Cataloging-in-
Publication Data

Maiorana, Sal, 1962–
Ivy League athletes : profiles in excellence
at America's most competitive schools /
Sal Maiorana.
       pages   cm
ISBN 978–1–55553–790–6 (cloth : alk. pa-
per) — ISBN 978–1–55553–840–8 (ebook)
1. College athletes—United States—Biog-
raphy. 2. Ivy League (Athletic conference)
I. Title.
GV697.A1M272 2014
796.0922—dc23
[B]   2013040924

5   4   3   2   1

Basketball court, pages ii – iii and 107:
Ulrich Mueller | Dreamstime.com

Soccer field, page 1:
pinkbadger / 123RF Stock Photo

TO IVY LEAGUE STUDENT-ATHLETES PAST AND PRESENT.
We may not see you very often on ESPN, but you embody the true
definition of what student-athletes should be: noble in the often-corrupt
world of college sports.

CONTENTS

FOREWORD

Legendary Harvard football coach Joe Restic stood before me and said, "Ryan, your time begins now." This was one of the biggest days of my football career. It was the day of the East-West Shrine game, an all-star showcase that would allow me to measure my abilities against Division 1-A players from across the country. This was the day I would prove to the NFL scouts that an Ivy League quarterback was worthy of a draft pick.

The week of the East-West Shrine game consisted of practices that were being viewed by NFL scouts. Every drop-back, every throw, and every decision I made that week had been scrutinized and would play a large role in determining my future in football. The big knock on a small school guy such as me was the level of competition I played against. Teams were concerned that having success against lower-level competition wouldn't translate when making the jump to the NFL. Throwing alongside guys like Kyle Orton and Derek Anderson provided an excellent platform for me to prove that I belonged.

Unlike the powerhouse college sports conferences, the Ivy League isn't seen as a steppingstone to the world of professional sports. A large majority of the athletes don't have the opportunity to continue playing at the next level. I came to view this as a positive. There are no scholarships being held over the heads of the athletes, forcing them to play. The games aren't nationally televised each week or, in most cases, at all. And in Ivy League football, there are no bowl games or playoffs to compete in at year's end. As a result, a certain purity exists because each athlete is competing out of a love and passion for his or her sport. This creates the common bond all athletes in the Ivy League share: an unbridled commitment to the sport they love, knowing that the end is near.

When I made the decision to attend Harvard, I did it for the challenge. It offered me an opportunity to live and learn with some of the brightest people in the country and also to continue to play a game I was passionate about. The recruiting pitch didn't revolve around the state-of-the-art athletic facilities or the athletic dorms or the preferential treatment you would receive being an athlete at the university. The recruiting pitch was the challenge. It was the fact that you were expected to graduate in four years just like the other students. It was the fact that, like all collegiate athletes, you would spend twenty hours each week at the football facilities, but the classroom always came first. And it was the fact that, with all the exogenous pressure that came with being a student at Harvard, you were still expected to perform on the football field. To me, that expectation provided a challenge that was too good to pass up.

During the week leading up to the East-West Shrine game, the difference in being an Ivy League athlete was never more apparent. A majority of the players were already done with school. While some had already graduated, most had left school early to focus all their efforts on making it to the NFL. When practice concluded and we put the pads away for the day, most players rested for the next day or buried themselves in the abbreviated playbook we had to learn for the upcoming game. For me, things were different.

When Coach Restic said, "Ryan, your time begins now," he wasn't encouraging me to perform well and take the next step in advancing my career as a football player, he was administering a final exam. I had the single most important game of my life on the same day I had a final exam for Econ 1813 — The Indebted Society. In the Ivy League, student always comes before athlete, and that meant I had to take the exam the same day it was being administered to my peers across the country in Cambridge. As a result, immediately following the game I was bused to my hotel and holed up in a conference room for three hours while I completed my economics test — a test I had been studying for throughout the week after practices, a test that sums up what it means to be an Ivy League student athlete.

My four years at Harvard gave me tremendous perspective and appreciation for what I do for a living now. I played with so many talented people that didn't get the opportunity to continue playing at the next level and I gain motivation each and every day thinking about the love and passion my former Crimson teammates showed in their commitment to football. As I catch up with some of them who are now bankers and entrepreneurs, real estate moguls and army commanders, I am humbled to still be playing a game that we all loved together. In my current role as the starting quarterback for the Buffalo Bills, I feel a responsibility to carry on the standards of dedication, passion, and commitment that all Ivy League athletes possess.

Ryan Fitzpatrick, Harvard '05

PROLOGUE

On a brisk but bright late-spring morning in June of 1852, James Whiton glanced out the window of his train making its way north toward the White Mountains of New Hampshire on the Boston, Concord & Montreal line and saw to the East a serene stretch of water that lay below the hillside track.

In the language of Chief Wonaton, Winnipesaukee means "beautiful water in a high place" and make no mistake, as Whiton and so many men before and after him realized, the state's largest lake was aptly named by the great Indian leader, who was captivated by its beauty as he presided there over the wedding of his daughter to a rival tribe leader in the mid-1500s.

So as Whiton gazed out at the scenic landscape, an idea came to the third-year student at Yale who was the son of James Whiton Sr., director of the BC&M Railroad. He turned to the man sitting next to him, James Elkins, who was the BC&M conductor as well as the local agent for the road, and proclaimed that it would be a perfect spot for a regatta.

Seeking respite from the study of physics and the tedious works of Plato, Whiton had become a rowing enthusiast and was by now the bow oarsman for the Yale Boat Club's newly built eight-oared barge named *Undine*. He regaled Elkins with stories of how crew had become such a popular endeavor at both Yale and Harvard, but when Whiton mentioned how he could see potential in bringing spectators up to Lake Winnipesaukee via the BC&M to watch a race between the two schools, that's when Elkins's ears really perked up.

Fascinated by Whiton's thought of excursion trains, which would create much-needed publicity and business for the railroad, Elkins told Whiton, "If you will get up a regatta on the lake between Yale and Harvard, I will pay all the bills." Whiton said he would be happy to bring the proposition back to his boat mates for approval, and would then issue the challenge to Harvard to come to Lake Winnipesaukee "to test the superiority of the oarsmen of the two colleges."

There was immediate enthusiasm from the men of Yale, who were anxious to take on their rival Harvard scholars in athletic competition, but also giddily cognizant that this could be an all-expenses paid summer road trip before the start of the next term.

Harvard seemed less interested, as the Crimson had only one suitable boat, the *Oneida*. Finally, after weeks of deliberation, and consultation with a member of the Eli crew who went to Cambridge to further pitch the merit of the match race, Harvard accepted.

And so it was that one man's love of rowing and another man's quest to build capital for a newly chartered railroad that was sagging behind already-established regional lines, led the crews of Harvard and Yale to Center Harbor, New Hampshire, to partake in an event that became etched in our country's sporting history. For on the afternoon of August 3, 1852, with the hillsides filled with hundreds of curious spectators who had been transported there by the BC&M Railroad — including New Hampshire native General Franklin Pierce, who three months later would be elected the fourteenth president of the United States — Harvard and Yale, to borrow a phrase from today's vernacular, got after it. And thus, the concept of intercollegiate athletics was born.

The Crimson entered their only boat, the *Oneida*, captained by Joseph M. Brown, who had been a classmate of Whiton's at Boston Latin School. Yale dropped two shells into the water, the *Undine*, captained by Julius Catlin, and *Shawmut*, captained by Robert Waite. Yet despite this imbalance in competition, the *Oneida* outpaced *Shawmut* by two lengths and *Undine* by six, covering the two-mile course in approximately ten minutes, or fourteen, depending on which account you read.

Three years would pass before Yale issued another challenge to Harvard, and again failed to back up its bravado, losing to the Crimson in a race contested on the Connecticut River. It would be another several years before the regatta became an annual event, but those original competitions began to spawn awareness that athletics could be a meaningful — not to mention healthy — part of a student's collegiate experience.

If nothing else, it sure beat the alternative.

Prior to the Harvard-Yale regatta, college presidents and deans did not believe organized sport had any place on their campuses. To their way of thinking, if students needed to release some pent-up physical energy, manual labor was a perfectly good outlet. After all, there was always some farming to do on undeveloped nineteenth-century university property, and it seemed there was always a pile of rocks that needed moving.

In an article he penned for the summer 1970 issue of *American Quarterly* magazine entitled "The Beginning of Organized Collegiate Sport," writer Guy Lewis described American college life in the early to mid-nineteenth century as, "dull, Spartan, well-regulated and academically rigorous. Austere faculty members, often former clergymen, exercised complete control over every aspect of the lives of their charges."

Eventually, students grew tired of this regimented lifestyle, and they formed associations that conducted intramural contests sometimes referred to as class rushes. The games were often violent, and injuries were common. Naturally, university leaders disapproved of this behavior and punished the participating students, though that only exacerbated a vicious circle because the students in turn took out their frustrations on their professors. Lewis wrote that, "riot and disorder were frequent, and each school year was marked by cases of personal assault upon members of the faculty." In some extreme cases, buildings were damaged by dynamite or set ablaze in protest of the steadfast administrative belief that academic institutions were solely for intellectual development and moral improvement.

Ultimately, the students won, and once athletics became an integral component of campus life, most of their aggression was channeled into winning competitions against rival schools.

The first recognized college baseball game was played in 1859, Williams against Amherst, and by 1870 many schools were playing regular schedules, leading to the formation of the first college baseball league in 1879. On a pleasant afternoon in early November 1869, in New Brunswick, New Jersey, Princeton (then called College of New Jersey) and Rutgers took to the field to play a game that would ultimately be called football. In 1873 students from Cornell, Williams, and McGill University of Montreal ran a two-mile foot race against each other, constituting the first track and field event. And in 1874 at Harvard's Cambridge campus, the Crimson squared off with McGill in the first intercollegiate rugby match.

That day on the banks of Lake Winnipesaukee, hundreds of spectators cheered on the crews from Harvard and Yale. Today, hundreds of millions of spectators attend collegiate sporting events every year, so it would appear that a New York City newspaper's prediction following the inaugural regatta in 1852 that intercollegiate sports would "make little stir in a busy world" was ill-conceived.

What is interesting about that published premise is that while college sports have actually become an overwhelming presence in an exponentially busier world, and athletic programs are typically the most recognizable aspect of America's universities, it is not that way in the Ivy League.

Just as in 1852, sports in the Ivy League are today what they were then — merely one aspect of the collegiate experience, an enjoyable and rewarding diversion from the rigors of class work. However, while we rarely see athletes from Harvard, Yale, Princeton, Cornell, Columbia, Dartmouth, Penn, and Brown night after night on the highlight shows, or gracing the cover of *Sports Illustrated*, it does not mean that their pursuit of athletic success means any less to them than it does to the kids who are doing their thing at the well-known sports factories from conferences such as the Big 10, the Big East, the ACC, the SEC, the Big 12 and the Pac-12.

"We are recruiting the kind of athletes who are coming to school to get an education that will prepare them for the rest of their lives," said Cornell athletic director Andy Noel. "And while they're in school and really invested in their academics, they also want to achieve athletically at the highest levels. These are first-class men and women who have athletic goals, but really understand that the four or five years that you're in college you're preparing for maybe the next fifty years. It's a very serious enterprise and we have quite a lot of teams and quite a lot of young men and women who are excelling."

For example, the nine students you are going to meet in the pages of *Ivy League Athletes*, who will share their triumphs and defeats, their laughter and their tears, and their personal stories of achievement.

As the 2011–12 school calendar began:

MELANIE BASKIND was heading into her senior year at Harvard on a premed track which would likely result in her enrollment in medical school a year, maybe two, after graduation. Melanie sheepishly admitted that in coming from a stable, happy, middle-class family from Framingham, Massachusetts, she had never really had to deal with any type of notable adversity. But this was not a silver-spoon-fed kid coasting through life. She was a fiery competitor and natural-born leader who wouldn't have any problem filling her days if they were thirty-six hours instead of twenty-four. Not only was she a member of two varsity collegiate teams, soccer in the fall and lacrosse in the spring, she was the captain of both teams, and she was doing so at Harvard. Some might call her an overachiever, but more accurately, she was an achiever.

ONA MCCONNELL was a junior at Yale and a would-be goaltender for the field hockey team who hoped to one day work in the medical research field and find a cure for the disease that afflicts her. An American who was born and raised in England and Germany, she had never lived in the United States until she came to Yale in 2009. After riding the bench her freshman year because there were two experienced goalies on the roster in front of her, Ona was excited about what her sophomore season would bring. And then, fate intervened. She began to experience unusual physical difficulties, and ultimately she was diagnosed with myotonic dystrophy, the most common form of adult muscular dystrophy. With the disease weakening her muscles by the day, Ona would never get the opportunity to be the goaltender for Yale, yet she remained with the team and provided a beacon of inspiration for her teammates. As a way to fight her condition, this driven twenty-year-old was granted a position on the board of the Myotonic Dystrophy Foundation, and with the help of her coach and teammates she played an integral role in fund-raising efforts that she hoped would play a role in someday finding a cure.

LUCKY MKOSANA of Zimbabwe was beginning his senior year at Dartmouth, still shaking his head in disbelief over the circumstances that had transported him from the dilapidated and dusty soccer fields of his economically challenged native land to the hills of New Hampshire. After high school he was aimlessly seeking a career in professional soccer when he was discovered by Jeff Cook, the head coach at Dartmouth. Cook had gone to Zimbabwe in 2007, inspired by the charitable work being performed there by an organization founded by Dartmouth graduate and former Big Green soccer star Tommy Clark. Grassroot Soccer was using soccer to help educate children about the horrors of AIDS and the HIV virus, which had decimated the country. Cook went to the African continent to see for himself what was going on in Zimbabwe and to offer his coaching expertise at clinics, but also to identify potential recruits for Dartmouth. After watching Lucky play, and then learning that he had a chance to qualify academically in the Ivy League,

xvii

PROLOGUE

Cook arranged for Lucky's life-changing trip to the United States, where he had become one of the greatest players in Big Green history.

ALEX THOMAS was a senior at Yale who would be one of the leaders of a football team that expected to contend for the outright Ivy League championship, a feat the Bulldogs had not achieved since 1980. Alex came to Yale on the heels of an astounding high school career during which he set all-time Connecticut rushing records playing for Ansonia High, just twenty minutes from Yale's New Haven campus. There were scholarship offers to play football elsewhere, but he decided to go to Yale because he felt academics were just as important as athletics. He quickly learned that his high school success on the field and in the classroom didn't mean much at Yale. He struggled mightily as a freshman, both as a student and a player, and there was doubt whether he'd be able to continue attending. But he persevered, was on track to graduate, and would be a vital member of the Bulldog team that not only hoped to win the Ivy championship, but would be seeking its first victory since 2006 against arch-rival Harvard in The Game, the annual season-ending contest that stands as one of the oldest and most historic rivalries in collegiate sports.

SHEILA DIXON was going into her junior year at Brown and would be one of the key players for the women's basketball team. Sheila was born to a drug-abusing mother who abandoned her at a hospital in Schenectady, New York, after giving birth. After spending the first couple weeks of her life without a mother, Sheila was taken in and eventually adopted by a woman who already had fourteen children, eleven of whom she had adopted (one of which was actually Sheila's biological brother). Phyllis Dixon didn't have much material wealth, but she had a heart filled with love, and from the time Sheila was very young she recognized that her adoptive mother had likely saved her from a life of bouncing from orphanage to orphanage, something not all of her step brothers and sisters understood. From that start, Sheila crafted a wonderful life story as she went on to excel both academically and athletically in high school, earning her way into the Ivy League.

KEITH WRIGHT would be entering his senior year at Harvard with the weight of expectations squarely placed on his broad shoulders. The center for the Crimson men's basketball team, named Ivy League player of the year in

2010–11, Keith was about to embark on what was expected to be an unforgettable year. The Crimson returned their entire roster from the squad that came within a gut-wrenching buzzer-beating loss to rival Princeton of advancing to the NCAA tournament for the first time since 1946. With Keith — who grew up in a one-parent home and didn't start playing basketball until the tenth grade — leading the way, the Crimson would have a chance to be a national story in 2011–12 as they pursued the first outright Ivy League championship in school history under coach Tommy Amaker, the most recognizable athletic department personality at Harvard. An All-America candidate who would likely generate interest from NBA scouts, Keith would be in the eye of the storm all season, and he cherished the challenge of leading the Crimson into uncharted territory.

ANDY ILES was the sophomore goaltender for the Cornell men's hockey team, and he was a kid with a different type of pressure. He was born and raised in Ithaca, New York, which also happens to be the address on Cornell's letterhead. He grew up a stones' throw from the campus, and while he had scholarship offers to play at other Division I schools, he chose to stay home and play for the team he grew up following, even though that meant his family would have to pay for a part of his cost of attendance. Already a local hero after having led Ithaca High School to a New York State championship when he was just a freshman, Andy continued his primary education in prep school in Connecticut before returning to Ithaca to don the Big Red jersey. Oh, and he'd also worn another prominent jersey as a freshman, the letters USA blazoned across the front. Andy was the backup goaltender for the United States team that competed in the World Junior Championship tournament that was held in Buffalo in 2011, and he would be in the running to play again for his country in the 2012 tournament in Calgary.

GREG ZEBRACK was about to start his second and final year at the University of Pennsylvania after having transferred to the East Coast to play outfield for the Quakers baseball team in the fall of 2010. It was an unusual move, to be sure, as he was born and raised in the baseball breeding ground of Los Angeles and began his collegiate career on scholarship at the University of Southern California, one of the storied programs in college baseball. Greg had been drafted out of high school by his hometown Los Angeles

Dodgers in 2008, but playing for USC had long been a goal, so he put a hold on his professional aspirations to wear the Trojan uniform. However, Greg endured a disappointing freshman season, and seeing that his situation wasn't going to change as a sophomore, he decided he needed to leave the only school he truly wanted to play for. After a non-playing semester at Santa Monica Junior College and then a mandatory period of inactivity at Penn due to NCAA transfer rules, Greg tore up the Ivy League in the spring of 2011, and was hoping that his final season would not only propel Penn to a championship, but also impress scouts going into the 2012 Major League Baseball First-Year Draft.

KYRA CALDWELL was beginning her senior year at Columbia, hoping that the injuries that had slowed her down for much of her junior track season were healed, thus allowing her the opportunity to lower her personal best times in her primary events, the indoor sixty-meter hurdles, the outdoor four-hundred-meter hurdles, and the indoor and outdoor four-by-four-hundred-meter relay. Born and raised in Ypsilanti, Michigan, Kyra's parents divorced when she was very young because her father was a drug-abuser, but Kyra decided that nothing was going to prevent her from reaching for the sky to achieve her dreams. School was her number one priority, and nothing short of attending a top-notch university was going to be acceptable. Through hard work on the track and in the classroom, Kyra was deemed Ivy League worthy by Columbia, and after some early trial and error picking her major, she settled on medicine, and would be spending the year finishing off her degree and getting prepared for the medical school application process.

Through these nine men and women, who come from different backgrounds and have varied interests and pursuits, the goal is to provide a behind-the-scenes look at the life of student-athletes in the Ivy League, the one athletic conference in America that can boast without hesitation that while sports are a vital part of each of the eight schools' culture, they are just one aspect of a holistic college education and experience.

INTRODUCTION

In the October 1953 issue of the *Rotarian*, legendary Kansas University basketball coach Phog Allen and his fellow Rotarian, University of California football coach Lynn Waldorf, debated whether the NCAA should hire a czar to police intercollegiate athletics.

Waldorf didn't think the idea had merit, but Allen argued in favor, writing, "I don't like the word 'czar' but I'll settle for it if the term means a high commissioner with ability and power and authority to clean up college athletics — even to fire the janitor if he thinks it's necessary! We have tried everything else and the mess is getting worse."

Allen went on to explain that what college athletics needed was someone like iron-fisted Major League Baseball commissioner Judge Kenesaw Mountain Landis, "equipped with a big stick, willing and ready to crack down on all those who spoil sports."

Clearly, he was a man ahead of his time, not only with his basketball strategies, which to this point had produced three national championships, but in how he could — more than sixty years ago — detect the erosion of morality and sportsmanship creeping into the college sporting society. Further, how the rise of commercialism and the lure of the almighty dollar were already starting to skew the lines of amateurism and tear at the fabric of what was supposed to be the purest form of athletic competition.

Allen proposed, in fact, that whoever was tasked with such an overwhelming albeit noble responsibility should earn a whopping salary of $75,000 per year, maybe even $100,000, a preposterous amount of money at that time. Though, as Allen said, he would be "worth every penny of it" because he would have jurisdiction over every school, every conference, and be allowed to "fire any athletic director, any coach, or any employee of a member school's athletic department who gets his nose dirty."

Can you imagine if Allen's idea ever took hold, and the NCAA did indeed create an all-powerful czar whose sole job was to keep athletic programs above reproach? A salary of several million dollars per year might not be commensurate with the duties that person would be asked to perform in this maddening, upside-down twenty-first century.

If Allen were still alive, what would be his reaction to what has happened to college sports, a multibillion-dollar industry that has run amok, a rudderless ship adrift in a sea of seemingly endless scandal? Since that day on Lake Winnipesaukee more than a century and a half ago when Harvard and Yale rowed those two miles, it seems as if the list of infractions and improprieties committed by this country's collegiate athletic programs stretches for about two miles. Single-spaced. Individual compliance officers at most schools can barely keep their heads above the roiling cesspool. For one person to rule over every institution would be a sheer impossibility.

"It's certainly out of control," said Andy Noel, who has been athletic director at Cornell since 1999, after serving the same school as wrestling coach for fifteen years. "I don't think anybody who is immersed in intercollegiate athletics today would debate that it's not out of control. It's gotten to a place that's really, I don't think, very healthy."

At the time of Allen's call for a sports czar, the firestorm created by the infamous college basketball point-shaving scandal uncovered in 1951 was still smoldering. The 1919 Black Sox scandal, where members of the Chicago White Sox were found guilty of fixing the World Series against the Cincinnati Reds, had reigned for decades as the undisputed champion of sports corruption. But when fresh-faced amateurs, who were supposed to be going to school to get an education and competing in athletics for the fun and love of the games, were coerced by members of the New York City mafia to alter point spreads, it rocked not only college basketball, but a nation of stunned and previously naive sports-loving fans who couldn't believe such a thing could happen.

At the heart of the opprobrium were members of the defending national champion City College of New York team, though they were hardly alone, as thirty-three players from a bevy of teams — including two prominent players from Kentucky's 1949 national champion squad — were ultimately found to be involved in the fixing of more than eighty games. Embarrassed officials at CCNY voted to deemphasize athletics in the wake of the tumult and dropped down to Division III, while Kentucky had its 1952–53 season cancelled.

Back then, this was a huge story, and clearly was one of the factors in Allen's impassioned plea to clean up the college landscape. Today, sadly, no one who follows sports would even bat an eye if that story led the eleven o'clock *SportsCenter*, so inured are we to such shameful behavior by our nation's collegiate athletic programs.

How did we get here?

"That's a great question," said Dr. Jason Lanter, an assistant professor of psychology at Kutztown University and president of the Drake Group, an advocacy organization whose stated mission is to help university faculty and staff defend academic integrity in the face of the burgeoning college sports industry.

Lanter believes that cheating among NCAA schools is "rampant" and he pointed to 2011 as a prime example:

- That was a year when Auburn won the Bowl Championship Series football title amid allegations that it gave money to former players in the program who came forward in interviews conducted for a piece on HBO's *Real Sports*. And, in a separate allegation, it came to light that the school may have paid for the services of quarterback Cam Newton, who led the Tigers to a 14–0 record, won the Heisman Trophy, and went on to be the number one overall pick in the 2011 NFL Draft.

- That was a year when Connecticut captured the men's basketball championship after the NCAA had ruled that coach Jim Calhoun committed violations in the recruitment of a player named Nate Miles, who ultimately never played for the Huskies. Calhoun was also reprimanded for having failed to create an "atmosphere of compliance" within his program. He was slapped with a three-game suspension during the 2011–12 season, and then retired at the end of that year, thus stepping aside before the team was deemed ineligible for the 2013 NCAA tournament because of its substandard graduation rates.

- That was a year when Jim Tressel, head coach of football powerhouse Ohio State, lied about knowing that five of his players — including star quarterback Terelle Pryor — had sold Buckeye memorabilia that had been given to them by a Columbus-area tattoo parlor owner. Tressel was suspended for the first five games of the 2011 season, and later resigned from what he had often called his "dream job."

- That was a year when the University of Miami's football program was brought to the brink of extinction when longtime booster Nevin Shapiro, imprisoned for his role in a $930 million Ponzi scheme, documented to Yahoo! Sports how he had been providing illegal benefits to Hurricane football and basketball players for nearly a decade. It was a stunning list of transgressions that included cash payouts, hosting athletes at his mansion or on his yacht, and providing prostitutes.

- And of course, that was a year when an American icon, Penn State football coach Joe Paterno, took a remarkable, shocking, and prodigious free fall from grace. His longtime defensive coordinator, Jerry Sandusky, was arrested and charged with fifty-one counts of sexually abusing boys during a fifteen-year period — most of which allegedly occurred on the premises of the football facility — and was later found guilty at trial in June 2012 on forty-five of the counts. Several Penn State officials, including Paterno, athletic director Tim Curley, and senior vice president Gary Schultz, allegedly had varying extents of knowledge of what was happening and did not act, in what would appear an attempt to cover up the scandal, but also to protect the viability of the almighty football program. Paterno was fired days after the news broke, and sadly, he died barely two months later of lung cancer.

"I hesitate to point fingers at everybody, but if it's happening at major programs, and with teams that are winning national championships," Lanter said, "then wouldn't the other teams that are eager and hungry to get there try and take whatever means is necessary to get there?"

What was disturbing about the nature of the incidents in 2011 is that none of it — perhaps with the exception of the Penn State horror story — was really all that unusual. Going back through the years, you could fill a computer hard drive with the instances of schools found guilty in the illegal recruitment of players, most prominently in the prime revenue-generating sports of football and basketball. And you could fill another hard drive with the violations that go undiscovered.

The list of violations is astoundingly broad-based, and Miami's Shapiro is only one of hundreds, perhaps thousands, of people with illicit intentions. For years college athletes have quietly been given merchandise ranging from iPods to automobiles; given monetary payouts anywhere from tens of thousands of dollars to $50 handshakes in the quad; or benefited when their parents were provided free housing or unwarranted employment. And guilt is just as widespread on the part of college coaches, athletic department officials, school administrators (sometimes reaching as high as the president's office), overzealous alumni associations and booster clubs, high school coaches, mentors, sports agents, and yes, the parents and even the kids.

"If you look at it right now, it's a major arms race in terms of intercollegiate athletics, with the emphasis dramatically and probably not surprisingly, on winning," said Lanter, making the point that universities will do almost anything to procure the services of some athletes. "There seems to be a correlation between violations and that win-at-all cost mentality."

Carolyn Campbell-McGovern has worked in the Ivy League athletic office, housed on the campus of Princeton University, since 1993, originally as the senior associate director and, since 2009, as the deputy executive director. She also serves as the chairman of the NCAA's Legislative Council, and in her involvement at the national governance level she has become all too familiar with the issues that have burdened the NCAA.

She says the train started veering off the track when athletic departments, succumbing to the pressure of winning at all costs in the revenue-generating sports, and sparing no cost in that pursuit, "got more into the entertainment business than in the education business." She thinks that when schools are paying football or basketball coaches millions of dollars a year to deliver victories and hopefully championships, but perhaps even more important, churning out enough money to fund the rest of the athletic department budget, that's the type of pressure that leads to cheating.

"The financial incentives to be able to get one of those jobs is pretty well-established," said Campbell-McGovern, who starred in lacrosse as an undergrad at Bates College in the mid-1980s, and later spent some time as an assistant lacrosse coach at Temple before ascending to the athletic administrative level. "If you get one of those jobs, you have essentially hit the lottery. However, people know they are going to be fired if they don't win, so the things that they have to do, and the decisions they have to make every day, are done with that in mind. Sometimes when push comes to shove, the entertainment part prevails over just trying to recruit players for the team."

To be fair, the root of the corruption begins before the kids are even thinking about what college they would like to play basketball or football or some other sport for. Countless high schools push academically challenged star athletes through their curriculum for the dual purpose of keeping them eligible to play for their own teams, and to ultimately help them gain entrance to college.

Showing leniency in grading to pad a report card is pretty easy; falsifying scores on standardized tests such as the SAT and ACT presents more difficulty, but it can be done, and has been. Case in point, Derrick Rose, now an all-star for the Chicago Bulls and the NBA's MVP in 2011. Rose accepted a scholarship to attend Memphis starting in the fall of 2007, and as a freshman he helped lead the Tigers to a school-record thirty-eight victories and a runner-up finish in the 2008 NCAA basketball tournament. However, it was later discovered that the university had knowledge that Rose's SAT score was likely invalid because he'd had someone take the test for him. The school did not report the incident and allowed Rose to play the year when he should have been ruled ineligible. The NCAA vacated all thirty-eight of Memphis's victories, placed the school on probation, and required it to pay back $615,000 in tournament revenue it earned by advancing to the championship game.

According to the College Board, which owns the SAT, cheating schemes like this occur every year, though it certainly isn't limited to athletes. The Educational Testing Service, which administers the SAT for the College Board, said there are a few thousand questionable scores each year out of more than two million tests that are taken.

Sometimes even this chicanery at the high school level isn't enough, so university athletic departments work with admissions officers and, if necessary, provosts and/or presidents, to lower the standards to get academically deficient athletes admitted.

A study in 2009 conducted by the Associated Press, using admissions data submitted to the NCAA by most of the one hundred twenty schools that play Division I football, showed that athletes typically enjoyed a prodigious advantage over the regular student body when it came to the softening of admissions standards. At twenty-seven schools, the study showed that athletes were at least ten times more likely to benefit from special admission programs than students in the general population. One example cited, though there are so many more to point to, was the University of Texas. During a period from 2003 to 2005, the average SAT score for incoming freshmen football players was 945 — about 320 points lower than the average for other first-year students at the school.

Once an institution can celebrate a recruiting victory and the coveted athletes are on campus, the next obstacle to clear is making sure they maintain their eligibility. One common practice is for counselors to advise athletes to take the easiest courses in the least-demanding majors to give them at least a chance of achieving the minimum grade point average needed to continue playing.

"This is something we call academic clustering," said Lanter. "There are teams where you see many of the players majoring in the same subject. Maybe it's sociology, and that's fine, it's a great major. And so is criminal justice. But are they truly interested in those majors, or have they been directed to them? Is it an academically rigorous program, or is it something that's easy to get through? There's a lot of Division I athletes who are majoring in eligibility in their first year or two. They make sure they take courses that will keep them eligible in future years."

If this approach doesn't work, there have certainly been some interesting schemes perpetuated to keep athletes in uniform.

- The University of Minnesota took a novel approach when a school academic advisor was found to have written more than four hundred term papers for basketball players over a period of five years in the 1990s, and was paid for that service by coach Clem Haskins. This episode cost the school four years of probation and five scholarships over a period of three years.
- In 2003, corruption infiltrated tiny St. Bonaventure, a cozy, pristine campus nestled in the Allegheny Mountains of southern New York. School president Robert Wickenheiser, at the urging of basketball coach Jan van Breda Kolff and athletic director Gothard Lane, admitted a junior college transfer named Jamil Terrell even though they knew he was not academically eligible. Terrell had never earned the associates' degree from Coastal Georgia Community College that St. Bona indicated in the admission process, only a vocational welding certificate. When the violation came to light in March of 2003, Terrell was immediately ruled ineligible, and the Atlantic-10 banned the Bonnies from participation in

the conference tournament. As a form of protest, the remaining players voted to boycott — and therefore forfeit — the final two regular-season games. The administrators were vilified, the players were called quitters, and the university was swathed in shame. Wickenheiser, van Breda Kolff, and Lane were all fired, and it took nearly ten years for the basketball program to recover before it finally earned an NCAA tournament berth in 2012.

- And while it was much smaller in scope than the Minnesota and St. Bonaventure fiascos, it's hard to forget the academic impropriety at the University of Georgia in the early 2000s. There, assistant basketball coach Jim Harrick Jr., the son of head coach Jim Harrick, taught a class in the principles and strategies of basketball, and granted credit hours to several players, even though none of the players ever attended the class. Of course, one wonders why they didn't just show up and "earn" the credits because one of the multiple-choice questions on Harrick Jr.'s final exam was, "How many points is a three-point field goal worth?" and another asked, "Who is the best Division I assistant coach in the country?" with one of the answers being Jim Harrick Jr.

A basketball coach teaching an obviously bogus course is one thing, but tenured professors or other faculty members bowing to the pressure heaped upon them by athletic departments and boosters to assist in the quest to win is what really boils the blood of Lanter and his colleagues at the Drake Group.

"I think what has happened is that the focus on academics has been pushed aside, and I think, with all due respect, the faculty have allowed this to happen," said Lanter. "They haven't stood up to say these students who are participating in athletics need to be in their classes. So there's complicity on some level."

What frustrates Lanter and other champions of academia is that this coddling does wonders for these kids during their time in the protective cocoon of the athletic department, but once the gym lights are turned off and they come to realize that their athletic talent is not expansive enough to ensure a career in the big-money world of professional sports, they are ill-prepared to go out into the real world with the knowledge and skills needed to succeed.

In addressing the media during a press conference in Houston prior to the 2011 Final Four, NCAA president Mark Emmert went to predictable lengths to espouse his theory that college athletics aren't as academically fraudulent as had been perceived, pointing to the increases that had been made in graduation rates and grade point averages among athletes.

"I've heard concerns expressed by people all around the country about the integrity of intercollegiate athletics right now, that people are seeing things that they don't like and that I don't like and that many people are concerned about," said Emmert. "As they see those things, they extrapolate across a whole enterprise of intercollegiate athletics. On the face of that, that's inherently unfair because the vast majority of what goes on inside intercollegiate athletics is done by people who have extraordinary integrity, who have extraordinary concern for their student-athletes, and by people who want nothing more than to have intercollegiate athletics be successful in all the ways we all want it to be.

"We have long ago established some of the core values of what collegiate athletics stand for and what they really mean. This is an enterprise that is fully embedded in the experience of higher education, that it's a part of our universities and colleges. It's not just an ancillary activity that goes on on the side, but it's something that's fully part of it. And that the role of the integrity of these games and the role of fair play and providing as high a level of competitive equity as we possibly can, really, really makes a difference. That is all worth preserving and working hard at."

The Ivy League has been preserving those tenets and working hard at it for nearly sixty years, building what it believes is an unbreakable model where student-athletes are students first and athletes second. If only the other athletic conferences would stand up and take notice, perhaps the world of the NCAA wouldn't be littered with the refuse of scandal from sea to shining sea.

In his closing argument in that 1953 magazine piece about hiring a sports czar, Allen suggested the NCAA, "return to the original purposes of college athletics . . . the development of healthy bodies and the promotion of the ideal of sportsmanship. Properly conducted, athletics should at least build up in the boy the moral fiber which makes him able and willing to say 'no' to the temptation to take money improperly, either as a subsidy or to throw a game. Let's give sports back to the players."

In the Ivy League, the sports have always belonged to the players. Not to the coaches, not to the administrators, and not to the boosters and alumni. The sports belong to the kids who play them.

It has been that way since the Ivy League officially organized and began play as an athletic conference in 1956, and it remains that way because for the Ancient Eight, sports are viewed as nothing more than extracurricular activities in the context of a full and rich collegiate experience.

No one is paying a street agent under the table to steer a particular athlete to a particular school; no one is providing a free house for a recruit's parents to live in; no one is having a test taken or a term paper written for them. In other words, no one is cheating, because, as Andy Noel, Cornell's AD, asks, what's the point?

"I just think the culture in the Ivy League is such that nobody believes that's an appropriate way to go," Noel said. "It goes back to the philosophy of, 'If you have to cheat to win, you're not winning.' If you have to buy athletes, do you really want those athletes representing your program and your university?"

It's all relatively simple in the Ivy League: If you have the grades to gain admission to one of the eight institutions, and your parents can afford to pay whatever is determined to be the family's portion of the cost of attendance (with or without need-based financial aid, of which plenty is available due to the large endowments at each school), you can call yourself an Ivy Leaguer. Just know that whatever talent you bring to the university — whether it's basketball, football, fencing, polo, playing the tuba, singing, solving physics problems, or creating business plans — you are not going to receive preferential treatment. Not in the admissions process, nor during your time at any of the schools.

"The athletes are representative of the students in the student body," said McGovern-Campbell. "And it's a student-athlete model that's very successful for us. Part of it is because of the long history and tradition where the institutions themselves are so established and respected, their names are much more valuable and the university is so much more valuable than the individual athletics programs. So athletics are treated just like any other department, the same as they treat the English department or the Chemistry department."

When the Council of Ivy Group Presidents sat down to outline the Ivy Presidents Agreement, defining the standards by which the Ivy League would operate as an athletic conference, they decided on a set of simple but non-negotiable tenets:

Each Ivy school would admit all candidates, including athletes, on the basis of their achievements and potential as students and on their other personal accomplishments; they would provide financial aid to all students only on the basis of need, as determined by each institution; and, they decreed that no student be required to engage in athletic competition as a condition of receiving financial aid.

Originally crafted in November 1945 to govern football only, the Agreement was extended to cover all sports in 1954 for the purpose of creating the Ivy League, which began round-robin scheduling among the eight universities in 1956. The key paragraph in the document reads as follows:

> The Group affirm their conviction that under proper conditions intercollegiate competition in organized athletics offers desirable development and recreation for players and a healthy focus of collegiate loyalty. These conditions require that the players shall be truly representative of the student body and not composed of a group of specially recruited athletes. They further require that undue strain upon players and coaches be eliminated and that they be permitted to enjoy the game as participants in a form of recreational competition rather than as professional performers in public spectacles. In the total life of the campus, emphasis upon intercollegiate competition must be kept in harmony with the essential educational purposes of the institution.

Through the years, the Group's membership has changed, but the spirit of the Agreement has never been altered, and that's what sets the Ivy League apart, and why it has avoided the type of corruption and scandal that has blighted other athletic conferences. And here's the thing: The Ivy League — so named by *New York Tribune* sports writer Stanley Woodward in an article he wrote about the eight schools leading into the 1933 football season — does not think it has the market cornered on morality, nor does it project a holier-than-thou attitude just because it has kept its nose clean for the better part of six decades. Players, coaches and administrators just understand that rules are rules, and they're not changing, so they deal with it.

"I don't think there's a pride factor in it, it's just a recognition that this is the way to do it," said Noel. "I don't think anybody feels like they're special; it's just obvious to us that this is the way that educators should be implementing their programs. I know this is an exaggeration, but you don't take pride in not robbing a bank, you just know you shouldn't do it. The administrators in our league know there's a right way to carry out their responsibility and that's what they do."

Noel made reference to the fact that like everything else in life, the Ivy League isn't perfect, and McGovern-Campbell concurred that there are numerous violations that come across her desk as director of the League's compliance program. However, she said, "In our world, 99 percent of the things I see are definitely honest mistakes. The rules are really complex so everyone breaks them because they're not that easy to follow, but it's almost always a situation that is easily fixable and not a major violation."

Since 1953 when the NCAA began keeping track of transgressions — right around the time of Phog Allen's published call for the cleansing of collegiate athletics — the Ivy League has been deemed to have committed a "major" infraction four times. Yale basketball in 1969, Cornell ice hockey and men's basketball in 1974, and Princeton women's tennis in 2008. The NCAA imposed two years probation on Yale because some of its players participated in unauthorized, outside, organized basketball competition during the summer of 1969; both Cornell teams were given one year of probation for recruiting improprieties and unethical conduct by members of the coaching staff; and Princeton was forced to vacate all of the matches won by a student-athlete who had $33,000 of her educational expenses paid by an alumnus who was merely trying to help because the girls' family was unwilling to cover her costs above and beyond what she received in financial aid, and did not think he was violating any rules.

Four incidents. None of which could even be considered in the same breath as the aforementioned transgressions at other Division I schools. Four incidents.

Why? McGovern-Campbell has a simple theory.

"Our institutions are lucky to be in a situation where they can afford to fund athletic programs through tuition fees and their well-established endowments," she said. "They do have to raise money from donors, but not by being in the entertainment business. The donors are also the type who are alumni or connected to the program in a way that they value what we do and they value the student-athlete model, the model where the athletes are representative of the students in the student body. That's part of the reason why the financial incentive is different in our places."

Many Division I universities, McGovern-Campbell said, "are required to raise revenues on their own. When you put money into the mix that means there's always going to be people who are willing to take more chances and more risks and live on the edge of the rules in order to get that competitive advantage and be able to make more money. Generally, our institutions look far less than other Division I institutions into raising revenues in order to enhance their athletic programs. That's not how our schools are operating. Our schools see the mission of the university as being enhanced by having an athletics program that is for student-athletes, that supports their educational development. Other places are not in the same position."

FALL

MELANIE BASKIND

HARVARD WOMEN'S SOCCER

The one thing Melanie wasn't going to do was cry, because, geez, how lame would that be? "Yeah, well, I opened my mouth and I started bawling," Melanie recalled, laughing at the memory of those tears pouring out of her brown eyes and running down her cherubic cheeks.

Rarely has she failed as resoundingly as she did that night just before Christmas break in 2008 when Lizzy Nichols, who would be selected captain of the Harvard women's soccer team for the 2009 season, came to visit her first-year teammate in her dorm room for a heart-to-heart discussion that turned into a commercial for Puffs.

It was a beautifully warm, sunny, cloudless August 2011 day on the periphery of Boston and, for the most part, a quiet one on the campus proper, too. Most of the students had not yet returned for the fall term, and the only noticeable activity was across the Charles River on the south side of the historic property, "over the river," as the students like to say, where the athletic facilities are located and the fall teams were in preseason training.

Melanie had just finished a longer-than-normal morning walk-through as coach Ray Leone covered a little more ground than the women expected. After showering and changing into a T-shirt and gym shorts, she was sitting on a comfortable leather sofa in the upstairs lounge of Dillon Fieldhouse, which houses the soccer and lacrosse locker rooms and the main training room and rehab facility for Harvard student-athletes, recounting the reason for that evening sit-down three years earlier with the now graduated Nichols.

It had been quite a debut soccer season for Melanie, who made the travel squad as a freshman in 2008 and never relinquished her spot. All players dress for home games in college sports, but some teams in some sports don't take their entire roster to road games because of travel budgets. The travel squad can vary, depending on which players are performing the best during practice and games, and Melanie was always on the list, and for good reason. She was one of the key figures helping to lead the Crimson to a 10–3–5 record, the Ivy League regular-season championship, and an appearance in the 2008 NCAA tournament. She'd scored a team-high nineteen points (four coming in a 3–1 victory over archrival Yale), and tied for the lead in goals with six. She won the League's Rookie of the Year award, earned second-team All-Ivy, made the League's weekly Honor Roll awards list five times, twice was selected as rookie of the week, and was named to Soccer America's All-Freshmen second team.

Even though the season came to a heartbreaking end with a loss to Northeastern on penalty kicks in the first round of the NCAAs, Melanie had exceeded even her own lofty expectations for how her freshman season would go. The fact that she was playing Division I college soccer had fulfilled a dream she'd first started having before she'd hit double-digit age. More amazingly, she was doing it at Harvard. Yes, Harvard, a place that was twenty miles away from her hometown of Framingham, but might as well have been twenty states away because she barely even gave the world-renowned university a thought at the start of her college selection process, so remote did she think were her chances of acceptance.

"It was kind of like a joke—yeah, Harvard, no way, absolutely not," she said. "Even though I was born and raised around here, I'd only been to the Square a couple times. I never thought I'd be here, I can definitely say that."

Yet she was there, and she was doing better than she ever could have imagined both on the field and in the classroom. So, a few weeks after that first soccer season had concluded, why was she sitting in her room crying on the shoulder of a respected team leader? Because playing her favorite sport at the varsity level, while adjusting to living away from home for the first time, and trying to make new friends in a wildly diverse culture, and handling a rigorous Ivy League curriculum, just wasn't enough for Melanie. Nope, something was missing, and she had a pretty good idea what it was: Her second-favorite sport, lacrosse.

"I'm a very competitive person, I've been a type A my whole life, and I just like to be busy," she said. "I played the two sports in high school (in addition to ice hockey her freshman year), and I was so used to playing so many games. You come to college and you play eighteen soccer games or whatever in the fall, and that's it, and it was starting to eat at me. Even though I really never intended to play lacrosse, and I'd told my soccer coach that, I really thought I could play both."

DOUBLE DIPPING

There was a time when it wasn't wholly uncommon for college students to play two varsity sports, and it was even more prevalent in the Ivy League because the Ancient Eight schools don't give athletic scholarships, so the kids don't feel as if they're bound to one particular sport. Obviously, it takes a special person to do it because you not only have to be proficient at both sports, you must be a tremendous student with wondrous time management skills to pull it off, but it was being done.

However, the number of two-sport athletes has dwindled, certainly in the past decade, and it's not because the kids aren't as talented or as scholarly. The issue is the increasing specialization of sports at the youth and high school levels. Kids are now focusing on one sport and they play it and train for it year-round, primarily in the hope that they can excel enough to enhance their chances of getting into their preferred colleges via scholarships or grant-in-aid packages.

Melanie didn't specialize, though. She was equally adept at soccer and lacrosse, and while soccer was her first priority and ended up being the vehicle that drove her to Harvard (OK, the fact that she was the Valedictorian in a class of about four-hundred-fifty, and a score north of 1,300 on the SAT probably helped, too), she began to realize once she was in Cambridge that she wanted to play lacrosse, too. There were fewer two-sport athletes across the Ivy League than there ever had been, but she knew she could push the meter ever so slightly the other way.

But oh goodness, what a drama-filled dilemma just the mere thought of doubling up created for her as her freshman soccer season came to a close. She'd made a commitment to the soccer team, and if she chose to play lacrosse, would her soccer teammates resent her? Would they be upset that she wasn't participating in the off-season training sessions? Would missing out on the social team bonding activities have an adverse effect on her standing within the team? Would Leone bury her on the bench? And what about the lacrosse players, would they even accept her, this girl who hadn't been recruited initially to play for their team?

"I didn't really have a clear answer for anything," she said. "If I tried lacrosse, is that bailing on my soccer team or turning my back? I had established myself as an up-and-coming leader and hopefully a player that people would look up to the way I looked up to the older players on the team when I was first coming in. Can you be the Ivy League rookie of the year and then just turn around and play another sport? I was really confused, I was a mess."

That's when she summoned Nichols to her room and cried enough to flood the Charles River. "Her take was that because I was so riled up and emotional about it, that meant that I really wanted to play lacrosse," Melanie remembered. "I was thinking that's really interesting, because that's what made me think I wasn't going to do it, for that very reason. I was a stress case."

She entered her sophomore year convinced it was soccer and soccer only, and that seemed like a good decision given her performance on the field. Melanie scored four goals and fourteen points to trail only teammate Katherine Sheeleigh in both categories, and it was her goal in overtime that gave Harvard a 3–2 League championship-clinching victory over Columbia. Lacrosse was not on her mind at all; she seemingly had put the idea of playing two sports to bed. But once again, when there were no more soccer games to play, she started to think about it.

"Sophomore soccer season I still had no idea I would play lacrosse," she said. "It wasn't until I resumed workouts in December of sophomore year that I thought maybe I should reevaluate. I had that whole, 'If I can keep up with soccer I'll do it—if soccer suffers I'll probably drop lacrosse' conversation."

Well, clearly, she was keeping up with soccer, so she decided to take the plunge.

"After her freshman year there was a conversation that we're doing something special here and the off-season training is important," Leone said. "I wanted her to develop a relationship with Sheeleigh (who had been Ivy League rookie of the year in 2007). I said 'We've got to develop this together' and she decided to stay with us and she and Sheeleigh practiced together almost every single day. I'm absolutely convinced that made a difference in us (defending the Ivy title in 2009) because I remember situations in games where they were playing to each other, and if they don't do that outside of September through November, I don't think it happens.

"I wasn't thrilled (that Melanie wanted to play lacrosse), but it wasn't as bad when she left after her sophomore year. Mel wanted to do it, and I care very much about all of my players, and I want them to reach their full potential in every avenue that they can. You can't do everything, but if you can prove you can do most things, then you have to let them do it. And she can pull it off, in the classroom and on the field, and not many people can do that."

CAPTAIN, MY CAPTAIN

As she sat in her motel room in Garden City on Long Island on the afternoon of September 2, 2011, a few hours before her senior soccer season at Harvard was to begin, Melanie couldn't shake the unsettling feeling in her stomach.

"I'm really nervous," she said as the hours and minutes ticked away toward the kickoff against Long Island University at a field located in the borough of Brooklyn. "This really feels different this year, being a senior. I'm more nervous than I have been the past couple years, for sure. There's all these expectations, and as a senior and a captain, people are looking up to you. Before big games I get anxious with anticipation, but you want to make sure you're doing everything right and not have any regrets. I guess that's where the nervousness is coming from."

Melanie is a natural-born leader, and had been since she was a little kid playing in the youth leagues in and around Framingham. But a situation came up just prior to the team boarding its bus for the trip to New York that she really didn't know how to handle, and it provided a glimpse of the type of responsibility she would be shouldering this season. Because Hurricane Irene had blown through New England the previous weekend and messed up the team's practice schedule, a chalkboard meeting was pushed back to the day the team was supposed to depart. The problem with this was that the six players who were not part of the twenty-woman traveling squad had to sit there in the locker room while their teammates were packing their bags and changing into their travel clothes, and Melanie, for one, could not ignore the disappointment in their faces.

"I texted a captain from last year (Gina Wideroff) to ask for advice on how to handle it," Melanie said. "It's awkward and you feel bad for those girls who have put in just as much training as you have the last few weeks and aren't able to be here to experience this. And what's hard for me is that the natural thing is to say, 'I know how hard it is,' but I can only imagine because I was always on the travel roster, even as a freshman. Both of the captains this year

(Lindsey Kowal was the other) have been starters since freshman, so it's hard for us to know how to say the right things and to make people feel like we're there with them even if we haven't necessarily been in that spot."

So as coach Ray Leone went over the teams' goals and expectations for the season, and discussed the details of the first road trip, the girls who weren't traveling sat there, trying to be enthused but, ultimately, failing to mask their disappointment.

Without the six players, the Crimson left for Long Island at around six in the evening, got held up by the never-ending New York City–area traffic, and finally pulled into the motel in Garden City at around eleven, tired and ready to get some sleep. "It was a long trip, and it was pretty boring," Melanie said. "We watched *Mean Girls* for about the five-hundredth time, and they teased me about the article in the *Globe*."

That would be the one-thousand-word feature story on Melanie that appeared in the *Boston Globe* the day before the game in which Leone was quoted as saying his cocaptain is "so small and so young looking, you're like, 'This kid is the player and competitor that she is?' Just don't underestimate her."

"I get so much crap for looking small, so people really liked that line where he said that," Melanie said. "My friends got a good kick out of it. It's a little embarrassing because I get a lot of attention and don't know what to say. I'm getting e-mails and congratulations on the article, so I guess it was pretty cool."

Well, yeah, it was.

Game night wasn't as cool, though. LIU took a 1–0 lead in the first half, and after Peyton Johnson pulled Harvard even early in the second half, the Blackbirds, who had already played three games and lost every one, netted the winner in the fifty-sixth minute. Ruby Leon worked herself free and fired a shot from right in front of the cage past Harvard goalie Bethany Kanten, who had taken over for starter Alexandra Millett. Melanie played all ninety minutes, took three shots, two of which were on net, and her last, in the seventy-ninth minute, was turned aside by LIU goalie Jennifer Bannon, one of the eight saves she made.

Not the beginning the Crimson were hoping for, and the long bus ride back to Cambridge gave Melanie and her mates plenty of time to decipher what had gone wrong.

LATE-GAME HEROICS

Let's face it, soccer can be dull. There's usually very few goals scored, and in some games, there are no more than a handful of shots. Soccer fans rail against those who criticize their sport and their argument almost always ends up being that the soccer-haters just don't understand the inner beauty and intricacies of the game. The counterpoint is that 1–0 is 1–0, and it's a tough task to convince the masses that 1–0 can be exciting. But three games into their season, the Harvard women seemed intent on proving that the pitch was the place to be.

Following the season-opening loss to Long Island, Harvard came home to Soldiers Field and defeated Elon, 2–1, in a thrilling game during which Melanie managed to get off ten shots. "I can't ever think of a game where I had that many shots," she said. One of them found the back of the net for her first goal of the year, and another led directly to Lizzie Weisman's game-winning goal with less than four minutes to play.

Five days later the Crimson were cruising along on their home turf, clinging to a 1–0 lead against UMass, when all of a sudden drama began unfolding faster than the Red Sox collapse that was currently in full flight over at Fenway. "It was a crazy game," Melanie said of the eventual 2–1 victory that she personally delivered.

It all began when starting goalie Alexandra Millet came out to play a fifty-fifty ball just outside the goal box and got kicked right in the face, the force of the blow breaking her nose in two places. She was helped off the field, and Leone was forced to send in his third-string goalie, sophomore Jessie Wright, because his number two keeper, Bethany Kanten, was sidelined by a shoulder injury suffered in the win over Elon. Moments after entering, Wright inadvertently tackled UMass forward Erin McGaffigan in the penalty box, resulting in a penalty kick, and having just come in cold with no warm-up, Wright had no chance as McGaffigan scored to tie the game.

Melanie, pissed about that sequence of events, took matters into her own hands—or feet, as it were—the way any good captain with a fire in her belly and a flair for the dramatic would. A few minutes after the penalty kick, Peyton Johnson gained possession and played the ball along the ground to Melanie who was about ten yards outside the penalty box. With one UMass defender trailing her, Melanie separated herself with a burst of speed, and then dribbled between two defenders as if they weren't even there, leaving her one-on-one with UMass goalie Emily Cota. Cota had played a strong game, with eight saves, but she was no match for Melanie, who ripped a left-footed shot into the right side of the net for the winning goal with just 1:40 remaining.

"I think I had a girl on my back, I turned the first touch inside and then put my head down and started dribbling and I realized I was all by myself so I just took the shot," Melanie explained. "Their defense is probably beating themselves up over that. I think they weren't expecting me to do what I did and I caught them off guard. It was pretty exciting."

DEEP ON THE DEPTH CHART

Ray Leone had been coaching college soccer for about two decades, and between Melanie managing ten shots in the win over Elon, her scoring the winning goal against UMass in the dying moments, and having to deal with injuries to three of his goalkeepers, he was at a loss to explain the chaotic opening to the season. When asked by the *Harvard Crimson*, the best he could offer was, "It's been a crazy couple games."

Melanie had never heard of a team having four goalies on the roster, but luckily this team did because there was freshman Cheta Emba, pressed into duty and playing well enough in her Harvard debut to enable the Crimson to pull off a 2–1 upset at home over UConn.

First-stringer Alexandra Millet was out because of the broken nose she suffered against UMass; second-stringer Bethany Kanten was sidelined by a sore shoulder; and third-stringer Jessie Wright took a blow to the head in the twenty-fourth minute against UConn that sent her to the hospital for observation and concussion tests. So here came Emba, and wouldn't you know it, after making a superb, game-saving stop in the final minute, she face-planted into the ground and the trainers had to come out to tend to her. Thankfully, she was able to finish. Of course, a couple hours earlier, Melanie was just hoping Emba would show up for the game.

"We thought she was over-sleeping before the game because she walked in like five minutes before we were supposed to meet," Melanie said. "We're all calling her on her phone, 'Cheta where are you?' I gave my bike key to Lizzie to go find her because we were meeting and no one knew where she was and we're thinking we need to find her because she might actually play in this game. And sure enough she got in."

Not only did Emba get in, she was a revelation as she made four saves and was in total control of her game and her emotions.

"We didn't know what was going to happen (after Wright departed), but Cheta just turned it on," said Melanie. "She was so confident, grabbed the ball, kicked the crap out of it, she was barking orders just like you want your goalie to do, and she came up huge. She made a couple really nice saves to keep us in the game, and then this girl hits a rocket and it's going in, and Cheta lays out of nowhere and made the save. I was on the bench and we were doing laps up and down the bench, screaming, and the coaches were going nuts. Her nickname is Sauce, and we're chanting her name after the game. It was like a movie, just crazy. It was such a great team win."

Emba wasn't the only freshman standout. There was also Lauren Urke, who scored the first goal off a nice pass from Melanie less than two minutes into the contest, and after UConn tied it, Urke's perfect left-footed cross was headed home by Alexandra Conigliaro ten minutes into the second half for the winning goal. "She just responded to whatever pressure there was and whatever nerves she had, and really stepped up for us," said Melanie.

One of the unique aspects about the Ivy League is that so many of the student-athletes are accomplished in pursuits other than the sport they play, and for Urke, it's her ability to play the violin. At Wayzata High School just outside Minneapolis, Minnesota, Urke lettered in soccer, hockey, and track and field, and as a senior she won her school's prestigious Athena Award for outstanding athletic and academic performance by a female. Soccer was her best sport and for four straight years she was voted by her soccer teammates as the hardest worker, an honor she cherished. Yet as talented as she was with her feet, she was even more proficient with her hands wrapped around a bow and the neck of her violin. For nine years she was a member of the Greater Twin Cities Youth Symphony, and her way of giving back to other musicians was to start her own volunteer mentoring program to provide violin lessons.

"She's an unbelievable violin player," Melanie said. "She put these videos on YouTube from her senior recital, and they're amazing. I was thinking here's this girl who got into Harvard on her own (not as a soccer recruit), she's an unbelievable violin player, and she's a freshman walk-on who takes down UConn. If they knew, they'd probably be in shock that this girl took down their team."

HECTIC SCHEDULE

Mondays were usually a day off from practice and games, and following a week in which the Crimson lost three games in a row—"a brutal week" as Melanie said—this day off couldn't have come at a better time. Losing to Boston University, Hofstra, and Rhode Island dropped the Crimson record to 3–4 with the start of Ivy League play looming with a Friday-night home against Penn.

"Everyone needed a day off; we'd gone through five games (in ten days) and that's pretty crazy for college soccer," she said. "It's not unheard of for Ivy League teams to do poorly early in the season. We try to pack in a lot of games in a short period of time and try to play catch up with teams who started practicing twenty days before we did. We haven't practiced much and it's starting to show. I'm not worried, but it's always frustrating to lose because these are games we could have and should have won."

Just because there was no practice, though, Melanie's day was still jam-packed because she took advantage of the soccer-free Mondays to load up her class schedule and therefore lessen the burden later in the week when there were practices and games. And on this Monday, in addition to four classes that had her occupied either in lectures or in labs from eleven in the morning to nine at night, she took time to write in the journal that she had decided to keep recounting her senior year, and she attended a meeting with the lacrosse team that she'd be rejoining in the spring.

"We just went over some of the team rules and expectations, and I wanted to show my face and say hi to those girls," Melanie said.

It was good to touch base with the lacrosse team because it briefly took her mind off the disappointment of the previous five days on the soccer field. The Crimson were soundly defeated at Boston University, 3–0, as the Terriers got a pair of goals from Kylie Strom, and their defense limited Harvard to a mere nine shots, only four of which were on goal.

Back home to play Hofstra, a scoring frenzy broke out in the second half, but when it was over, Harvard was on the wrong end of a 5–4 final, the highest-scoring game the Crimson had been a part of since September 9,

2001, when they lost by the same tally to Colorado College. "Hofstra was kind of a low point," Melanie said. "We gave up a lot of goals in that game, had a lot of breakdowns." Melanie's lone contribution was an assist on a goal by Alexandra Conigliaro that gave Harvard a 2–1 lead in the eleventh minute of the second half before Hofstra scored three times in the next five minutes to blow it open.

Melanie was a little more active in a 3–2 double-overtime loss at Rhode Island as she attempted four shots and drew an assist on a goal by Lizzie Weisman. But in the second overtime, Rhode Island's Megan Rauscher ripped a laser from about twenty-five yards to win it. "I don't think Hope Solo would have saved that ball," Melanie said. "We came back from a 2–0 deficit to tie it so that was pretty good. The captains had a meeting trying to recollect ourselves and starting fresh (after the Hofstra debacle). People are frustrated, but there wasn't any big speech by anybody. Ray is a pretty positive coach; every once in a while he'll get on us, but he knows being Harvard girls we tend to overanalyze things and we're pretty tough on ourselves, so he's aware of that. He points out things that we need to work on, but the tone is usually pretty forgiving and looking at the positives."

Riding a three-game losing streak was no way for the Crimson to go into their Ivy League opener at Soldiers Field, especially given that their opponent was Penn. The Quakers were the defending League champions, and this game would be pitting the two teams that had won the past four Ancient Eight titles in women's soccer. However, trying to take that glass-half-full approach, Melanie said, "The Ivy League games are a whole different ballgame, so you don't really think about what has happened in the past whether you've done well or not. We were really excited and not thinking about the past games. We know we're a good team and this is a huge game because they won the League last year, and we came out flying."

They sure did. The Crimson defense, "played out of their mind and it was like someone lit a fire under our asses," Melanie said. And on the other side of the rain-soaked field, Melanie was on fire, too, as she scored a pair of goals in the first twenty-four minutes and that's all Harvard needed for a 2–0 victory that the Crimson knew could prove to be critical in the Ivy standings by the end of the year.

"It was definitely the best performance I've seen this year, if not a couple years," said Melanie, who matched her goal output from the first seven games. "It was one of those nights where everyone was feeling it. We watched a ton of video, fixed some defensive issues, and the energy wasn't even comparable."

Melanie's first goal came after a long pass from Peyton Johnson that was right on her foot and from there it was one touch in the left side of the box and then directly into the net, a hard, low shot that Penn goalie Sarah Banks had no chance to stop. Her second goal came off a corner kick taken by Johnson. The ball was cleared off the goal line, but it came right to Melanie and she wasted no time banging it into the net off a Penn defender.

That's all Harvard needed as Cheta Emba and Bethany Kanten combined on a shutout, and just like that, those three losses were wiped from the Crimson's memory.

LOCAL YOKEL

Ray Leone traveled thousands of miles to recruit the twenty-seven players on his roster, and no region was ignored, as twelve states were represented including California (seven players), Massachusetts (six), New York (three), Hawaii, Florida, Utah, Nevada, Minnesota, Virginia, New Jersey, Maryland, and Illinois, plus Belgium and Canada. But he didn't have to go very far to find his best player.

Melanie happened to be playing in a Boston-area high school showcase tournament shortly after she'd sent a letter to Harvard, and Leone—who had just taken the Crimson job in February of 2007—came to check her out.

"I was looking through the people who had written to Harvard, and there weren't that many on the list when I first got the job," said Leone, who had spent the previous six years at Arizona State where he'd become the Sun Devils' all-time-winningest coach. "I saw Mel's name so I wanted to go out and find this kid. The previous coach (Erica Walsh) had known about her and mentioned she was a skillful player, but she said, 'You'll have to make your own decision on her.'"

Without knowing anything about Melanie, right off the top Leone liked the fact that she was a Boston kid because it's always good to have locals on the squad, in effect to show you are protecting your own recruiting turf. And when it's a soccer hotbed like Boston, even better because that means this potential recruit must have some talent.

"I went to see her, this tiny little thing, but she was just a natural winner, you could see it," he said. "I remember her warming up her own team. She's like sixteen or seventeen at the time, and she's warming up the team while the coach is giving me a little feedback on who Mel is as a player. I'm listening to the coach as I'm watching her run the show for the team and I'm like, 'Who the heck is this kid?'"

At first, Melanie was shocked that Harvard was interested.

"I knew very little about their soccer program, but they found out I had pretty good grades and it could probably work if it was good for both of us," she said. "I knew I'd be helping them out because I was local, I came from a good school, and I had a good GPA. But I didn't know how it was going to work out with the team. I didn't know what they wanted from me soccer-wise; I felt like I was about their fifth-best recruit because I hadn't played at the top levels. But I knew that if I could get in and if they'd have me, I wanted to be here."

She even rationalized that if she didn't make the team, or she made it and was relegated to bench-warmer, she'd be OK with it because she was still at Harvard. And if she wasn't good enough to play at Harvard, she probably wouldn't be good enough to play at other Division I schools anyway, so she'd focus on school and move on with her life because, "It's Harvard, that's pretty cool to put on a resume, and for me it was always about the academics first. But I think I definitely surprised them."

Her words, not Leone's. He knew Melanie could play, he saw very clearly that she was a leader, and when she strutted onto the practice field that first August in 2008 Leone knew he'd pegged her correctly. "It didn't take long to notice her," he said. "She was starting and she was a main player right away. I remember the older players, they wanted a shot at a championship and one of the seniors, Erin Wylie, a great kid, I told her, 'You're going to start sometimes and other times you're not' and she said, 'Hey, I don't care, I just want to win an Ivy League championship and Mel is good.'"

Melanie was good. Ivy League rookie-of-the-year good, and Harvard won the League championship for the first time since 1999 and earned its first berth in the NCAA tournament since 2004. Now four years later, with two Ivy League titles earned since Melanie arrived, and a big League-opening victory over Penn in the books, there was a great belief that her last year on the pitch could be special, too.

You know the old Dan Patrick line from his days at the ESPN mothership? "You can't stop him; you can only hope to contain him." Well, that was Yale's plan as it assigned sophomore defender Anna McCahon to shadow Melanie throughout the game at Reese Stadium in New Haven, Connecticut, on the first day of October.

The Bulldogs' hope was to limit the number of touches Melanie would get, and make someone else beat them. "I had a girl following me around the whole game to prevent me from getting the ball," said Melanie. "She was really fast and she was doing a good job."

Just not good enough. With Harvard trailing 1–0 in the sixtieth minute, senior Patty Yau dribbled up the right side and whipped a pass across that Melanie was able to get her left foot on and steer into the net just inside the near post. "Awesome pass," Melanie said.

The two teams played through regulation without a goal, and then 2:16 into overtime, the Crimson caught a huge break. Following a corner kick, Johnson gained possession in the box and attempted a shot that struck a Yale defender on the hand, warranting an automatic penalty kick. Johnson, a fiery sophomore from Catonsville, Maryland, drilled the winning shot to beat the archrival Bulldogs, 2–1.

"Yale is a big deal," said Melanie, who finished the soccer portion of her two-sport career a perfect 4–0 against the Bulldogs. "I mean it's not like the football game, because that's The Game, but there's definitely the Yale factor. And really, in terms of the Ivy League, you play every game like it's a championship, so that makes it big, too."

Melanie, who had two assists in a non-League 4–1 victory over New Hampshire the Sunday after the Penn victory, enjoyed the postgame tailgate before the team piled back on the bus for the trip home, but she did so in some discomfort. Because she had been marked the entire game, she did an awful lot of running and cutting in an effort to break free, and by the end she had some pain in her hamstring that had stayed with her for the next couple days. If the next game had been against an Ivy League foe, Melanie likely would have suited up and played. Instead, Fairfield was the opponent, so Leone sat her out and let her rest, and the Crimson were still able to earn a tough 2–1 victory, their fourth straight.

"I think I overdid it a little against Yale so I just stayed out as a precaution," she said. "It's one of those injuries where if you just rest it quickly, it can be fine, but if you don't take time off, it can get worse and cause you a lot of problems down the road."

This was one of the few times since the calendar flipped to October that she'd stood still. Her class load was lighter than normal—this was the first semester in her time at Harvard where she had no labs or problem set classes. And because the bulk of her requirements for her neurobiology major had been filled, she was able to back off just a bit and take four classes instead of five, and physics wasn't one of them, which was a good thing. However, her time was still precious, and the day before the Yale game was a stressful one because she did an on-campus interview for a position at the Advisory Board Company, a global research, consulting, and technology firm based in Washington, D.C., that helps hospital and university executives better serve patients and students.

Less than seven months from graduation, Melanie was pretty sure she was going to wind up in medical school, but her plan was to take a year or two off from studying, get a job, and then start back into school. "The interview went pretty good, easier than I thought, so now I'm waiting to hear back," she said. "I was a little nervous, didn't know what to expect, wasn't sure what kind of questions they would ask me. I was happy because it was more of a behavioral interview than a case one. I felt pretty good walking out. If I don't get the job it will be because there were better candidates and not because I didn't come off the way I wanted to."

REVENGE WEEK

There was no arguing with the headline in the *Harvard Crimson* the morning of October 10: "Harvard Fails to Maintain Lead Twice in Deadlock at Cornell."

"Yeah, that was kind of negative, so that sucked," Melanie said in reference to the article in the school paper that recapped Harvard's disappointing 2–2 tie two days earlier on a balmy Saturday afternoon in Ithaca, New York.

However, it was true. After a scoreless first half, Aisha Price headed one into the net off a corner kick from Lindsey Kowal to give Harvard its first lead, but just sixteen seconds later, Cornell tied the score on a goal by Abigail Apistolas, which, amazingly, was the first goal the Big Red had scored against

Harvard since 2004. The Crimson regained the lead with less than six minutes to play when Lizzie Weisman converted a pass from Price, but again it was short-lived. With just 1:42 remaining, a defensive lapse allowed Cornell's Maneesha Chitanvis to get open in the goal box and she beat Harvard goalie Bethany Kanten to force overtime.

"Being ahead twice and letting up a goal right after each time was just a total lapse in concentration, and we paid for it," coach Ray Leone said.

When regulation play ended, Cornell was clearly riding a wave of emotion, so Melanie huddled the team in front of the scorer's table just before the start of overtime and tried to inspire her tired teammates with a few words of encouragement, then took her water bottle and started squirting everyone, eliciting shrieks of joy. When junior Taryn Kurcz did the same, the suitably soaked Crimson were stoked, and they carried the play for both ten-minute periods. Unfortunately, it did not result in a goal, and when the final horn sounded, Cornell, which entered the game with a 2–9 overall record, celebrated as if it had won the Ivy League championship.

"It was disappointing, but they played really well," said Melanie, who had two shots on goal, but did not figure in the scoring. "A couple of our girls knew some of their players and they said it was their fall break and they were preparing for this game like it was the World Cup final and they played like it. So the general consensus was that it was props to them. I think in the end it will be a very good thing for us, a wakeup call that makes us reevaluate rather than think that we're cruising."

When the Crimson took the pitch for their next game against Siena College, the last non-League game on the schedule, there wasn't the slightest possibility that they would let the Cornell tie linger, nor would they overlook the Saints. "It's revenge week," Melanie said of the game against Siena, and the next one against Brown, both in Cambridge. "We lost to Siena and Brown last year in really close, hard-fought games. So far, so good on that."

So dominant was Harvard in its 2–0 triumph over Siena that Kanten wasn't even required to make a save on the four shots the Saints attempted. Melanie assisted on Hana Taiji's goal in the forty-ninth minute, and Weisman added an insurance marker in the seventy-seventh minute.

After the game, there was some eating and talking at the tailgate party, and then it was back to her dorm room where she found her roommate in the midst of pulling an all-nighter. So, like a good roommate, Melanie didn't rub it in. She just hauled out a textbook and did some studying of her own because, as she said, there's always something to do.

GUEST SPEAKER

The coaching fraternity at Harvard is knit tighter than one of grandma's quilts, and it's not uncommon for these men and women to visit each others' offices to talk strategy or philosophy or to just shoot the bull. Or, in the case of men's basketball coach Tommy Amaker, to stop by Dillon Fieldhouse to say a few words to Ray Leone's women's soccer team the day before its showdown with Brown.

"I think he and Ray are pretty friendly, so it was a nice surprise for us and really cool to see him because he's like a celebrity around here," Melanie said of Amaker, a former star point guard during his playing days in the mid-1980s at Duke University. When he went into coaching, he was the head man at Seton Hall and Michigan prior to coming to Harvard and resurrecting the Crimson program in 2007.

With Melanie and her mates sitting atop the Ivy standings at 3–0–1, just ahead of Penn and Yale, who were both 3–1, and getting ready to host 2–2 Brown in the second half of its self-proclaimed "revenge week," Leone thought his squad would benefit from listening to Amaker's message.

"He came and talked to us about things he tells their team about being composed and confident, finishing strong, things like that, so it was cool," Melanie said. "And then we got to ask him some questions."

Melanie had a question, but she wasn't looking for some deep motivational response that would help Harvard get mentally prepared for Brown the next day. As a captain she was always trying to find new and better ways to manage the environment of the team, and who better to turn to than the coach who completely transformed Harvard basketball? She asked Amaker what it was like inside the Harvard locker room the night of last March 12, and what he said to his crestfallen players when the Crimson lost a one-game playoff to Princeton on a buzzer-beating shot that denied Harvard its first berth in the NCAA tournament since 1946.

"He said usually he doesn't address the team right after the game because sometimes coaches will get in trouble saying things based off emotion, and he likes to see the film first to get a better sense of what he should say," Melanie explained. "But obviously that was such a crushing loss, so he let them collect themselves and he told them he's been there, he lost in the national championship before (1986 with Duke), and it would take a while to settle in, but it doesn't take away from the unbelievable season they had. When he said that, I agreed with him because it really didn't take away from the season they had. I think that when everyone talks about last season, it isn't necessarily the thing that people think of, that buzzer beater. It's the fact that they won (a share of first place in the League, which was also a school-first) and got Harvard basketball on the map."

On game day, Leone knew exactly what to say to his players after they gutted out a 2–1 victory over Brown at wind-blown Soldiers Field with Melanie and freshman Mai Le scoring goals in the second half to overcome an early 1–0 deficit. "We're really fortunate to get out of here with this win, because we didn't play our style at all," Leone said.

And he was right. With a strong gale blowing through Cambridge, both teams struggled to maintain control of the ball, and what was really weird is that all three goals were scored by the team that was going into the breeze.

"We wanted the wind in the second half, but we lost the coin toss to start the game so we had it in the first half, but then they scored," Melanie said. "So that was kind of unfortunate, but we felt fine at halftime, people weren't freaking out at all, it was very calm and composed. We'd had a ton of scoring opportunities, I hit two crossbars and we hit a post, but we just didn't put one in."

The teams switched sides and, go figure, Harvard scored twice in a span of just over five minutes. Melanie got the first one as she slammed in a loose ball off a corner kick, and then Le, who didn't even dress for the first four games, took a pass from Meg Casscells-Hamby and deposited a shot just inside the right post for the first goal of her career.

From then on, the Crimson held on for dear life. The wind hadn't been a factor on the goals, but it was at the end of the game when Brown smothered Harvard and dominated territorially. "It felt like the last ten minutes we couldn't even clear our side so we were pretty fortunate they didn't score," Melanie said.

SENIOR MOMENT

The memories Melanie had accrued during her time at Harvard will last for the rest of her life, and if she ever gets around to ranking them, perhaps in a David Letterman Top Ten kind of way, the sheer excitement of what took place on the afternoon of October 29 may be awfully difficult to keep out of the number one slot.

"Just a crazy day," Melanie said. "I can't believe it happened the way it happened."

When it was done and she crawled into the bed in her Quincy House dorm room, sleep did not come easily as she lay there staring at the ceiling, the emotion of the day buzzing about her brain as she tried to comprehend that for the third time in her four years on the soccer team, Harvard was the Ivy League champion and would be playing in the NCAA tournament.

On a cold, rainy, raw afternoon at Soldiers Field, the Crimson pulled out a pulsating 2–1 victory over Dartmouth when sophomore Peyton Johnson scored off a free kick from about twenty yards out with a scant ten seconds left in regulation. And then a few hours later, a second round of celebrating commenced when heavily-favored Penn—needing a win to stay alive in the chase for the championship—could not score a goal against Brown and settled for a 0–0 tie, thus clinching the title for the Crimson.

"Unbelievable," Melanie said, describing the scene in the common room of Quincy where the entire team had gathered to follow the Penn game on a laptop computer, first via the Gametracker feature on the Penn website and then through the available live audio. "We were going crazy, screaming and hugging each other."

This was Senior Day, the final home game for Melanie and the other five seniors, and there were tears flowing from sun-up to sun-down. Before the game the team watched a video that had been made to celebrate the careers of the soon-to-be graduating players, and then prior to kickoff each girl was introduced to the crowd and their parents and family members presented them with flowers and joined them on the field.

Then the game started right around the time the nor'easter that had already dumped several inches of snow in some parts of the Northeast arrived in Cambridge. The wind began to blow, the temperature began to plummet, and the mood was dampened, not only by the bursts of rain, but by a Dartmouth goal ten minutes into the first half.

That's when Melanie, the captain—who'd helped put Harvard in the position to clinch by scoring the winning goal in a 2–1 victory over Princeton the previous Saturday—delivered the way she had always delivered. About two minutes before halftime, Erika Garcia crossed the ball from the left flank to Melanie who was coming from the top of the box. Melanie was knocked off balance as she took the pass, but she managed to get a shot off with her left foot that slipped past Big Green goalie Tatiana Sanders just inside the right post to tie the game.

During the second half the Crimson played with the gusty wind at their back, but they couldn't get the tiebreaker as the conditions worsened. "It was so cold and it rained to the point where you couldn't see the ball coming," Melanie said. "I was running during the game and I wasn't sure if my shorts were falling down. I looked down because I couldn't feel anything on my legs, I was so cold. It looked like nobody was going to score."

Until Johnson did. The play started with a long ball through the middle, Melanie advanced it further into the Dartmouth zone with her head, and ultimately Johnson had control and was trying to get off a shot when she was fouled just outside the box and the official, who had been letting some rough stuff go, blew his whistle. The day before, Melanie had seen Johnson with a bag of balls before practice working on her free kicks, and that sure seemed to pay off. She lined up, took her run, and lasered one with her right foot that cleared Dartmouth's blockade and soared just over the outstretched hand of Sanders. Ballgame.

"We pretty much went nuts," Melanie said. "We didn't know at that point that would clinch the Ivy League, but we knew it would put us in a good position. People were crying, there was so much emotion, and then we got back to the locker room and we were crying because all of our bodies were just frozen."

Once they showered, thawed, and ate some food at their tailgate party inside Dillon Fieldhouse, they trooped over to Quincy to monitor the Penn game.

"We started off on Gametracker because we didn't know there was live audio available, and it was 0–0 and then the Gametracker kind of froze, so we were calling people to see if anyone knew what was going on," Melanie said. "Then I called my dad to see if his Gametracker was working and he said there was live audio, so I had my phone on speaker for a bit and then we picked it up on the laptop. So we're there with the rosters and we were trying to follow along. We were all yelling, and I wasn't even thinking that they might not score, but then there was about twenty seconds left and I was like, 'holy shit, we're gonna win the League!' At that point we all stood up and we're in these concerned positions and when they said 'that'll do it' we went crazy."

Just before sleep finally came that night, Melanie reflected on a wish she'd made two years earlier.

"We write letters to all the seniors each year and I remember specifically writing to the senior class when I was a sophomore after we'd just won two Ivy League championships in a row," she recalled. "I was so jealous and I said I could only hope that I could leave here with a championship as a senior, feeling like I went out on top, and that's what it will be now. I really feel like I have no regrets, and to put in all the time and energy and to have it pay off is so awesome."

ALONE AT THE TOP

As athletes, part of Melanie and her teammates' responsibility to the team is to take care of their bodies when they are away from the field. You know, work out, eat right, keep the partying to a minimum, at least during the season. Except, of course, after you've just clinched the outright Ivy League championship with a 1–0 victory at Columbia, you're on a long bus ride back to Cambridge, and it's Lizzie Weisman's birthday.

"Someone Googled up Cold Stone and we drove completely out of the way, but it was worth it," Melanie said of Cold Stone Creamery, a chain that bills itself as "the ultimate ice cream experience" and is known for its extravagant sundaes which, under ordinary circumstances, would be banned from any athletic training table.

The Crimson deserved some indulgence after ruining Columbia's Senior Night when freshman Lauren Urke scored in the twenty-first minute, and then fellow freshman Bethany Kanten made two saves to make that goal stand up. With Penn winning its final game against Princeton, Harvard's win prevented the Quakers from grabbing a share of the crown, and the Crimson finished unbeaten in the League for the first time since 1999 with a 6–0–1 record. Penn ended 5–1–1, that loss coming at the hands of the Crimson a month and a half earlier when Melanie scored both goals in what proved to be a title-deciding 2–0 victory.

Two days after the Columbia game, Melanie received great news on a couple of fronts: She found out she was getting a final-round interview with a San Francisco-based company called Acumen LLC, which provides government agencies with high-quality, impartial research and analytical tools to inform decision making. "I didn't get the job I applied for at The Advisory Board and they referred me to another job in the company, but I didn't want it, so that fizzled out. So I applied for this through career services, and it went really well. I would be a writer and research analyst, so I have to go to San Francisco sometime around Thanksgiving."

However, first things first, and that was the NCAA tournament, where the Crimson would have an opportunity to gain some revenge on Boston University. When the draw was announced, Harvard was listed across from the Terriers for a first-round game at BU's Nickerson Field, and that was fine with Melanie.

"They're a really good team," Melanie said, recalling that the Terriers blew out the Crimson, 3–0, earlier this year, and by that same score in a 2010 match. "We've always played them early in the year so it will be interesting to see how both teams have developed, and I think it will be very different this time. I think it will be a close game."

Still, BU was a clear-cut favorite, and even though Harvard was red-hot and riding a ten-game unbeaten streak, Melanie knew the challenge ahead would be daunting. "They're having the best season they've had in a long time, they're ranked about twelfth right now, so it's hard not to look past us after they beat us 3–0. I'm sure their coach is saying we're a better team now, so we'll see if they believe it."

This would be Melanie's third NCAA tournament game; she hadn't won one yet, and now as a senior, she realized this was her last opportunity. "I guess I don't really remember much about the other years, but I know it's a big deal and I'm very excited."

At some point Melanie figured the mourning for a season cut shorter than she'd hoped would begin and the tears would flow. But in the immediate aftermath, there was just a sense of numbness to the finality brought on by Harvard's 3–0 first-round NCAA tournament loss to BU.

"It's sad, but it's more just a mellow sadness," Melanie said a couple days after her soccer career came to an end. "I guess I'm surprised I haven't cried yet, but there will definitely be a time. Obviously it was a big bummer because I was really excited and I really thought we were going to win and I think that was the team's mentality."

The Crimson did not win, even though they played a much better game than the lopsided score indicated. Unlike the 3–0 loss to the Terriers early in the regular season, this was a much more evenly played game and Melanie would argue that in the second half Harvard was actually the better team. However, all BU would say to that is "scoreboard," and it would be right. Kylie Strom and Anna Cuffia scored first-half goals for the Terriers, and then with about twenty-eight minutes left to play Harvard's Hana Taiji had the misfortune of having a BU corner kick deflect off her head and into her net for an own goal that sealed the Crimson defeat.

"It was a very different game than the first one," said Melanie, who acknowledged that BU had owned Harvard the first time. "We held possession very nicely, we out-shot them, we out-cornered them. We were in their end most of the second half, but they scored on their opportunities. It was frustrating because we played well."

Just not well enough to defeat an opponent ranked fourteenth in the National Soccer Coaches Association of America poll, that had now won fourteen games in a row and nineteen of its twenty-two games this year, and that had outscored Harvard, 9–0 in the last three meetings dating back to 2010. Still, Melanie was not going to let the loss detract from what she called "a hell of a season," and neither could coach Ray Leone, whose only regret was that this senior class, led by Melanie and her cocaptain and close friend, Lindsey Kowal, did not get to taste victory in the NCAA tournament. They had won three Ivy League championships in their four years, but lost in the first round of the NCAA each time.

"I just can't say enough about the kind of kids that they are," Leone said.

"Remarkable four-year run. Three championships. The only thing that was not on our resume was winning an NCAA game, and that's what we really wanted them to experience. But that doesn't erase away the excellence that they've demonstrated the last four years."

Melanie would eventually cry, but unlike fellow seniors Kowal, Taiji, Sophie Legros, Rebecca Millock, and Patty Yau, whose varsity athletic careers were finished, Melanie's was not. She would wipe her ducts dry and after a couple months off to refresh herself mentally as well as physically, she would rejoin the Crimson lacrosse team for one more chance to represent Harvard.

"That definitely helps to ease the pain," said Melanie, who in the week before the BU game was voted the Ivy League player of the year, and was also named to the Capital One Academic All-District team for the third year in a row. "I'm in the soccer funk right now, and I thought about this maybe being my last soccer game, but it didn't strike me as much as you would think and maybe that's because I know I'm still going to be playing lacrosse."

Soccer was now a closed chapter in her life, one that she would never forget. She left the Harvard pitch as one of the school's greatest players, ranking seventh in goals (twenty-seven), sixth in assists (twenty-five) and tied for sixth in points (seventy-nine). Yet despite all her accomplishments, she remained humble from the time she was handed a Crimson uniform in the summer of 2008 until she handed that uniform back to Leone for the final time.

"I came to Harvard thinking that I wouldn't even play, being pretty intimidated by the idea of playing Division I college soccer. So to go from there to where I am today, it's kind of unbelievable. It doesn't even feel like it was me, it's like I'm happy for someone else. That's the best way I can describe it; it feels like someone else did that and it's hard to believe that's me. I guess I tend to underestimate myself, but now looking at what I've done, it's kind of of shocking."

ONA McCONNELL

YALE FIELD HOCKEY

Ona was no different than any other goaltender who had been recruited by coach Pam Stuper to play for Yale's field hockey team. During her freshman year in the fall of 2009, Ona, like other first-year goalies before her, had one primary duty on game day: Videographer.

Quite a comedown from her days as a school-girl whiz when she was the most valuable player on the teams she played on while growing up in England and Germany.

"What happens to the new goalkeepers, unless you're really good and you play right away, which usually isn't the case, is that you film the games your freshman year," said Ona on a late August 2011 Monday morning that was filled with tedious tasks before she had to head over to practice after lunch. "So that was me. I didn't really expect anything else because there were two other goalies on the team at the time, so it was a nice easy start for me, but it was definitely hard because I didn't like sitting on the bench."

After a moment of reflection, Ona remembered how she really felt about her role, and she amended her comment by saying, "Actually, I wish I could have just sat on the bench because then I could at least watch the games and enjoy it with my teammates. When you're filming you can't really even watch the game because you have to follow the ball."

Such was life as the newbie on the squad, but deep down, while she wasn't enamored with her non-playing status, Ona was nonetheless ecstatic to be at Yale, because it was a place she never thought she'd end up.

"I had no clue where I wanted to go," said Ona, who did all of her primary schooling in Europe and never lived in the United States until she moved into her dorm on Yale's New Haven, Connecticut, campus. "My counselor said to start looking at schools, and I knew I had a chance to play field hockey so I printed out my field hockey resume and sent it out to about fifty schools, and then I waited for e-mails. Yale, at that point, said they had a walk-on goalie (recruit) and they didn't need a goalie, so they were off the list."

Only briefly, as it turned out.

Ona, whose impeccable grades and test scores were her assurance that admission would not be a problem no matter where she applied, looked into two other Ivy League schools, Dartmouth and Princeton, and also went to check out Bowdoin. Princeton would have been her choice, "But by the time I went there, they said they were taking two other players and couldn't fit a third (goalie) in."

On a lark she called Stuper one last time to see if anything had changed in Yale's recruiting class, and lo and behold, it had. The walk-on goalie had apparently walked off and accepted an opportunity somewhere else, so yes, Yale was looking for a third goalie. Ona showed up for an official visit on Halloween 2008, and, "Once I was here, it wasn't much of a choice. I loved it. I went to a game, loved the team, it's a beautiful campus, and everyone I met was very welcoming and nice. And what I really love is that everyone here has something specific that they do, either a sport, an instrument, a great writer, there's something about them that they have that's unique to them. I love that, and there's always something new to see every day. And it also seemed like everyone was having fun as well. The early application date was November 1, so the next day, I knew this was the place for me and my dad hit the submit button from home and that was it."

Count Ona among those smiling faces, even though it was usually hidden behind that video camera. She made the decision that if she couldn't get into the games, she was going to make the most of practice. Every time she waddled onto Johnson Field in her bulky goalie pads, she brought a vigor and spirit to her work because she recognized that practice was her time to play, her time to shine, her time to show Stuper and goaltender coach Tamara Durante that, come next year, she wasn't going to be doing the filming, she was going to be the one being filmed.

At least that was the plan, but Stuper and Durante weren't so sure, because, for whatever reason, as the season progressed, Ona simply wasn't showing in practice that she could someday be the number one goaltender for the Bulldogs.

"We brought her in as a freshman, and we didn't think she would contribute much that season just because it was her first year," said Stuper, a member of the USA Field Hockey Hall of Fame and the head coach at Yale since 2005. "We thought she had some athleticism and had some skill, but she needed some training and needed to have the opportunity to go to college practices, see what it's like at the next level, and get used to it. But Ona wasn't making the saves or even reacting to the shots. Tamara would come up and say 'Something's not right, I don't understand it. We're doing A-B-C, and she's not reacting, or the ball is in the net and then she's reacting.' And then we learned why."

LIKE MOTHER, LIKE DAUGHTER

Jerry and Karen McConnell were both born and raised in America, Jerry in North Carolina, Karen in California. He attended the University of North Carolina and was a Morehead Scholar, then went on to Yale Law School. She did her undergrad studies and also earned her MBA at the University of California, Berkeley. Both wound up in Munich, Germany, Jerry working for Bain Management Consultants—which was cofounded by 2012 Republican presidential candidate Mitt Romney—and Karen as an investment banker, and they were introduced by a mutual friend. Married not too long thereafter, they relocated to London, England, where all three of their children—the oldest, Joseph (whom the family has always called Alec), and the twins, Ona and Sam—were born.

The McConnell's lived in England for the first eight years of Ona's life, and though her parents spoke in their native American accents, Ona developed a British accent. "I was very English," she said with a smile. That is, until she had to become very German. By now Jerry was working for Goldman Sachs, and the firm asked him to move to Germany to operate an office near Frankfurt in the centrally located state of Hessen, and this thrust the McConnell children into a nearly untenable situation.

"My siblings and I got sent to a German school immediately without knowing a word of the language," Ona recalled. "And I can tell you the teachers really didn't care much that we couldn't speak the language."

There were many nights when she would sit on her bed and cry because it was difficult to make friends without the ability to communicate, not to mention the challenge it created to keep pace in school. But as kids are wont to do, Ona began to adapt, and pretty soon she was managing quite well.

"Amazingly, and I still don't know how it happened, but without anyone translating, I just started picking it up," she said. "I guess when you're thrown into a situation where no one speaks a word of English, you don't really have a choice and you just pick up the language. Within two months I was having conversations."

Speaking German came easier than reading it at first, so one day when a classmate handed out fliers to the kids in her grade, Ona took one to bring home so her mother could decipher what it said. "They were looking for players for the field hockey team," she said. "That's where it started for me."

Karen McConnell had quite a field hockey history that her daughter never knew about. The sport had been dormant at Berkeley for more than thirty years, but Karen, who had played in high school in Marin County, spearheaded an effort to bring it back, and she succeeded. This was in 1972, right around the time Title IX was voted into legislation to provide equal opportunities in athletics for women. Karen not only captained the team she reinvented, she was the treasurer of the schools' Women's Athletic Association and was part of a group of officers who secured money (about $50,000, she recalled, while the football team alone was getting around $650,000) to be used to fund women's athletics. "We were the first university to have a real budget for women's sports," Karen said. "And this will make you laugh, but in our original press statement, we didn't want scholarships for women. The way we looked at it, we saw the men and thought, 'only the elite men can play,' and we wanted sports for women to be available to everyone, so no scholarships. That didn't last long, but it's funny that that was our idea at the time."

So when Ona brought home that flier, Karen perked up and said, "I played field hockey for Berkeley. So yes, you're going to play."

Early on it was evident Ona had her mom's field hockey gene, and she took to the game immediately. At first Ona played forward, but in her second year she found herself in the goal crease, and she never wanted to leave. "The team needed a goalie," she remembered. "We had a game and there was no one to play. Nobody raised their hand to be the goalie, so I was thinking 'What could be so bad?' The coach said they'd give a bag of candy to anyone who wanted to play, so I went in and I absolutely loved it. I loved the adrenaline rush; you're nervous, but at the same time it's exciting. My mom said, 'Ona, don't you want to be on the field running?' and I said, 'No, not really.'"

Ona eventually captained the grammar-school team to the Hessen state championship, and she was in line to become a member of a select team representing Hessen in regional and national tournaments when her father broke the news to her that the family was moving back to England, primarily because he and Karen felt the children needed to get back into a better educational system to properly prepare them for college, which they were always going to attend in America.

"They had never written English, so they had no writing capabilities," said Karen. "The only reading they did were books for fun that we had at home, and the only English they heard spoken was among us. And honestly, the German school system had gone downhill fast and we saw all three of our kids losing interest in learning, so that's why we went back to England, to get them revved up about learning."

Not surprisingly, Ona was upset to have to relocate again, especially since she had finally learned to communicate in German, had made friends, become part of a team, and had enjoyed success in the only sport she played. And then, upon enrolling in the American School in London, her disappointment grew when she learned that she would not be eligible to play for the high school field hockey team because she was only in eighth grade.

The team at the American School was several notches below the one she played on in Hessen, and once she was able to play, she was its undeniable MVP. "I played every minute, and I was always busy in goal," she said with a chuckle.

Ona was so good that at the age of fourteen she joined a ladies club team based in the northwest London suburb of West Hampstead and played with women in their mid-twenties, easily holding her own. "They didn't have any goalies, but I also was good enough to play," she said. "They don't care how old you are, if you're at that level, they let you play. I was shy at the beginning, I didn't say that much, but they made me feel at home. I got to know everyone and I was like the mascot of the team, but I played so it was awesome."

It was while she was with the West Hampstead team that a coach named John Hurst, who had trained England's men's field hockey goalies for the country's Olympic team, took an interest in Ona, believing she could potentially be an Olympic performer.

"He was saying I looked pretty good, and the Olympics were always a dream of mine," she said. "He said I had something, and his colleague said the same thing, but it sort of went downhill after my junior year and I wasn't sure why. But now I do."

THE DIAGNOSIS

With her first season at Yale behind her, and having not played a single minute, Ona knew the offseason would be critical to her chances of competing for playing time, and perhaps a starting berth, as a sophomore. She had noticed a downturn in her performance during her last season of high school when she was slow to react to even the most routine shots and wasn't making the saves she normally made, and she hadn't been able to extricate herself from what she believed was just a slump during her initial year at Yale. While she wasn't sure what was going on, she was intent on working as hard as she could to make the necessary improvements. However, she began to experience some strange physical problems, and it was alarming, to say the least.

"We were in the weight room lifting, and my hands would get stuck to the bars," she said. "Whenever I grabbed something it would take ten or fifteen seconds to let go; my hand wouldn't respond to what I was doing. So I thought that was pretty odd, why is that happening?"

It was the same thing when she tried to release a doorknob or a fork or a pen, so when she went home to England for Christmas break, her mother took her to a doctor for an examination and it was determined that Ona likely had some nerve damage that could be corrected with surgery. Of course that didn't fully explain why her performance on the field the past two years had slipped. Not satisfied with the original diagnosis, Karen accompanied her daughter back to Yale for the start of the second semester with the intention of having doctors at Yale delve into the case.

"It was when I went back to Yale with her and they started doing extensive tests that she talked to a friend who said her symptoms sounded like what her mother had," said Karen. "I started doing research online and we thought, 'My goodness, this might be it.' The doctors agreed so they did more extensive testing where they have to stick needles into your muscles and do electric impulses."

The diagnosis came back, and it was what the McConnells feared: myotonic dystrophy, the most common form of adult muscular dystrophy, an inherited disorder affecting approximately one in eight thousand people worldwide. The disease causes muscles to weaken and progressively deteriorate in the heart, brain, and gastro-intestinal tract as well as the endocrine, skeletal, and respiratory systems.

OK, Ona thought, what do I have to do to get better? "That's when they told me there was no cure," she said.

So, what does an eighteen-year-old college freshman, with so much life in front of her, do when she's told that her body is going to begin failing her to the point where she may be wheelchair-bound, her life expectancy will be chopped by years and perhaps even decades, and there's no cure for what afflicts her?

"That was definitely hard news, but the first question I asked was, 'Can I still play?'" Ona said, laughing at the thought. "My mom and dad were like, 'Ona, this is a little more important.' But I really wanted to play. It's a downer, yes, your life might be shorter, you're going to get weaker, everything is going to get worse and we don't know what's going to happen. And yes, I definitely have days where I say, 'Yeah, this sucks.' But honestly—and I kind of surprised myself by thinking this—there's nothing I can do about it. So I'm not going to sit here and just be unhappy. I continued to stay positive and, you know what, I'm going to do exactly what I was going to do before and keep it up."

Which impressed the hell out of her mother. "I was devastated and crying my eyes out, and she was taken aback and a little bit depressed, but she got into a better place within three to four weeks and she started to come around saying, 'I'm not going to let this stop me.' She called me one night and she said, 'I'm going to go into medicine, and I'm going to find a cure and I'm going to win the Nobel Prize.' That was her attitude, it was amazing. That made me feel like, 'OK, I've got to stop moping around here and crying my eyes out.' We had to move forward and find a way to deal with this."

GET A GRIP

When Ona broke the news to Pam Stuper about her diagnosis back in March of 2010, the coach admitted to being floored. "It was hard to hear, and I felt so bad for her," Stuper said. But as she listened to Ona explain what myotonic dystrophy was, and that there was no cure, Stuper quickly came to attention and asked what she and the team could do to help.

"The first thing you need to do with any crisis is to be calm and be there for the student-athlete, hear the news and help her out from there," Stuper said. "And then it was trying to understand the disease and how to help her continue with training and playing, if that was possible. And a lot of that was learning from Ona, learning what she was hearing from the doctors, to understand what was being affected, and how we could manage her training. Once we got through that part, it was, 'What can we do to raise awareness and support Ona?'"

Ona and Stuper met about once a week for breakfast and discussed a number of potential fund-raising ideas, and they settled on a campaign entitled "Get a Grip," which they hoped would shine light on the disease, procure funding for research, and offer support to those afflicted.

The centerpiece of the program was the Goal-A-Thon, where people could pledge to donate money for every goal the Bulldogs scored during the season, and they kicked it off with events surrounding the first game of the 2010 season against Sacred Heart at Johnson Field. The team sold T-shirts in front of the main dining hall on campus, Commons, and then the day of the game other Yale athletes pitched in with the T-shirt sales, and handing out blue wristbands to those making Goal-A-Thon pledges.

"We had a great crowd," Ona recalled. "I basically harassed people to come, and my teammates did the same thing."

And in an absolute Hollywood script end to the day, the Bulldogs opened an insurmountable 5–0 lead and Stuper sent Ona into the game for the final ten minutes, the first live action of her Yale career. "I was smiling for the next week after that," said Ona, who appeared in two other games and finished the season without allowing a goal in just over thirty minutes of playing time. "My mom told me afterward that everyone was yelling when I went in, and I didn't even hear them, I was just so excited to play. It was unbelievable, a great feeling. I was really proud of my school and my team for being part of it, so the pride I have for playing for Yale is amazing."

By the end of the year, the Bulldogs scored fifty-two goals, tied for second-most in team history, and the Get a Grip campaign raised more than $50,000, all of which was donated to the Myotonic Dystrophy Foundation, on which Ona had already become the youngest board member.

"It was really a neat thing to be a part of," said Erin Carter, the 2011 team captain. "Our goal was to raise money, but we really wanted to get the word out and make sure people know that this is something people suffer from, like our teammate. To raise that much money really put it into perspective for us because as college students, a research position is something very tangible; we know people who have worked over the summer as research assistants, and the fact that we could fund a whole position and that person might be able to contribute to the cure for myotonic dystrophy, it was great."

Now, expectations were soaring in 2011 for the second Get a Grip initiative. Two days before Yale's September 3 season opener against nationally ranked Stanford in a game that would be about so much more than just field hockey, the first batch of T-shirts—which were designed by Carter—were already sold out, so Stuper had to place another order to meet the demand for game day. And with fliers being handed out around campus, a Facebook event page created, tweets via Twitter, and e-mails being sent to alumni and friends of the program, the team was stoked about playing in front of a potentially big crowd, all the while raising more money for a great cause.

The only foreseeable problem for Stuper was the game itself. Even though her top seven scorers from last year's 12–5 team were back, there was no question that twentieth-ranked Stanford was the stronger team. That being the case, Stuper was already dealing with the inevitability that she probably wouldn't be able to get Ona into the game.

"It'll be tougher to do it this time," Stuper said, alluding to the fact that Ona's condition had also deteriorated since last year. "Last year Sacred Heart was a weaker team than Stanford and we were ahead comfortably enough to do it. I would love to get her into the game, but I always put the best players on the field. If the moment arises, I'll get her out there."

A SPECIAL DAY

As Karen McConnell sat in the stands with her husband, Jerry, and their two sons, Alec and Sam, she could not resist the mist that formed in her eyes as she gazed down at Ona standing on the sideline in her bulky goaltending equipment, so eager and ready to play in a game that she had no chance of playing in.

"I saw Ona on the bench and I thought about how hard it is for her," Karen said, not meaning the physical difficulties that confronted her daughter. "The thing that bothers her the most is the fact that her teammates and her coaches at Yale have never seen her play at the high level she used to play at. When she and I watched Yale play (when Ona was being recruited), we both felt she was easily at that level, maybe even better."

Karen was right. A healthy Ona would have been starting, and starring, for the Bulldogs on this warm and sunny opening day of the 2011 season. Karen was also right that Yale would never know how good Ona once was.

This was her daughter's day, no one else's, yet Ona was one of only three Elis (the other two were freshmen, one being the backup goaltender) who did not see action in the 3–1 loss to Stanford. As happy as Karen was to see the Yale community once again come out to support Ona in her fight against myotonic dystrophy, it was offset by the sadness regarding why this day was necessary in the first place.

As team-oriented as Ona is, she would never put herself or the Get a Grip campaign ahead of the team, but in reality, the game was secondary to the cause. Sports are a vital part of American culture, and they are often the lifeblood of the university experience, whether it's 100,000 people at the Big House on an autumn afternoon in Ann Arbor, Michigan, or 331 folks, most adorned in blue Get a Grip T-shirts and accessorized with blue wristbands, hanging out at Johnson Field. This wasn't about field hockey, and it wasn't about the fact that Yale was now 0–1 on the season. The next day's game at Quinnipiac would be about trying to get that first win, but this day was about raising awareness of a horrible disease for which there is no cure, and to keep alive hope that someday one would be discovered.

"My emotions were everywhere," Karen said. "The *Yale Daily News* interviewed me and I almost started crying. It was a terrific day. For field hockey, usually the stands have a few parents and friends, but they were packed, it was a huge turnout, and it was wonderful. And I think her team is now really understanding what she's going through. When they put on the fund-raiser last year, she had been diagnosed after her freshman season was over and they weren't playing hockey, so nobody really noticed anything. They knew in theory she was ill, but they couldn't physically see the problem. Throughout the course of the last year they really saw how Ona suffered and how difficult it was for her to do a lot of the stuff they were doing. I think this fundraiser, it was in the minds of the team much more, and it was significant for them, so that was very exciting for her."

As expected, the days leading up to the game were hectic. Classes had begun, and that meant instantaneous homework. At Yale, and the other Ivies, there's no break-in period at the start of a term. "Oh yeah, we get right into it," said Ona, whose fall semester consisted of Fundamentals of Neuroscience, Physiological Systems, Media in Modern America, and a statistics course. "I had a quiz my second day."

When game day finally arrived, things couldn't have started much better, as Ona's best friend on the team, junior forward Maddy Sharp, scored just 1:56 into the contest, and that stood as the only goal of the first half as the Bulldogs rode that early momentum with sophomore goalie Emily Cain holding the Cardinals at bay. However, Stanford broke through early in the second half with a decisive three-goal flurry in a span of seven minutes to win the game and dampen the enthusiasm of the day, though only slightly.

When it was over, and the Bulldogs had gathered at their post-game tailgate party, coach Stuper summed up the day best when she said, in effect, she knew it was going to be a tough battle and Yale would have to really fight hard to win the game, but that's what Ona does every day when she comes out to practice or simply goes to a class. Every day is a fight.

"It definitely made me feel good," Ona said. "I'm not a teary-eyed person, but my mom, I think she was definitely close to it."

RIDING THE BENCH

After the excitement of the start of the season and the Get a Grip fund-raiser had died down, Ona reflected on that busy weekend—which had also included a surprising 3–2 shootout defeat to neighboring rival Quinnipiac the day after the loss to Stanford—with her typically upbeat attitude.

Last year, with Yale comfortably ahead against Sacred Heart, coach Pam Stuper had sent Ona in to play the last ten minutes, but as Stuper had feared, the opportunity did not arise against Stanford, and Ona was fine with that.

"I wasn't disappointed," she said. "I had thought about it before the game and I asked myself if I'd be disappointed, because I knew we probably wouldn't be up in the game. But I wasn't disappointed. Even though I'm sitting on the bench, I feel so much a part of the team. I'm cheering for them and you feel like you're in the game. And the thing is, I guess it is my day, so I almost felt fine that I wasn't playing because the game was for myotonic dystrophy, so I felt a huge part of it."

She didn't have that same warm and fuzzy feeling, and she figured coach Stuper wouldn't either, after the Bulldogs lost to Quinnipiac. "We were clearly the better team, we just didn't execute," said Ona. "We had a huge advantage in shots and corners, so it was a heartbreaker."

Emily Cain had done her job, but like all goalies in the penalty stroke shootout, she was pretty much helpless. After two scoreless overtime periods in field hockey, the game is decided much the same way penalty kicks break a tie in soccer. Shooter versus goalie, one-on-one, and as in soccer, the shooter has a tremendous advantage with the ball placed a mere seven yards from the goal line, and the goalie having to guard a net that measures twelve feet wide by seven feet high.

It's a nightmare for a goalie, though Ona has a different take. "Nobody really puts pressure on the goalie because they know how tough it is, so there's actually more pressure on the shooters because they're supposed to score," she said. Unfortunately, two of Yale's shooters did not score, and Quinnipiac put four behind Cain to win the game.

A week removed from that letdown, the mood was decidedly happier after the Bulldogs traveled to Long Island and wiped out Hofstra, 5–3, for their first victory of the year. "Everyone's face lit up," said Ona. "We needed a win; we knew we were good enough to get it against Hofstra, so we were very happy."

This was a game Ona thought she'd have a chance to get into when Yale opened a 4–0 lead early in the second half, but Hofstra scored twice and the victory wasn't secured until Erica Borgo scored with sixteen minutes to go. "Every time I see someone get up and get ready to go in, I'm like 'Man, I wish I could be doing that.' I always hope for the fact that we're up 5–0 or something because I might get a chance if we're winning by a lot and the coach would put me in."

HERO WORSHIP

Ona's wish came true the following weekend, which, as it turned out, wound up being a weekend for the ages for her.

To recap:

In the locker room before the annual alumnae day game against Harvard, a former Yale field hockey goalie and team captain named Lorraine Pratte-

Lewis, class of 1978, who had been invited by Stuper to say a few inspirational words to the team, certainly struck the right chord with Ona when she said, "Ona, you're my hero." The Bulldogs stormed onto Johnson Field and Harvard never had a chance as Yale cruised to a 5–1 victory in its Ivy League opener.

The next day, Sacred Heart came to town, and with her team comfortably in front in the second half, Stuper sent Ona in for her first game action of the season, and while Ona gave up her first goal as a Bulldog, she also made her first save, as Yale ran away to a 9–1 victory.

In the two games, the team scored fourteen goals, so that was going to look awfully good on the Goal-A-Thon tally sheet, not to mention the two victories got the Bulldogs back on track following a loss to Albany and evened their record at 3–3.

And then later Sunday evening, Ona was strolling down the brick sidewalk along Broadway Street in the heart of campus on her way to get a bite to eat at Gourmet Heaven, known around campus as G-Heav, when she bumped into her teammate, Taylor Sankovich, a senior from Short Hills, New Jersey. "I was already thinking my weekend couldn't get any better, and then I saw Taylor and she said to me, 'Ya know, Ona, I thought it was amazing and very exciting to see you out there today. I thought it was really inspiring.' I was like, 'This is the best weekend ever,'" Ona said.

So yeah, that qualifies as a pretty good weekend, for Ona, and for anyone, really.

When Stuper took over the Yale program in 2005, one of her off-the-field priorities was to reach out to the alumnae, so she designated one game to be the centerpiece of an alumnae day function. That day in the odd-numbered years was the home game against Harvard, and in the even-numbered years when Yale had to travel to Cambridge, Stuper picked another game.

Pratte-Lewis and her former teammates Emily Bateson '80 and Carol Roberts '81 bought into the idea and had been making the sojourn back to New Haven each year. In 2010, Pratte-Lewis learned of Ona's medical condition and she was deeply moved by the story.

"I had a chance to meet Ona after the announcement of her situation and the (Get a Grip) campaign, and I just wanted to introduce myself," said Pratte-Lewis. "We talked and she told me about what it was like going through her days and the difficulties. It was very compelling, and she was just very thoughtful, told us about her situation in a way where she wasn't looking for any sympathy or sad faces, and I was incredibly impressed."

For the next year, Ona was fixed in Pratte-Lewis's thoughts, and she couldn't wait to get back to Yale to touch base with her.

"One thing that really struck me was how she talked about how difficult it was for her to sleep at night because of the cramping, and that really stayed with me all year," Pratte-Lewis explained. "I would be tired late at night, looking forward to a good night's sleep, and I found myself thinking about Ona and how she didn't get that luxury often."

Stuper invited Pratte-Lewis, Bateson, and Roberts into the locker room before the game to speak to the team. When Pratte-Lewis took the floor, she congratulated the senior class on the success it had enjoyed, she told goalie Emily Cain how important it was to play for the seniors, and then she closed with a message for Ona. "I just turned to Ona who was standing right next to me and I said that she was my hero, and what an honor it was to meet her last year and that I thought about her so much. I don't know if she was surprised that I was talking about her, but I felt a nice connection that I had a chance to say something directly to her right from my heart. She's out there every day in those pads, and she's a part of the team, and you can tell that there's an enormous amount of respect for her from her teammates. It was a very emotional moment for me."

It was for Ona as well, and with a big smile she said, "That was very cool."

Ona admitted to being a little disappointed that she didn't get to play against Harvard, even when the Bulldogs opened a 5–0 lead with twenty minutes left. Stuper opted to relieve Cain with freshman Heather Schlesier because she needed some game experience, and Ona understood why, but still, she said, "I wish I could have had a part of that win."

However, there was hope for a chance against Sacred Heart—the team she had played against in 2010 on the day of the inaugural Get a Grip game. And she was right. Yale scored the first nine goals, and after Cain and Schlesier had taken their turns, Stuper signaled down the sideline for Ona to get her mask on and get in there.

"It was awesome," Ona said. "Last year I got to play a few minutes, but I never touched the ball in any of the games I played. So this year I wanted to go out there and be more confident and stronger than I was last year. The assistant coach (Tamara Durante) pulled me aside and said, 'Be confident, be strong, you've got this,' and I was like, 'OK, I can do that.' I was way overjoyed, smiling, happy, almost laughing because I was so excited."

Ona was on the field barely a minute when the play came down into the Yale end. One of the Sacred Heart players broke free and fired a shot, Ona dove to her right, stopped the ball with her upper body, and the crowd screamed in delight. However, the rebound got away, another shot was attempted, and it glanced off a Yale defender inside the box, which necessitated an automatic penalty stroke for Sacred Heart's Leah Salindong.

Penalty strokes are tough enough for completely healthy, mobile goalies, so Ona was really at a disadvantage, and sure enough, Salindong scored. "I was pretty calm, and it was a very good shot. I almost got there, I was very close to it, but it would have been tough for any of the goalies on our team to stop that shot."

That goal mattered little, only to finalize the 9–1 Yale victory, and after bumping into Sankovich later in the evening, that goal was the last thing on Ona's mind. Foremost, she was thinking, wouldn't it be great if we could play Sacred Heart every week?

EYE OF THE TIGER

What wouldn't be great is playing Princeton every week. Not unless you're some kind of masochist.

Princeton is far and away the dominant Ivy League field hockey team, and had been since the players on its current roster were in diapers. Entering 2011, the Tigers had won or shared the League championship in sixteen of the previous seventeen years, and had won their last twenty-four Ancient Eight games dating back to September 2007.

However, as the Bulldogs prepared for their annual attempt to knock off the bully, they were emboldened by the fact that this particular Princeton might be ripe for the taking. Playing without four of their best players who were on leave from school to train with the United States national team, the Tigers lost games on back-to-back days the previous weekend. They went up to Dartmouth and saw their Ivy winning streak end with a 2–1 defeat, and then traveled to Syracuse to meet the fifth-ranked Orange and were embarrassed, 5–0.

Now, the other way to look at this was that rather than playing a suddenly vulnerable team at the right time, it might be Yale's misfortune to be catching the Tigers at the absolute wrong time, when they were in an ornery mood and loaded for bear.

"We were feeling very confident, and our coach wanted us to play as if it was just any other game, which I think is the way she should have done it, but I could tell the team was more excited than usual to play them," Ona said. "Last year we were more frightened to play them because they've been known as the number one unbeatable team, but this year after Dartmouth beat them and they were missing four of their best players, we were more excited to play them."

Sure enough, the Bulldogs did not back down and they played with confidence, but they made just enough of the little mistakes that make the difference and Princeton prevailed, 3–2. Allison Behringer beat Emily Cain with a shot from the top of the circle 17:23 into the game, but ninety-one seconds later freshman Jessie Accurso tied it for Yale off a rebound, her first collegiate goal. Yale then gave up a backbreaking goal just twenty-three seconds before halftime as Sydney Kirby scored, and twenty-one minutes into the second half Kirby tallied again to make it 3–1. The Bulldogs inched closer when Erin Carter scored off a corner with 3:47 remaining, but they couldn't get the tying goal.

Ona stood on the sidelines, watching helplessly, as she usually does, and she could see Stuper growing angrier as the game went on because the Bulldogs were in the game but were wasting opportunities to turn the tide in their direction, and it cost them.

"I've never seen our coach so upset," said Ona. "She said, 'I did everything possible in my power to prepare you for this game; we were prepared and we should have won, but I don't know what goes on in your heads. I don't know what else I can do, there's nothing else I can do.'

"I have to agree with her. I swear I don't know what goes on inside some of these kids' heads. And what's frustrating, since I'm not playing, I have no control over anything on the field. If I'm on the field, I can yell something, which I do from the bench, but it's not the same thing as being on the field. Everyone was upset after the game, but Dartmouth lost, so the championship is really up for grabs and that's our major goal, the Ivy championship, and we're still in the game. If Princeton hadn't lost last weekend, we'd be way more depressed than we are right now."

The Bulldogs bounced back the following weekend and continued their Ivy push with a one-sided 7–2 victory over Cornell, then put forth a great effort before losing a non-League game to UConn, the fourth-ranked team in the nation, 1–0.

And then it was time for midterms, and what little time Ona had for a social life was officially wiped away. This week her days consisted of classes in the morning and early afternoon, field hockey practice, and then lengthy evening study sessions in Bass Library. "Yeah, I'm pretty much secluded in the library at night," she said. "I don't like to study in my room, I like to separate sleeping from studying, so I go to the library with all my stuff and do my work. Bass isn't my favorite spot, but it stays open the longest."

This was a difficult week for just about every Yale student, but it's particularly challenging for the athletes who, in addition to their course load, invest a sizeable portion of their day to their chosen sport.

"It's a very big stressor for some people," Ona said. "Field hockey takes a huge amount of time and you don't have as much time to study when you need to. And it's not like we can say to our coach, 'Hey, I have this test tomorrow, I need the time.' That doesn't fly with her. She expects us to manage our time and do well. I mean, we're at Yale, we work hard, and it's up to us to do it. We're all adults; we need to figure out what you're going to do to study and get the material done before or after hockey."

Now factor in the obstacle that myotonic dystrophy presented for Ona as she studied for this week's exams in her physiological systems and statistics classes. "It takes me much longer to do things," she said. "I have a tremor so it's harder to type, and when I'm tired I shake a bit more. And for one of my classes you have to write on note cards or you're not going to do well and that's hard for me. It hurts to write, it takes me much longer to write than anyone else, so the time thing is a factor."

Early in the practice week, as the Bulldogs prepared for their lengthiest road trip of the season to play against nationally ranked opponents Michigan and Northwestern in Chicago, Ona had already noticed the toll midterm week was taking on the team.

"What's hard for most of the players, they get out to the field and all they can think about is the midterms," she said Thursday. "What I like to do when

I'm on the field, I like to literally forget everything else and just play. You can tell when they're out there they're thinking, 'Oh my God, what am I going to do?' I just think it's not worth stressing out about because it's not like you're going to study better by stressing out. You can tell on the bus (riding from campus to the practice field) if someone had a hard day, and then they say, 'Oh my god, we have practice.' And I'm like, 'Do you know what it means to have practice? You get to play a game you want to play. That's why you signed up.'"

Of course, Ona had a slightly different perspective on this. Because she rarely played in the games, every practice meant something to her. This was the only chance she had to put her mask on, stand between those goal posts, and compete in the sport she loves. For those two hours, it doesn't matter what's happening elsewhere in her life; she's there to play field hockey. The rest of the team sometimes takes practice for granted and often thinks of it as drudgery, but that's because they know come the weekend, they will be playing.

The Cornell game was a bit different, though. Ona knew she wouldn't be playing against UConn, but when the Bulldogs jumped to a big lead against the Big Red, and every player on the team was involved in the victory except Ona, she was perplexed and disappointed.

"I was upset about that game," she said. "It's disappointing to come off the field with a huge win, everybody is happy, and everybody had a part except for you. I'm happy for my team that we won, but for me, it's kind of hard to feel like we won."

Not playing had become more of an issue this year for Ona, because while she understood her condition was worsening and it was hard for coach Stuper to trust her in a game situation, she was now an upperclassman, and watching freshman Heather Schlesier get playing time ahead of her was frustrating.

"It's hard to see a freshman overtake me," Ona said. "I think I'm getting better, but the rate I'm getting better is less than the rate that the other goalies are getting better, so no matter how much I try, I'll never overtake them."

Still, when Yale was winning 5–0 against Harvard a couple weeks ago, and 7–2 against Cornell the other day, it was clearly the better team in both games, and when there were less than twenty minutes to play in each, it seemed pretty obvious—at least to Ona—that those games were no longer in doubt. So why not let her play? "It is getting harder and harder to deal with it," Ona said.

TEAM BONDING

For anyone who happened to be strolling around the outer edge of the North-western University campus on the sunny afternoon of October 8, there was quite a sight to see as the Yale field hockey team, decked out in its Spandex shorts and sports bras, was frolicking around in not quite icy, but certainly uncomfortably cold, Lake Michigan.

"It was freezing, but that was a pretty good bonding experience," Ona said the following Monday in recalling the ten or so minutes the team spent in the lake after its disheartening 7–1 loss to thirteenth-ranked Michigan.

When the Bulldogs are at home, they often conduct their postgame debriefing sessions while taking ice baths in the training room of the Smilow Field Center. "It holds about eight people so we get into groups and we talk about the points that our coach told us to concentrate on before the game and we decide how we think we did on them during the game and we give them a score from one through ten," Ona explained.

Well, this was a game that definitely needed to be talked about—the worst loss of the season by far—so the team figured Lake Michigan, chilled by Chicago's crisp autumn air and located a few hundred feet from Lakeside Field where the game had been played, was as good a place as any.

"She basically killed us," Ona said of Stuper's voluble speech in between the Lake Michigan excursion and the team dinner at California Pizza Kitchen later in the evening. "Pam hates losing, and she hates losing when she thinks we could have won. Losing 7–1 should never happen, and she told us in the meeting, 'I've tried to take it down a notch, I've tried to be positive and talk to you guys nicely, and that isn't working, so I am not going to do this anymore. Now it's going to be tough love. If I want someone to go left it's going to be go left, God damn it. And if they have a problem with my tone, then they come off the pitch, cry and get back out there when they pull themselves together.'"

Well, Ona wasn't sure if Stuper's verbal assault was the difference or not, but the next day the Bulldogs were a completely different team and they upset their Northwestern hosts, 3–2. Stuper had been at Yale for eight years as an assistant and now six as the head coach, and she told her team afterward that the Bulldogs had never beaten an opponent ranked as high as number fourteen Northwestern.

"We played like we did when we played UConn," Stuper said. "This was just an incredible team effort, and everybody followed the game plan. [Against Michigan] we didn't play like we could have and should have. We recognized that, went back to the drawing board, and came out playing to our strengths. We haven't traveled like this in five years; the players on this team had never been on a plane trip together. This is also a busy time of the year academically, with lots of midterms, so to be able to get a split against teams from a strong conference like the Big Ten is a tribute to the players' ability to focus."

BOARD MEMBER

When Ona learned in early 2010 that she was suffering from a disease for which there was no cure, the first question she asked the doctors was, "Can I still play field hockey?" The second was, "What can I do to help find a cure?"

In that initial period of sadness when Ona came to understand that her life was never going to be the same, she never once felt sorry for herself. She had an indomitable spirit, whether it was stopping a slap shot on the field, studying for an exam, or logically debating friends on whatever the hot topic of the day was. So once the shock of her situation began to dissipate, which wasn't too long after her diagnosis, she knew she wasn't going to sit idly by as myotonic dystrophy continued to claim victims.

"My parents and I did a lot of research and we found the Myotonic Dystrophy Foundation website," Ona recalled. "My dad called up and there were some overlapping things. The chairman of the board (Jeremy Kelly) was a Morehead Scholar, like my dad; they were based in northern California near where my grandmother lives; and they also told us there was a position open on the board."

Intrigued by the interest the McConnells showed in wanting to be active in the search for a cure, the Foundation asked if someone in the family would like to step up and fill that vacant board position. Ona jumped at the opportunity and the board openly welcomed her because it knew that as a young person dealing with the disease, she would provide a unique and invaluable perspective, not to mention an energetic passion to the cause.

"I wanted to be active, I wanted to do something about this, I hate sitting back and not being able to do anything about a situation, so I definitely wanted to be involved," she said.

Once a month Ona joins a conference call with her fellow board members to discuss various ways to raise money and awareness, and she'll spend an hour to an hour and a half brainstorming with some very accomplished and influential people, among them: Kelly, a native of England who lived in Mill Valley, California, and was on the management team of Provident Funding who had two young sons diagnosed with myotonic dystrophy; Tim Kaine, the former governor of Virginia and now the chairman of the Democratic National Committee, who became aware of the disease through his relationship with a Virginia family whose sons are afflicted, and he decided his experience with health care reform legislation and his skills as a fund-raiser would be well suited to the Foundation; John Brekka, a managing partner of a law firm in Fort Lauderdale, Florida, who, like Ona, suffers from the disease; and Todd Stone, a defense attorney in Richmond, Virginia, who joined the cause because his wife and two sons all have been diagnosed and started the 501(c)(3) nonprofit Stone Circle of Friends which raises funds as a subgroup to the Foundation.

One of the talking points on the agenda for this month's call was finalizing the search for someone to serve as the chief point person for fund-raising, and one of the key parts of the discussion was figuring out which qualifications for that position were most important. And at the end of the call, plans were made to attend the Empower 2011 Myotonic Dystrophy Family Conference in Clearwater Beach, Florida, in early December. Ona was excited because she would be able to make it, as the conference fortuitously fell at the end of Yale's reading week and just before the start of finals, so she wouldn't miss any class time.

"We need to have a presence there and to be more visible," she said of the conference, where she would be asked to deliver a speech. "And it's great that I can go because I do take pride that I'm representing the younger people who are affected by this. The important input that I give to the board is that I'm a different generation, and we need to approach people from my generation and make them understand what this disease is."

THE SAVE

As the clock wound down to end the first half of Yale's October 30 game against hapless Holy Cross at Johnson Field, Ona couldn't believe what she was witnessing. The red-hot Bulldogs had built off their big, season-changing victory over Northwestern by winning their next four games against Dartmouth, Fairfield, Penn, and Columbia by a cumulative score of 16–3. With a 9–6 record, and 5–1 in the Ivy League, they were firmly in contention for the League championship, yet they were barely beating the Crusaders, a team that had won just one of its seventeen games.

"We were horrible and we were only winning 3–0," Ona said. "Our coach was basically swearing at us at halftime and saying this was pretty embarrassing."

Ona was none too thrilled, either. She had expected this to be a blowout, and given that inevitability she was certain that Stuper would let her play at the end, but with Holy Cross still so close, Ona feared her opportunity would be gone. "I knew this was the game I'd have the best chance to play in because Holy Cross has been losing all year, so I was a little worried," she said.

With Stuper's tongue-lashing still ringing in their ears, the Bulldogs got serious and, coupled with the cold reality that Yale was simply a far better team than Holy Cross, the second half was the mismatch everyone predicted. Yale scored five times in the first twenty-two minutes after intermission, so Stuper gave freshman Heather Schlesier about fifteen minutes of playing time, and she sent Ona in for the final 6:32, setting the stage for the on-field highlight of Ona's Yale career.

Yale was so dominant that it hadn't even allowed Holy Cross to attempt a shot against starter Emily Cain or Schlesier, and as the final seconds were melting away, the shot count was an eye-popping 44–0. "Neither of our goalies had touched the ball, so I was thinking it was pretty unlikely that they'll come down, but at least I got a chance to play so I don't care," Ona said.

But then there was a slight crease in Yale's impenetrable wall and here came the Crusaders, driving toward the net for the first time all day, and Ona was the last line of defense.

"Before the game, one of our goals was how about we get a shutout, we've only had one this season," Ona said. "We knew we were going to win, so we made that our goal. So when they were coming toward the net, it was almost like it was in slow motion in my mind. It was so funny because there were two Holy Cross players literally fighting for the ball; they were like 'I got it, no I got it' so finally one of them decided to shoot and I managed to stop it, and the ball was right in front of me and I was able to clear it. So when it was gone from the circle, it was the best thing ever because I made the save, I kept the shutout, and I did exactly what I was supposed to do. It was awesome. I was very excited and all the parents were excited and they came up to me after and said, 'You got the most action and you made the save.'"

Stuper remarked afterward, "That was one of our goals for today, to get a shutout. I was very proud of Ona for making that save."

Ona was obviously overjoyed by her contribution to the game, and she also had another reason to be smiling brightly. Yale's eight goals pushed its season total to a school record sixty-two, shattering the mark of fifty-five set in 1998. Of course for every goal the Bulldogs scored, money was donated to the fight against myotonic dystrophy through Yale's Get a Grip campaign.

"Yes, it was a very good day," Ona said.

The victory stretched Yale's winning streak to six, and it kept the Bulldogs tied with Princeton for the top spot in the Ivy standings with one game remaining, Yale hosting Brown and Princeton traveling to Penn. Because the Bulldogs lost to Princeton, the only way they could win the Ivy outright and advance to the NCAA tournament play-in game was to beat Brown and hope Penn could shock the Tigers. Still, if both teams won, Yale would gain its first piece of an Ivy title since 1980.

"We're all hoping, but we know it's pretty doubtful they'll lose," said Ona. "We're focused on winning our game, and if we do that we'll be Ivy champions. It would be disappointing because the NCAA was one of our goals, but I know we'll be very happy if we can get part of the Ivy League championship."

SILVER LINING

The e-mail came early on the afternoon of November 8, and it contained the one sentence every player on the Yale team expected, but was nonetheless disappointed to read: "We didn't make it."

Stuper was informed that the Bulldogs, despite finishing tied for first with a 6–1 League record thanks to their season-ending 7–0 win over Brown, would not be receiving one of the at-large bids to the NCAA tournament.

"Coach had told us if we weren't going to get a bid, she was supposed to be on the conference call (to determine the bids)," Ona explained. "If we had a chance for a bid, then she wouldn't be on the call. Well, she was on the call, so she let us know, and everybody was pretty sad. We're actually ranked ahead of Princeton, but they're going to play. We reached one of our goals, being Ivy champions, so we're all going to be happy, but it would have been exciting to play in the tournament."

That e-mail signaled the official conclusion to Ona's junior season, and it left her struggling with clashing emotions regarding what had transpired over the previous three months.

"I knew that I probably wouldn't play much due to the fact that my condition is a progressive disease and I'm going to continue to get worse and not better," she said. "Last year I played about thirty minutes of the season and I didn't touch the ball, and this year I played about fourteen minutes, but I actually made two saves and that made a world of difference for me. So to be honest, when I look back on this season I'd rather have this season any day. In that one game (against Holy Cross) where I made the one save of the three goalies and saved the shutout, I couldn't have been more excited, so I'm not feeling too disappointed."

However, there were moments of undeniable disappointment when Stuper passed on opportunities to let Ona play, opting instead to give much of that backup playing time to the freshman goalie, Heather Schlesier.

It happened again in the last game of the year, Yale's easy victory over Brown on Senior Day at Johnson Field. The outcome was never really in doubt, and after Yale had opened a 5–0 lead, Ona began to think about playing in a historic game where the Bulldogs would be clinching a tie for first place in the Ivy League, something they hadn't done in field hockey in thirty-one years. However, as the minutes were ticking away, Emily Cain was still on the field and Ona didn't understand why.

"With about fifteen minutes left we were way ahead and I was thinking I'd play," Ona said. "And then there was five minutes left and she turned around and said, 'Oh my God, Heather, I forgot to put you in. Warm up and I'll put you in.'"

That was like a proverbial punch in the stomach, and a wave of anger flooded over Ona because she knew she wouldn't be playing.

"That was really disappointing. I would have expected they would put me in for the last five minutes. It's like I've worked three years for that one day, and Heather has worked three months. I would have been OK with ten seconds, just to be able to say that I played in the game where we won the Ivy League championship. Heather has three more years, and I think I should have been given that opportunity. I was so happy we won, but I had the feeling that I

50

FALL

didn't even play and everyone else did. I was torn, I had these two feelings at the same time, and it was upsetting for me."

Ona was uncertain what her athletic future held. Her condition was worsening, and she said, "You never know what's going to happen, and that's the worst part; I don't know what the next year is going to be like, or even what each day is going to be like."

Class work was already a difficult endeavor. Yale allows a student in each of Ona's classes to be her note taker, and she had been working with voice-recognition technology to assist her on the computer because she has a tough time typing, especially for long stretches. But when it came to exams, she had to do everything herself, and there was no escaping the pain in her hands or the fatigue that often overcomes her.

Field hockey had been her passion, her joy, her escape from the rigors of a Yale curriculum, and a way to prove to herself and to the world that she could fight the disease that afflicts her, and maybe, just maybe, beat it.

"It is harder to play, it takes more energy and effort to play and practice, and I feel much more tired than the other kids, but there's no way I'm going to give up," she said. "My parents say I should think about quitting hockey, it's a big-time commitment, maybe I shouldn't do it, but I said, 'No, I'm going to do it exactly the way I would have done it without this problem.' My condition is going to stay the same or get worse until we find a cure, and so I might as well do what I love to do. I love field hockey, I love it every day. I can't stop living my life, and every day I play is my way of fighting this disease. I feel like every time I'm out there it's like I beat this disease today. It's like, I'm here, you're not gonna stop me."

LUCKY MKOSANA

DARTMOUTH MEN'S SOCCER

Lucky Mkosana was ready, although he wasn't quite sure what he was ready for. Over the course of several late-August 2011 days, the northern New England region, including the picturesque town of Hanover, New Hampshire, where Dartmouth College has lived and breathed for more than two centuries, had been on high alert because Hurricane Irene was on her way, and she'd been in a nasty and destructive mood for nearly a week.

"I was ready for it; it was going to be my first hurricane," said the native of Zimbabwe, who'd come to the United States in 2007 to attend prep school for a year with the goal of eventually qualifying academically to enroll at Dartmouth and play soccer for the Big Green. "I was a little bit disappointed."

Irene first made landfall down in Puerto Rico before starting a terrifying track through the Caribbean and then up the Eastern Seaboard, creating panic in the major metropolitan areas of Washington, Philadelphia, New York, and Boston. There were mandatory evacuations; mass transit systems and airports were shut down; and by the time Irene had blown her last breath up in the Canadian Maritimes, more than seven million homes and businesses had lost electrical power, flooding had reached record levels in many parts of New England, significant property damage had been inflicted, states of emergency had been declared in eleven states, and the cost of the carnage was cresting at about $10 billion, all of which paled in comparison to the nearly sixty deaths blamed on the storm.

"I was kind of excited about it because I wanted to see how it would feel, even though it's not a good thing to be excited about," said Lucky, who clearly understood the severity of the storm and the havoc it had wrought, but nonetheless was intrigued by what it would be like to experience a hurricane. "We just got pretty hard rain, and it was a little windy, but that was it. When it started I thought it was going to be the calm before the storm, but then nothing really came."

It was hard to tell what Lucky was more disappointed about, though—the fact that Irene had petered out by the time she reached Dartmouth, or that she forced the cancellation of the Big Green's scrimmage against neighboring Franklin Pierce College. It may have only been a scrimmage, but it was going to be a chance to play a soccer game, and Lucky has lived to play from the time he was restlessly knocking around in his mother's womb twenty-four years earlier.

"Yes, my mother said I was always kicking, which I think is pretty funny," Lucky said with a smile that can only be called infectious.

If all that kicking was the first clue that he was going to have a future in the game, the second surely was when his mother, Ayda, returned home from the hospital in Bulawayo, Zimbabwe, and the nursery already contained a prominently displayed soccer ball. "My dad bought me a soccer ball before I was even born, which was kind of ridiculous," Lucky said with another smile and a roll of his dark brown eyes, knowing that it actually wasn't all that ridiculous, not in a place like Zimbabwe.

Yes, people in Zimbabwe are passionate about their soccer, and the game is like a religion there because, as Lucky said, "There's no other big sports, no football or lacrosse. We have soccer, cricket, and maybe some rugby, but most kids grow up watching and playing soccer. That's just the way it is."

Lucky was raised in the town of Plumtree, located in the state of Matabeleland South in the southwest portion of Zimbabwe, only a few miles from the border of Botswana. Barely two thousand people reside in this place, where there's very little industry besides grain milling and brick making, but many folks pass through Plumtree, as it serves as the last major Zimbabwean station on the Bulaway-Cape Town railway.

And while there isn't a whole lot to do there, the suburban-like feel of the neighborhood where Lucky grew up would probably shock many Americans, who only picture the African continent as a place where zebras and giraffes roam the wild and where famine and disease devastate impoverished villages. It is true that Zimbabwe was for a few years in the first decade of the twenty-first century one of the most troubled lands in either hemisphere. But no place is all bad.

"It's the same as everywhere else in the world," Lucky said with a shrug. "There's more affluence than people think. On TV people see the bad parts of Africa, but they don't see the good parts. We were fortunate."

The fourth of Hereinmore and Ayda Mkosana's five children, Lucky rarely wanted for anything. There was always a well-kept house to live in, food on the table, and clothes on the backs of him and his siblings. "It was pretty standard," he said. "I mean we weren't rich, but I guess you'd say we were middle class. For me, Zimbabwe was a good place to grow up."

Not all Zimbabweans could say that. Lucky, however, was truly one of the lucky ones.

PASSION PLAY

Lucky's love of soccer came from his father, who played the game in his youth, and perhaps could have gone on to play professionally had he not opted to take a job with the government of Zimbabwe, get married, and start a family with Ayda.

Hereinmore was a left-footed player who advanced through the school-aged ranks and ended up playing local club soccer, and Lucky remembered when he was young and kicking the ball back and forth in the yard that his dad "still had the touch."

Lucky could never get enough of the game. School in Zimbabwe is a year-long endeavor and there is no summer vacation. Students attend class for three three-month terms, each separated by a one-month interim, and on those breaks, it was non-stop soccer as Lucky would find a match wherever he could.

He'd leave his house barefoot—not because his family couldn't afford sneakers or cleats, but because barefoot was the way you played—and tell his mother he'd see her at dinnertime. Ayda needn't worry that Lucky was going to be running around finding mischief on the streets of Plumtree; she knew he'd be running around on a dusty field with perhaps as many as thirty or forty other boys, and her proof would be the dirty, sweaty clothes clinging to his lithe body when he returned.

"When I was a kid, I wasn't watching cartoons or playing video games like the kids over here (in America)," he said. "I was playing soccer. I'd get up in the morning, go out to play, and I'd be gone all day."

Unlike America where youth sports are generally well-organized—some might argue that they're too well organized and parent intensive—and kids are coached even before they learn to tie their sneakers, Lucky and his pals were pretty much on their own. There was no coaching, no pastel-colored team T-shirts, and there were no "soccer moms" pulling up in a minivan toting a cooler full of orange slices and Capri-Sun drinks.

In Zimbabwe, like the other soccer-loving nations of Africa, the kids would simply congregate at a field—hopefully somebody would have a ball or at least something that was suitably round—and they would have at it, enjoying endless hours of fun.

"I remember one day we had a ball and we kicked it so much it deflated," he said. "Then we had to make another ball with string and play like that. It didn't matter what we had to use; it was the love of soccer. We didn't have coaches when we were young. We just went and did whatever we wanted with the ball, but that's how you developed your skills. We'd have like thirty kids with one ball, and we'd be in pairs, teams of two. You'd try to get the ball and dribble through all those kids and score. That's the most different part about it from home to here. Kids (in America) are coached when they're younger, and they teach them plays and things, but I think they need that freedom when they're young; go get the ball and play with a teammate and develop your skills. It's OK to coach the kids later on, but when you're young, kids just need to enjoy it, and that's what we did."

Lucky's parents had different opinions on how much soccer he should be playing. Hereinmore was a fanatic who dreamed that perhaps his middle son would go on to the professional career that he did not have, so naturally, he encouraged Lucky to play whenever he could. Ayda was always harping on Lucky to pay attention to his grades rather than his dribbling or his corner kicks, and ultimately they struck the perfect parenting balance.

"My mom was afraid that soccer would come between [me and] my studies so she was always worried about that, and my dad wanted me to play soccer, so it worked out pretty good," he said. "If they had been on the same side, maybe I wouldn't be here."

Here would be on the other side of the world, at Dartmouth. It's a place Lucky knew a little about because his older cousin, Methembe Ndlovu, had graduated from Dartmouth and was a member of the Big Green soccer team through 1997. But never in a million years did he think he'd ever see it, let alone study and play soccer there.

That is until a series of cascading events unfolded that altered the course of Lucky's life.

While the rest of the Ivy League was back in session and taking a one-day break from classes to observe Labor Day, Lucky was still on summer vacation.

Of course, it wasn't quite a vacation when you consider coach Jeff Cook was gathering the Dartmouth soccer team twice a day—in the morning for a light workout that was focused mainly on technical work, and then a full-fledged practice in the afternoon. Still, due to the trimester calendar that Dartmouth operates on, Lucky wouldn't be hitting the books until the third week of September, so this had been a fun time to be practicing; hanging out and bonding with the team, particularly the incoming freshmen; and basking in the serenity of a relatively empty campus without having to worry about lectures and labs and tests.

There was no practice on the holiday, so Lucky visited the Norwich, Vermont, home of Alex and Susan Kahan—located just across the Connecticut River that separates Vermont and New Hampshire—and spent the day watching the U.S. Open tennis tournament on television and enjoying a cookout with the people he lovingly refers to as, "my white parents."

Among the many discussions, there was an unhappy recounting of the first two games of the season, which were played over the weekend. The Big Green traveled down to Worcester, Massachusetts, Friday and battled Holy Cross to a scoreless draw, then hosted twenty-fifth-ranked Boston College Sunday at Burnham Field and failed to score again, falling 2–0. It was a frustrating couple of games for Lucky because he'd totaled nine shots on goal (six against Holy Cross) and not one found its intended target.

"Holy Cross came out really fast, but we got control in the second half and we had the upper hand; we were just unlucky," Lucky said. "We had some good shots, and I had a really good opportunity, but it just missed the post and was about an inch from going in. The BC game, they've beaten us the last two years, so it was a really important game for me and the other seniors and coaches; we wanted to beat them really bad. We went in with that mentality, but unfortunately we didn't play well as a team."

The Kahans knew what Lucky was talking about because they were at Burnham Field, as they always were for Big Green home games, cheering on this young man who had become such an integral part of their lives ever since he showed up on their doorstep in the summer of 2007.

So many people had helped Lucky acclimate to life in the United States. Obviously, there was Cook, who discovered Lucky on a recruiting mission in Zimbabwe and was so wowed by his talent and personality that he offered him a chance to come to America. There was Chris Cheney, a teacher and soccer coach at Kimball Union Academy, a co-ed prep school located fifteen miles south of the Dartmouth campus in Meriden, New Hampshire. Cheney helped procure a Kimball scholarship so that Lucky could spend a year there basically training to be a college student and preparing for the all-important SAT exam that would help determine whether he could enroll at Dartmouth. There was Lucky's girlfriend, Nigerian native Fumnanya Ekhator, a political theory and government major and aspiring lawyer whom he'd begun dating in November 2010. And there were the Kahans, who were asked by Cheney to, in effect, be Lucky's surrogate parents while he was at Kimball, thus giving him a support system as he made the difficult transition to his new life.

"When we first met Lucky, Chris Cheney brought him by and said, 'Oh, by the way, can he stay with you guys for a while before school starts?'" Alex Kahan remembered. "It was no big deal, my son (Elisha) would be playing with him on the soccer team, so that was fine. But we really had no idea that he would essentially become our de facto son."

So days like this had become commonplace for Lucky, hanging out with the family he had lived with, gone on vacation with, spent holidays with, and borrowed the car from when he had needed to go somewhere. He was a world away from home, but he was right at home.

DARTMOUTH CLASSIC

And though Lucky was a world away, about six thousand miles and countless time zones, Hereinmore Mkosana was only a mobile phone call away and still able to provide some insight or lend an ear to Lucky.

"I talk to my dad on the phone, weekends mostly, and he asks me about soccer, and if I say it's stressful, he just says to enjoy it and think about when you were young and how you played," Lucky said. "That's what I try to prevent, thinking about pressure. The more pressure, the more bad things can happen. People expect things from you and that's when you don't play well."

It was easy to understand why Lucky would feel some pressure, especially this season when he was a senior, a captain, and a player who would be in the mix for many of college soccer's highest honors. But given his personality, it was also easy to understand why Lucky didn't have much problem with pressure. He played the game with such a natural grace, an understanding of the angles and the ebb and flow, and he had so much fun on the field that pressure never entered into his mind-set.

Of course, it helps when you're as gifted as he is, and that talent was on display in the annual Dartmouth Classic the second weekend of September, when the Big Green defeated South Carolina, 2–0, and then played the eleventh-ranked team in the country, South Florida, to a 3–3 tie.

"He's getting an awful lot of attention this season, and when South Carolina (Dartmouth's first-round opponent) came here, from a BCS conference, and then South Florida, I don't think they expected an athlete the caliber of Lucky on an Ivy League team, especially here in the woods of New Hampshire," said Dartmouth coach Jeff Cook. "Last year he was too much for the Notre Dame defenders to handle in the NCAAs. It's a combination of his speed and power that make him so dangerous, along with his ball skills. No doubt, any team in the country would take him."

On the first day of the tournament, the Big Green jumped all over South Carolina, scoring twice in the first ten minutes and then making that hold up. Lucky was the central figure on both goals. On the first, just forty-one seconds into the contest, he picked up the ball in the midfield, dribbled to the top of the South Carolina penalty box, and drove a shot that Gamecock goalie Alex Long stopped, but the rebound went right to freshman Alex Adelabu for an easy tap-in, Dartmouth's first goal of the year. Lucky then tallied his first when he pounced on a turnover in the box and was able to chip a shot past Long, who had come out to try and cover up the defensive mistake.

In the championship game, South Florida was the favored team, but the Big Green ran stride for stride with the Bulls, and when sophomore midfielder Patrick Murray converted Nick Pappas's pass for a goal in the eighty-ninth minute, Dartmouth earned the tie. Lucky had scored Dartmouth's first goal when he headed senior midfielder Aaron Gaide's perfectly-placed cross past South Florida goalie Chris Blais, tying the score at 1–1. And then Lucky drew an assist in the twenty-fourth minute on a goal by Adelabu. South Florida scored the next two before Murray's equalizer.

"South Florida was ranked eleventh and most people thought we'd get crushed," said Lucky. "Fortunately, we tied them. It was a tough game, but we played well. The young guys really came through this weekend."

DEEP IN THE HEART OF TEXAS

During his first three years at Dartmouth Lucky had seen quite a bit of the United States, traveling with the Big Green throughout the Northeast as well as to Florida, California, and Indiana. And now early this season, he added Texas to his itinerary. Dallas, to be precise, and his reaction was typical of anyone who visits Big D for the first time: "It's big," he said. "This was my first time in Texas and it's pretty nice, and everything is humongous. Everything is different from [Hanover]."

Actually, Texas was a new experience for most of the Dartmouth traveling party because their participation in the Southern Methodist University Invitational was going to be the first time the Big Green had ever played in the Lone Star State. And on their first night there, Lucky lay in bed reflecting on how fortunate he was to be in this beautiful hotel, in this dazzling American city, playing the game he'd been playing since he was old enough to walk, and wondering where he'd be if so many things hadn't fallen into place for him.

"I was going to forget about soccer," he said, recalling a period after high school in Zimbabwe when he couldn't figure out what his future held. "My mom wanted me to go to college in Zimbabwe and let this soccer thing pass. And I almost did that."

Lucky had made a name for himself in Zimbabwean soccer circles, first at primary school Alan Redfern, then at Plumtree High, later at Thekwane High, where he took his Ordinary Level curriculum, and finally at Mzingwane where he studied his Advanced Level courses. One year he scored fifty-two goals, which anyone who follows the often scoring-challenged world of soccer knows is a remarkable feat. He won athlete-of-the-year awards and League MVP honors, and led his teams to championships, yet despite that glowing resume, there didn't appear to be a future in the game, at least not right away.

He was an excellent student, and he knew he wanted to go to college, but in Zimbabwe, college sports are nonexistent. "Either you play professional soccer or go to college, you don't do both. There are sports teams in college, but they're not competitive and not recognized."

He had every intention of enrolling at National University of Science and Technology in Bulawayo, where he would have focused solely on school, but that plan was scuttled when he inadvertently missed the application deadline. Lucky, who in his heart did not want to give up soccer, claims it was an honest mistake. As it turned out, it was a wonderfully fortuitous flub.

Unable to attend college, and unattached to a professional team, Lucky was in a quandary until he received an invitation to play for the prestigious Aces Youth Soccer Academy in Zimbabwe's capital city of Harare, several hundred miles from home in the northeast sector of the Republic. Rodwell Dhlakama, the coach of Zimbabwe's under-nineteen national team, contacted AYSA on Lucky's behalf, and he joined the program and played with players such as Knowledge Musona, Darryl Nyandoro, and Khama Billiat, all of whom went on to play professionally in Europe.

It was a great nine months in Harare for Lucky, and he said his game was "ten times better coming out of AYSA," which prompted him to inquire about trying out for a pro team in Botswana. But once again, his timing was off and he missed the signing period and was told the next one wouldn't be for six months.

With his mother still pressing him to forget about soccer and go to school, and his father holding out hope that soccer would pan out, Lucky learned of an opportunity that could potentially satisfy both his parents' wishes, as well as his own. There was a showcase tryout being held in Bulawayo and organized in part by his cousin and Dartmouth graduate, Methembe Ndlovu. It was a chance to perform in front of college coaches from the United States, and perhaps earn a scholarship, enabling him to attend school and play soccer in America, far away from his now disease-ravaged, economically crumbling homeland.

"I was hesitant at first because I thought this soccer thing was not going to work out and my parents were getting tired of paying for my trips back and forth," said Lucky. "I begged them and said this was going to be the last time I tried anything concerning soccer. I called my cousin Methembe and asked about the tryouts, he filled me in with the details, and that's when I went to give it a shot."

THE POWER OF SOCCER

The story of Lucky's journey from the barren soccer fields of Zimbabwe to the lush green grass of Dartmouth's Burnham Field was actually rooted in Dartmouth coach Jeff Cook's original coaching stint at the school way back in the mid-1990s.

Upon graduating from Bates College in 1989, Cook went into coaching, and after three years as the top man at Division III Wheaton, he ascended into Division I by accepting Dartmouth head coach Fran O'Leary's offer to be his assistant. One of the Big Green stars at that time was Lucky's cousin, Methembe Ndlovu, and Cook and Ndlovu built a relationship that went beyond coach-player. They became close friends and stayed in contact even after Cook left Dartmouth to become head coach at the University of Cincinnati in 1996, and Ndlovu graduated Dartmouth in 1997.

Eventually, Cook made his way back to Dartmouth and replaced O'Leary as head coach in 2001, and shortly thereafter, he was asked by Ndlovu—who had stayed in the United States to play professionally and later coach—if he'd be interested in hosting a cookout at his home so that another Dartmouth soccer alum, Tommy Clark, could share an idea he had been formulating that almost certainly would help the people in Ndlovu's homeland who were suffering through the tragic outbreak of HIV/AIDS.

Cook happily agreed, and thus, in the living room of his home, the grass roots for the birth of a wildly successful 501(c)3 charitable organization called Grassroot Soccer literally began to germinate. That night, Cook and several prominent members of Dartmouth's soccer alumni base listened intently as Clark outlined a plan to use soccer for the purpose of educating, inspiring, and mobilizing communities to stop the spread of the insidious disease.

Clark was born in Scotland, where his father, Bobby, had been a soccer icon as a member of the national team. When Tommy was fourteen, Bobby moved his family to Zimbabwe because he had been hired as head coach of the Highlanders, a top-tier professional club that would later be coached by Ndlovu. It was a short stay, as political unrest in the country convinced Bobby to come to America where he accepted the head coaching position at Dartmouth in 1985. A brilliant student, Tommy was accepted at Dartmouth and played soccer for his father, captaining the team as a senior in 1991.

After graduation, Tommy wanted to give pro soccer a try, and he felt a pull to return to Zimbabwe, thinking it would be an enjoyable experience reuniting with friends from his youth soccer days, as well as older players who had played for his father with the Highlanders club. Instead, it was a year that would change the course of his life forever.

He learned that several of Bobby's former players and some of his young friends had either died, or were dying, of HIV and AIDS, and the pandemic was cutting a swath of death through the nation. At that time, an estimated 26 percent of the population was infected, a staggering number that Tommy could not believe was even possible. And what struck him most is that nothing was being done to teach children—or, for that matter, adults—ways to prevent contracting the disease. In the school where Tommy spent his days teaching English and coaching the soccer team, there was a deafening silence regarding HIV and AIDS, and it was then he knew his career path was about to spin in a direction he never would have imagined.

Tommy gave up on his dream of playing pro soccer, returned to Hanover to enroll in Dartmouth Medical School, and for the next four years he shuddered from afar as the death toll continued to rise in Zimbabwe and the southern regions of Africa. During the intern year of his pediatrics residency at the University of New Mexico, his concept of Grassroot Soccer began to take shape. The idea was to enlist Africa's revered professional soccer players to become educators in their communities and use their hero-worship status to teach people about HIV and AIDS through a rigid, soccer-themed curriculum established by Grassroot Soccer.

"At that first meeting Tommy talked about how when he went back there it really hit home seeing what a large percentage of the kids he played with had passed away from HIV," said Cook. "Having worked with some players from Africa, I knew what the power of soccer was in Africa, and I thought it was a way to grasp the power of pro soccer players. It made such sense to me because there was no one more powerful to a young African boy than a professional soccer player; they are their role models and their heroes."

Among the first people Clark shared his vision with were Ndlovu and an American, Kirk Friedrich, both of whom had also played professionally in Zimbabwe and had experienced the same eye-opening astonishment Clark had. A few months after the meeting at Cook's home, in the fall of 2002, the threesome traveled to Bulawayo to gauge the needs of the various communities and create the initial footprint of the program.

Later, another American who had played in Zimbabwe for the Highlanders named Ethan Zohn, became the fourth cofounder of the organization. Zohn, who had played his college soccer at Vassar, took time off from his pro career to compete on the 2002 season of the American reality television show *Survivor*, which was contested in Kenya. During the taping of the show, Zohn won a reward challenge and got to visit a tiny Kenyan village where he kicked a soccer ball around with children who he later found out were all HIV positive. Zohn ultimately won *Survivor*, and after being so moved by what he saw that day in Kenya, he contacted Clark, offered part of his $1 million prize as seed money for the organization, and used his new-found celebrity to shed light on the situation in Africa.

Since those early days, Grassroot Soccer has become a remarkable success story, and it has received financial backing from dozens of groups and companies including premier-level support from the Bill and Melinda Gates Foundation, Nike, the United States President's Emergency Plan for AIDS Relief, USAID from the American People, the Elton John AIDS Foundation, and the Clinton Global Initiative. Through 2013, Grassroot Soccer was operating in South Africa, Zambia, and South Africa, and had launched soccer-based development initiatives with more than forty governments, corporations, and civil society partners in twenty-three countries worldwide.

Starting with the original meeting at his home, Cook followed the exploits of the organization and tried to champion its efforts whenever he could. Somewhere along the way, it dawned on him that perhaps he could do more and, in the process, help his own program at Dartmouth. "I thought if there was a guy like Methembe in Zimbabwe who could come over here and do so well, there must be others," said Cook.

Turns out there were, and one of them was Lucky.

OUT OF AFRICA

Cook wasn't going to lie. "My initial motivation was to find a player for Dartmouth; that's my job," Cook recalled of his first visit to Zimbabwe in the spring of 2007.

But once he arrived, it became immediately apparent that bringing back a star striker to enhance Dartmouth's pursuit of Ivy League championships and potential NCAA tournament victories was secondary.

Cook knew the horror stories of how the HIV virus and AIDS had ravaged the country, and how hyperinflation had collapsed the economy and was depriving children of a proper education, not to mention the basic necessities of life such as food, water, clothes, and shelter. Hearing it and seeing it are two different things, and when he stepped off the plane, he saw what the term *third world* really meant. That trip was no longer so much about recruiting for Dartmouth as it was offering the hope and possibility of a new life.

"When I went there and saw the talented kids, their bright nature, their enthusiasm, it dawned on me that I couldn't take one guy every three or four years who would fit Dartmouth's academic requirements, to play for me," said Cook. "All these young men were trying to find a way out to build a better future for themselves and their families. When you see that, that really motivated me to help these kids. Once I was there I couldn't do anything else but to try and help them."

Cook contacted Ndlovu and asked for his help in putting together a soccer showcase where Cook could travel to Zimbabwe and not only offer coaching expertise to the kids, but evaluate potential recruits both athletically and academically to see if any were Dartmouth material.

Ndlovu, who had come to Dartmouth because Tommy Clark saw him play in Zimbabwe and suggested his father recruit him, which he did, was more than willing to do the ground work in the hope that he could help provide the same type of opportunity he'd had to other Zimbabwean boys. Fran O'Leary, the former Dartmouth coach whom Cook had replaced in 2001 and who was now at Bowdoin College, accompanied Cook on the trip, and the men were greeted by more than forty boys of varying ages, skill levels, and academic prowess.

The field at the sports club in Bulawayo was mostly dirt, with a few strands of straw-like grass sprinkled about. There were no lined boundaries, and the goal frames did not have nets. "It was like an untended pasture, a soccer field that your average U.S. club team would refuse to play on," Cook said.

By process of elimination the group was trimmed in half after the first day, and not only did Lucky make the cut, Cook believed he was the best player there. "He was something different than what we get here in this country in terms of being deceptive on the ball, his speed, and just the joy of using his natural gifts that I thought was so unique," said Cook. "I thought he'd be able to make a big difference at Dartmouth." That was Cook's assessment after only the first day, which consisted primarily of putting the boys through basic technical drills. Then he saw Lucky play, and he was certain.

"They told about twenty of us to come back," Lucky remembered. "We played a game (against a team put together by his cousin, Ndlovu) and it was probably the hardest game I ever played. I was so tired, but I scored about five goals and we won. After that they asked if I had any contracts with a team, I told them I was waiting for one next August, and they told me not to sign anything, come to the office the next day, and that's when I met Jeff Cook and he told me he was interested."

Lucky had done well in school and it was determined that, based on his transcripts, he'd have a good chance to get into Dartmouth, but there was much work ahead—namely, the American SAT exam. Dartmouth, like many schools around the country, preaches its holistic approach to admissions and says the SAT is merely one piece of the puzzle, but Lucky had obviously never taken it in Zimbabwe, so it was a hurdle he needed to clear. Prior to the trip, Cook had been in contact with his good friend, Chris Cheney, the soccer coach at Kimball Union Academy. They had discussed the possibility of whether the hierarchy at Kimball would agree to provide scholarships for any boys that Cook would bring back from Zimbabwe so that they could spend a year getting accustomed to school and life in America while preparing for the SAT, which would help determine whether they'd be able to attend Dartmouth, or any other college.

"Our head of schools, Mike Schaefer, was very supportive," Cheney said. "He had been at Middlesex School where he'd had some international students and he recognized how they could add another flavor to the community in a real positive way. It's a big investment by the school, but he agreed because he thought it would be a great thing to do. It's a great transition for an international kid who isn't used to America. Prep school is a lot like college; they live in a dorm, eat three meals a day in the dining hall, they're playing sports, traveling, and studying, so Jeff and I thought it would be a great thing to set up. And the other part was at that time, Zimbabwe was the worst country in the world, so for an institution like KUA to be able to offer an opportunity, that's a pretty good thing."

Cheney certainly enjoyed the fringe benefit of having Lucky on his team, too. Kimball enjoyed quite a 2007 season, posting a record of 16–2–1 and winning the New England Prep School Athletic Conference Class B

Championship. Lucky scored thirty-seven goals including one in the title match against Brooks School, and he was named a league all-star.

"He was electric and far and away the best player," said Cheney. "I've been around prep school and college soccer in New England, seen guys go to the pros, and that's the level he was at."

But that year at Kimball was about so much more than soccer, or even preparing for the SAT, which he ultimately did well enough on to be able to enroll at Dartmouth. Lucky's year at Kimball was a treasured one because he forged bonds with people that will last a lifetime.

"I'll never forget how nice everyone was to me," he said.

BACK TO CLASS

It was back to reality for Lucky and the Big Green soccer team. "Now we have to get up early and go to class and then go to practice," Lucky said following a September 19 practice, the first day of the new school year at Dartmouth. "We went from being like professional soccer players to now we're back to being students."

And that meant classes in the morning, practice starting at around four in the afternoon, post-practice physical training and film sessions, dinner, and then homework at night. In other words, the life of an Ivy League student-athlete. "We just started and I've already got a lot of work to do," Lucky said.

Coach Jeff Cook likes to break the soccer season into three equally important segments:

Phase I of the schedule is filled with games against non–Ivy League opponents and serves the dual purpose of getting the team ready for the coming grind of the League games, and providing the players the chance to begin meshing together and understanding each other's strengths and weaknesses and playing styles.

Phase II commenced right around the late start of Dartmouth's fall term when the League games begin, and this was a critical juncture. Cook had to be careful how he handled the team because he understood the difficulties they faced getting back into the swing of school, especially the freshmen who now had to juggle practice and games with their class schedule and figure out a time-management system that worked best for them.

Phase III encompassed the homestretch of the regular season when the

Ivy championship was up for grabs as well as a potential NCAA tournament berth.

The first of those thirds ended in Dallas as the Big Green lost 2–1 in overtime to host SMU, and then 3–2 to Tulsa, making the long trip back to New Hampshire a solemn one. Lucky, who scored a goal against Tulsa, said while the Big Green had gotten off to a 1–3–2 start, no one was "freaking out," because, "It's obviously not something we were expecting, but judging from our schedule, we're playing really good teams. We know losing these two games will help us."

Cook agreed, saying, "We have a young team and we're coming along; I think we're going to be all right."

It would seem Cook had his club pegged pretty well because Phase II got off to a great start. It began with a 2–1 come-from-behind victory over Massachusetts. It continued with a shockingly easy 4–1 romp over defending Ivy champion Princeton in the League opener which snapped the Tigers' twelve-game League unbeaten streak. And then there was a 2–0 victory over Vermont, which vaulted the Big Green over five hundred (4–3–2) for the first time this season.

Against UMass, Lucky scored the tying goal early in the sixty-sixth minute, and then assisted on Kevin Dzierzawski's game winner in the seventy-sixth minute, a performance that earned him a spot on the Ivy League's weekly honor roll.

"That was a really big game, and I feel like we really grew as a team because we were down 1–0 and we showed a lot of character," Lucky said, thinking back to the game that perhaps would turn the season around. "We fought until we were up, and we defended well, so that was important. We didn't come up with the results we wanted in Dallas, and everyone was kind of down and sad, but this win against UMass was really important."

The Big Green rode that wave of momentum to the blowout of Princeton, a game in which Dartmouth scored four goals in the first thirty-six minutes of play, the last two coming off the right foot of Lucky. "We followed the game plan and it worked out well," Lucky said. "We scored early in the game and we set the pace and made them come to us."

Against Vermont, the cocaptains, Lucky and Nick Pappas, scored second-half goals, both assisted by Dzierzawski, to put away the pesky Catamounts on a rainy night at Dartmouth's Burnham Field.

"The first half it was fifty-fifty, but in the second half we came out flying and we dominated them," Lucky said. "When you're playing like we were, it's relaxing and you don't have to worry about if you make this pass and give the ball away. When you're playing good, it gives you the freedom and confidence to just play."

PRACTICE MAKES PERFECT

And when you practice poorly, well . . .

There is an the old sports axiom that says, "You play how you practice" and it came to fruition for the Big Green in their next two games, a 2–0 loss at Yale, and a 2–1 victory at Penn on the second and third Saturdays of October.

"You train how you play," said Lucky, who scored on a penalty kick—the first of his career—in the twenty-second minute for what proved to be the game-winning goal against the Quakers. "That's how it was in both of those games."

Like any good captain, Lucky took the loss to Yale personally. The Elis gladly exposed Dartmouth's lethargy and scored a goal in each half, and the Big Green never had a response. "Everyone just seemed tired," said Lucky. "In the warm-up for the game we tried to get the guys up, but we didn't pass well, we were bad on second balls, didn't try to win the ball. It was weird. We just didn't show up the whole game and I feel like they took advantage of that. Jeff was pretty upset. We know it's an Ivy game and showing up like that is not going to win us the title. He said we needed to work harder, physically and mentally, and we did."

That's what they did in the days leading up to the trip to Philadelphia, and they dominated Penn to earn the five-hundredth victory in Dartmouth program history.

"We picked it up in practice and it was amazing how you play when you train properly," said Lucky. "We did a lot of one-on-one defending because we didn't defend well against Yale, and it was probably the hardest week of practice we had this season. We did a lot of running with the ball, high-intensity stuff."

Maarten van Ess scored on a header in the fourteenth minute to give Dartmouth the early lead, Penn pulled even in the twentieth minute, and then less than two minutes later van Ess was tackled in the box, a penalty kick was awarded, and Lucky stepped up to take it. "I was pretty nervous," said Lucky, who had deferred throughout his Dartmouth career on penalty kicks to upperclassmen, but now, it was his turn.

Penn goalie Max Kurtzman guessed correctly and moved to his left, but Lucky had enough pace on his mid-height right-foot shot to just sneak it inside the post. That proved to be the final goal, as Dartmouth played solid, lock-down defense the rest of the way.

CHASING HISTORY

Scoring goals is no easy task in soccer, but sometime in the next couple of weeks, Lucky was hoping to be able to lay claim to the fact that no one in the long history of Dartmouth soccer had scored more than he.

By producing Dartmouth's lone goal in its 1–0 victory over Colgate on October 25, two of the most hallowed records in program history were standing right in front of him. With thirty-three career goals, he was tied with 1954 graduate Bob Drawbaugh for number one on the all-time list, and with seventy-seven points, Lucky was tied with 1990 graduate Vladica Stanojevic. One more goal, somewhere in the next batch of games, and Lucky would be alone atop the mountain.

"To be able to do that is kind of unbelievable considering the kind of success Dartmouth's program has had in the 1990s and more recently with players like Craig Henderson and Daniel Keat," said Nick Pappas. "To be spoken [of] in the same company as those guys is awesome. It just reflects what an impact he's had on the program, these records that he's going to achieve."

When Lucky came to America in 2007 and set the single-season goal-scoring record at Kimball Union in his lone year at the prep school, it gave him the confidence to set some lofty goals when he moved on to Dartmouth. "When I was a freshman I wanted to be the top goal-scorer every season I was here," he recalled.

He did it as a freshman when he scored eleven goals and earned Ivy League rookie-of-the year honors and made the all-Ivy first team. But injuries short-circuited both his sophomore and junior seasons and he finished tied for the top spot with Keat in 2009, and was one goal behind Andrew Olsen in 2010. So heading into his senior year, Lucky needed to set a new individual goal and that was to become Dartmouth's preeminent career scorer. By scoring his ninth of the year against Colgate, he was on the brink of history.

"I was starting to think about it," Lucky said, referring to being held off the score sheet in the loss to Yale and then again in a 2–0 victory over Columbia. "When you start thinking about stuff, that's when you have pressure and stress and it's hard to control because it's always on your mind. I don't want it to distract me, and I'm trying to just take every game as it comes, but it's hard not to think about because I'll be honored to break these records if I can."

Pappas, who hails from Scottsdale, Arizona, had spent four years watching Lucky turn Ivy League defenders inside out, not to mention him and the other Dartmouth backs in practice every day. As their college careers wound down, Pappas thought about what it meant to have played with someone as gifted as Lucky.

"There hasn't been a marquee player like him who, from the day he stepped on campus, everybody knew he was going to play at the next level," said Pappas. "To have that ability day in and day out in practice, and some of the creativity that he brings, it's been an amazing experience. You don't see that on a week-to-week basis, at least not in the Ivy League. The forwards I've guarded, he's right up there in the top three players I've ever played with or against."

The Big Green had a great chance to qualify for their fifth consecutive NCAA tournament appearance. Before Lucky arrived in Hanover, Dartmouth had never played in more than two in a row, which is why Pappas said, "You can argue that during his four years Dartmouth has had as much success as it has ever had. He's one of the main reasons why we elevated ourselves to one of the elite programs in the nation. Not many teams have made the tournament four years in a row. It's been awesome."

REWRITING THE RECORD BOOK

Both records fell on the night of November 5, during a crucial 3–1 victory over Cornell at Burnham Field that not only vaulted the Big Green into a tie for first in the Ivy standings, but snapped the Big Red's thirteen-game unbeaten streak.

"It was an amazing moment for me," Lucky said of his goal with a little more than two minutes remaining that secured the triumph and allowed Dartmouth to have its destiny in its own hands in the season finale. If they could win that game at Brown the following Saturday, they would be Ivy League champions and thus earn an automatic bid into the NCAA tournament.

On what had already been an emotional day and night because of Senior Day activities feting the outgoing players, Cornell had just scored a couple minutes earlier to pull within 2–1 in a game Dartmouth had to win to keep its championship hopes alive. The ball was directed into the Cornell zone, Lucky tracked it down and passed it to Aaron Gaide on the left flank. Gaide then read the situation perfectly and he played it back through to Lucky, and the crowd of nearly one thousand rose to its feet because it was clear this was the moment history might be made.

Lucky, as talented a ball handler as Dartmouth or the Ivy League has ever seen, accepted Gaide's pass and ran past a Cornell defender, then dribbled around Big Red goalie Zach Zagorski who was all alone and had to come out to challenge. It was no contest as Lucky left him lurching at air before kicking the ball into the yawning cage for his thirty-third career goal and seventy-eighth and seventy-ninth points, touching off a raucous celebration on the field and in the stands.

"I was just thinking 'wow,'" Lucky said when it hit him what had just happened. "I had been thinking 'I have to do it today, I have to do it today.' But I hadn't scored and I was cramping pretty bad and I remember coach yelled at me before I scored because I didn't go for this one ball that I should have, but I just couldn't get to it."

Lucky had been feeling some pressure in his quest for the scoring record. He was held without a point in a 1–1 tie at Harvard, and he didn't play in a 3–0 loss to New Hampshire, a nonconference game in which coach Jeff Cook rested most of his front-line players so they would be healthy and ready for this showdown against Cornell.

"I talked to my friends and they were telling me they remembered my first game here and me saying that I wanted to break records and I don't remember that, but thinking back, it just shows how much I wanted it," he said.

Lucky's journey from Zimbabwe to Dartmouth had been almost movie-script worthy, and this would have provided a few notable pages. Because it was Senior Day and the last home game of his brilliant career, his heart strings were being tugged like a puppeteer almost from the moment he woke up. The team had breakfast together, and then Lucky walked over to the locker room and sat there in silence and solitude for a little while, memories of his time at Dartmouth washing over him. "I was thinking back on freshman year and it feels like yesterday, and it struck me how time really flies," he said. "It was pretty emotional for me."

After going back to his dorm room to chill out and listen to some music, he had lunch with friends, then went over to Burnham to watch the women's' team play and cheer on his classmates who were also celebrating Senior Day. After the women wrapped up their season with a 1–0 victory over Cornell, the men gathered for Cook's pregame talk, and to watch a video that had been put together for Lucky and the other seven seniors.

"It was emotional for us and that made it like, 'Wow, we are really graduating,'" Lucky said. "That video really got into our heads and it helped us in the game. There were six starting seniors in the game and we came out really wanting to win and we were playing out of our minds."

Still, all that energy got Dartmouth nowhere, and the game was scoreless at the break, prompting Cook to tell his team to "go out there and kick these guys off the field right now," and the Big Green did. Kevin Dzierzawski scored four minutes into the second half and Maarten van Ess appeared to put it away when he scored during a scrum in the eighty-fifth minute. Cornell would not go quietly, as Patrick Slogic beat Big Green goalie Noah Cohen less than a minute later, but then Lucky made sure Senior Day would be a happy affair when he scored his historic goal about two minutes after that.

Lucky's parents could not be there to cheer their son on his big day, but Alex and Susan Kahan and their youngest son, Elisha, were there, as was Kimball Union soccer coach Chris Cheney's wife, Lisa, and Lucky's girlfriend, Fumi.

"It meant so much to me," Lucky said. "They are my family and having people I love there was phenomenal. To know these people would support me when my parents couldn't be here, it meant a lot. I did call my dad, and he said they were going crazy and that they were really proud of me for working hard and breaking the record."

THE BUS RIDE

For two painstaking hours the Dartmouth soccer team sat in the darkness of its chartered bus as it chugged through New England on the way back to campus following a disappointing and potentially season-ending scoreless tie with Brown. The only light came from the glow of laptop computer screens scattered throughout the bus, all displaying the Gametracker feature on Cornell's athletic website. Every minute or two the screens would refresh, bringing the latest updates from Cornell's game against Columbia, and for the longest time there was nothing but unchanging gloom coming from cyberspace.

"It was a little stressful," Lucky said.

For good reason. The Big Green had blown a chance to win the Ivy League title earlier in the day when they failed to beat Brown, so the draw left their fate to be determined by what was happening in Ithaca, New York. If Columbia defeated Cornell, it would be the Ivy champ, but if the Big Red could pull out a tie or a victory, then Dartmouth and Columbia would tie for first and the Big Green would win the title based on tiebreakers and earn the League's automatic berth to the NCAA tournament.

Unlike sports such as basketball and football where each Gametracker refresh is a highly anticipated event, the low-scoring nature of soccer doesn't provide that drama and can make following along an exercise in tedium. That is until the news came that Cornell had scored late in the first half, and then the ongoing updates that revealed that neither team would score again.

"The bus ride was agony," said coach Jeff Cook, whose team would be playing in the tournament for the fifth consecutive year, making it one of only twelve schools to turn that trick since the advent of the tournament. "I desperately wanted the Ivy title for this group of players because I felt they really deserved it based on everything they put into the season. It was a terrible feeling because we were completely helpless. We were all pretending to read or listen to music or watch a movie, but you couldn't think of anything else."

Lucky said, "When we read 'game over' everyone just screamed. When it ended tied everyone stood on the bus and we were celebrating for the last hour of the ride, playing music and dancing until we got home. It was one of those moments that was really great to be a part of."

It had been an amazing couple of weeks for Lucky, breaking the school's all-time goals and points records, and now being able to complete a personal four-year run in the NCAA tournament, something only the seniors on the 2010 and 2011 teams could lay claim to achieving. "We didn't want to be a class that didn't make it," Lucky said.

When the team gathered a few days after the return from Brown to watch the NCAA selection show, there was some disappointment when it learned it wouldn't be hosting a first-round game at Burnham Field. The Big Green would have to go right back to Providence, this time to play Providence College.

"We were hoping to get a home game; unfortunately we didn't, but we were OK with that because we feel like we can play any team anywhere right now," Lucky reasoned.

If the Big Green could defeat the Friars, something they'd done in eleven of fourteen previous meetings, they'd be jetting off to Southern California to play UC–Santa Barbara in the round of thirty-two.

"Coach told us we deserved it," Lucky said recalling Cook's remarks on the bus. "He said to go have fun, but don't go crazy because we had lots more work to do."

AN UN-LUCKY ENDING

The Big Green did that work and were ready for everything Providence threw their way, but it wasn't enough to prevent a frustrating, season-ending 1–0 tournament loss. Afterward, Cook found Lucky sitting alone in the locker room, shoulders heaving, tears streaming down his face, trying to cope with the fact that the greatest chapter to date in his still-brief life was now complete.

"It was pretty emotional," Lucky said. "It was one of the most upsetting moments for me. I've known some of these guys for four years. We've been really close and there's nothing like a college soccer team. You have such a connection with a college team and that's the worst thing, that I won't have that now."

Lucky's tears flowed from his dark African face with a little bit more meaning than any of the other seniors Cook had coached during his eleven years at Dartmouth. These were no ordinary four years in New Hampshire's upper valley for the native of Zimbabwe; not for him, not for Cook, and not for anyone associated with the Big Green soccer program or the university.

Lucky's life changed in a way he never thought was possible when Cook found him at that showcase event on a dusty, dilapidated field in his homeland five-plus years earlier and arranged to bring him to the United States so that he could get a world-class education and play soccer for the Big Green. And

Dartmouth's life changed when Lucky arrived and brought his immense soccer talent and infectious spirit to the Hanover community.

"Lucky will go down as one of the greatest players to ever play at Dartmouth," Cook said. "But he meant so much more to us. We're a small region, but it's a great soccer area and people started hearing about this guy who was coming to Dartmouth and he was remarkably successful. And his coming here coincided with us opening our new soccer field, Burnham Field. His arrival and the new stadium came together at the perfect time. We now had a destination stadium with floodlights and a nice grandstand, and here was this tremendous player from Zimbabwe playing on a successful team. We get full stands every time we play at home, the program has continued to develop, and he's transformed our program from a visibility standpoint. It's not 100 percent because of Lucky, but he's contributed so much."

During his four years at Dartmouth, Lucky helped lead the Big Green to the NCAA tournament every year, the team won two Ivy League championships, Lucky set school scoring records, he won the League's rookie-of-the-year award as a freshman, and then was told the day before the Providence game that he'd been selected this year's Ivy League player of the year.

But in his last game, Lucky did not score a goal, did not register a point, and even though none of his teammates did either, his zeros across the stat sheet left him feeling like he hadn't done what Cook had brought him to Dartmouth to do, and now there were no more chances to get that accomplished.

"I was looking at Coach Cook and remembering when he came to Zimbabwe and brought me to this country and it was like I feel like I failed him," Lucky said. "I was crying most of the time because it sucks that this is my last game under him."

That premise couldn't have been further from the truth, but Cook, who had gone back to Zimbabwe a few times and had become educated on the mentality of the Zimbabwean people, understood why Lucky felt that way.

"There's a huge cultural influence in Africa of taking care of your elders, so when he becomes a pro soccer player, it will also be expected that he will help to support his family, and he will want to," said Cook. "With that kind of respect for elders, I think there's an expectation that's probably built into him that because I helped him come here, he had to produce X number of goals and X number of championships. That's part of what I was trying to say to him after the game, that he had done so much for Dartmouth soccer and for me as a coach, he should have no regrets. He has paid up his part of the bargain with incredible interest."

Just a few days earlier the Big Green had boarded a bus in Providence and returned to their rustic campus amid sheer glee after learning during the ride that their 0–0 tie against Brown had indeed been enough to clinch the Ivy championship and an automatic bid into the NCAA tournament. This journey back to Hanover was conducted in season-ending silence.

"Nobody really talked at all until we were about an hour away from school," said Lucky, who spent those four hours contemplating what he will do without a Big Green practice, or game, or training session from now until he graduated in March. "It's going to be weird because I'm so used to the routine."

Just as it was going to be weird in a few months to not have Lucky bouncing around the Dartmouth campus.

"He has that trademark hairstyle and no one else has it on campus," said fellow senior and captain Nick Pappas. "He's kind of a celebrity on the Dartmouth campus, so it's been really cool to have that on the team, and to be really good friends with him. I got to experience his personality on a day-to-day basis, which is great. He's one of the funniest people I've met so it has been a treat to play with him for four years. When I look back on Dartmouth, he's created a huge impact in my experience here, and I can't thank him enough for that."

ALEX THOMAS

YALE FOOTBALL

When Tom Williams was introduced in January 2009 as the new head football coach at Yale University, he stepped behind a lectern set up in a conference room at historic Ray Tompkins House, looked out at the gathered media and various members of the Yale athletic and academic communities, and proudly announced in his confident and boisterous voice, "Welcome to a new era in Yale football." Williams later went on to add that Yale's primary objectives were going to be, number one, to win Ivy League championships, and number two, beat Harvard, "And if we take care of those two things, we'll be in a pretty good spot."

At that moment in time, Alex was anything but in a good spot. It was midway through his freshman year, and his life was in disarray. He'd just endured a terribly disappointing first season with the Bulldogs, when he'd descended from record-setting, much-ballyhooed local high school super-stud recruit to benchwarmer on a middling Ivy League team, a comedown of epic proportion that dealt a mental blow to his confidence. Now, Jack Siedlecki, the head coach who had recruited him, was retiring, and most of his staff was being replaced, so Alex would have to start from scratch and try to impress Williams and his assistants who had no emotional attachment to any of the holdover players.

But none of that was even Alex's primary concern. As Alex listened to Williams outline his plan to get the Bulldog program back on track, he knew he needed to get himself on track in the classroom before he could even entertain thoughts of helping the new coach achieve those gridiron goals. As the fall term ended and Alex wobbled wearily back home for Christmas break to Ansonia, Connecticut, fifteen miles east of the New Haven campus, he was officially on academic probation because he hadn't completed the required course work for a semester as outlined by the Committee of Academic

Progress. It's no secret that at many Division I schools, academic problems have a way of getting swept underneath the carpet, but that wasn't the case at Yale.

Alex had dropped two classes during the first semester, an intro to microeconomics course and a first-year English course. Also, while he received a passing grade in Spanish, he did not earn the credit and to this day, it has never been fully explained to him why. You need to earn at least three credits per semester to stay off probation and eligible to play sports, and he only had one, so the only way he would be able to return to the team for his sophomore year was to make up those lost credits in the spring, and then in the summer.

"That first semester was tough for me because I was totally unprepared for what to expect here," Alex said. "I was in trouble, and that was definitely one of the hardest times of my life. There were many times when I didn't think I was going to make it here."

Had anyone who knows Alex heard him utter that comment, they would have gasped, because Alex had never failed at anything; not in the classroom, and certainly not on the football field. At Ansonia High School, Alex was an honor student who routinely compiled a ninety-plus average. The SAT gave him a little trouble, but he kept hammering away at it the way he used to pound on opposing defenders as Ansonia's star running back, and he finally produced a score of about 1,200 (he can't recall the exact number) that, along with his grade point average, class rank, and football prowess, would help in his quest to go to the one university he was aiming for: Yale.

"I took school for granted when I was younger because it came pretty naturally to me, and when it got a little harder in high school I put more time in," he said. "I always had a desire to succeed in school. I mean, why not do good in school? You're there for that reason, to learn."

As competitive as he was in class, it didn't compare to the brilliance he showed on Friday nights at Ansonia's Jarvis Stadium where Alex became the most statistically accomplished player in the history of Connecticut high school football. His iconic career would have opened up scholarship opportunities at some Division I football schools had Alex been interested, but early on in the process he zeroed in on Yale as the place he wanted to be.

"I was getting those superficial letters from a lot of the big schools, but who knows what that means," Alex recalled of his recruiting experience.

"And I was also getting a lot of interest from Patriot League teams and some other Ivy League schools. But I was pretty much Yale from day one, once I thought there was a possibility that I'd be able to get in here, and I owe that to my high school coach (Tom Brockett). He told me as a freshman that if I kept getting good grades, I could go to Yale someday, and I kind of laughed at him originally. An Ansonia kid going to Yale, yeah, that hasn't happened in years. Sure enough, they started recruiting me, and basically from where I stood, if I got accepted I was going to come to Yale."

Accepted he was, and Alex saw himself becoming the heir apparent to another former Connecticut schoolboy standout, Mike McLeod of New Britain, who would be a senior in 2008 when Alex came in as a freshman. McLeod had helped lead the Bulldogs to a share of the 2006 Ivy League crown, their first of the 2000s, and had been the League's player of the year in 2007, when he rushed for more than sixteen hundred yards and scored twenty-three touchdowns. McLeod ultimately finished as Yale's all-time leader in rushing yards, attempts, and touchdowns, leaving a sizable legacy for Alex to strive for.

"He was a Connecticut guy as well, had great success in high school and then here, so I started thinking why not Yale," said Alex. "Best of both worlds; Division I football and one of the best educations that anyone could get, so it was kind of an easy decision."

And from the moment he committed to come to New Haven to try his hand at being the hometown hero, that was the last thing that was easy for Alex that first year.

"I was hoping I could come in and get some carries on the varsity and to not be able to do that was a little disappointing," he said. "I'm thinking I was this big star, this hotshot in Connecticut, and then coming here and being kind of an average guy, living under the radar, was a blow to me. And the fact that I was struggling in school for the first time in my life, literally not knowing if I'd be able to get through the classes I was taking, not knowing how I was going to pass them, I was at a loss at one point. It was tough at the start."

With McLeod wrapping up his record-shattering Bulldog tenure, Alex spent most of the fall of 2008 on the junior varsity, where he gained 402 yards on fifty-five carries, totals he had occasionally surpassed on singular Friday nights in high school. He saw action in just two varsity games, getting one rushing attempt for a single yard at Dartmouth.

School was already dragging him down, football was flat-out depressing because he'd never been in a situation where he wasn't the star player, and then came the news of coach Jack Siedlecki's retirement, and the hiring of Williams.

"I definitely had some concerns," Alex said of his future.

However, it wasn't long before it dawned on Alex that perhaps this could be the fresh start he needed. He hadn't been given the chance to contribute by Siedlecki, and with McLeod now out of the picture, and Williams claiming that every position was up for grabs, Alex stopped worrying and began focusing on proving he was the best back on the team.

"I was ready to work," Alex said. "Fortunately, coach Williams is a great guy, I love him as a coach. I was very fortunate in that sense, and the fact that they were open to competition, they weren't going to recruit their guys and forget about the guys who were already here. Basically the best men were going to play and that was a good philosophy."

So when spring practice began in 2009, Alex was in a better frame of mind regarding football, and his head was no longer spinning in the classroom, as he was starting to settle in and work his way back into good standing, his fears over flunking out now subsided.

"I didn't have the proper work ethic that I needed," he said. "I was a hard worker in high school, but that didn't really transfer over here. The expectations were at a whole different level, and I wasn't where I needed to be. The second semester I took four classes and then I had to take three more in the summer to make up for the first semester in order to be eligible as a sophomore, and the summer classes really helped. That was my first taste of success here, really. All you're doing in the summer is focusing on those classes, and I was able to do better. The first semester was very tough, but then the second semester I started to adjust and get the hang of things."

And those good vibes transferred to the practice field where Williams immediately took notice.

"I didn't know much about any of the kids when I got here," said Williams, who'd played at Stanford, had a cup of coffee with the San Francisco 49ers, chose coaching as a profession, and bounced around in a variety of college jobs before spending the previous two years in the NFL with the Jacksonville Jaguars.

"I met with a few of the guys when I was interviewing for the job, and I had certainly looked over the roster and saw some of the game tape, but Alex didn't show on the tape because Mike McLeod was the featured running back. Alex was a young player on the team, and he hadn't quite emerged. So what we said to the whole group is that we're starting from scratch, clean slate. We're going to evaluate with fresh eyes, and as we go into spring practice, whoever emerges is going to play, and Alex was one of the guys who stepped up."

GEARING UP

Having watched the rest of the nation's college football teams start their schedules, some as early as three weeks ago, Alex was excited that game week had finally arrived for the Bulldogs with Georgetown coming to the Yale Bowl in a few days.

Unlike most of his teammates, who dreaded preseason training camp, Alex actually liked it. "It's an exhausting time, but it's really the only time you have to just focus on football, especially here at Yale with the academics we have to deal with," he said. "Football is something you love to do, so camp is almost like a refreshing aspect. I mean, it's definitely a grind, but at the same time you appreciate it. It's like a good pain."

Still, nothing is like game day, especially this season, because Alex expected to be a prime weapon in this offense, a role he had gradually built up to during his time at Yale.

Even though he'd impressed Tom Williams in spring ball, the new coach went with his upperclassmen early in 2009, Alex's sophomore year, and it wasn't until the third game that Alex finally got some meaningful playing time with three carries for five yards in a loss to Lafayette. His workload remained light until the final third of the season when Williams was finding it tougher to keep him on the sideline. Alex scored his first career touchdown in a victory over Columbia, and after forty- and fifty-five-yard rushing outputs in losses to Brown and Princeton, he earned his first start as a collegian in the traditional season finale against Harvard.

That day, in front of more than fifty-two thousand people at the Yale Bowl, Alex became just the fourteenth Bulldog back in the long history of The Game to gain over 100 yards rushing, but his 124-yard effort was wasted when Harvard scored with 1:32 left to play to pull out a 14–10 victory.

"That was a confidence-builder," said Alex, who wound up as Yale's leading season rusher thanks to that game, and set him up as the number one back going into 2010.

His junior year started well with 90 yards in an opening victory over Georgetown, and 124 as the Bulldogs started their Ivy schedule with a victory over Cornell. After a rib injury slowed Alex down, he was back in form with a career-high 137 yards in a victory over Columbia, and the next week he had 121 in a win over Brown. A 77-yard effort helped Yale defeat Princeton, 14–13, and that set up a season-ending showdown against Harvard, where a Yale victory coupled with a loss by Penn at Cornell, would give the Elis a share of the Ivy League title. Alex rushed for 71 yards and scored three touchdowns at Harvard Stadium, but it wasn't enough, as the Crimson came away with a 28–21 victory, their ninth win in the last ten meetings.

By losing that game, Yale's 2011 senior class became just the fifth in school history to fail to earn a victory over their archrivals from Cambridge, joining the classes of 1916, 1923, 2005, and 2006. This year, Alex's class would join that ignominious group, and while the Harvard game, the last of Alex's career, was more than two months away, it was hard not to think about what it would mean.

"It's really all about Harvard and Yale, and it kind of stinks in a way because that's all anybody seems to care about," said Alex. "You talk about it with people in May and they say, 'I can't wait until the Harvard game' and it's like we have nine games before that. It's for good reason; there's such great tradition behind it and it's always a great game. Even though we've lost the last couple years, they've always been great games. Losing sucks, I hate losing, always have in anything I do, but that game, just the magnitude of it makes it slightly worse."

MIXED FEELINGS

Alex isn't too fond of having the carpet yanked from under him either, and that's exactly how he felt following Yale's season-opening 37–27 triumph over Georgetown. It was a happy Saturday night in New Haven, and a bunch of the Bulldogs made their way to a frat house party to celebrate the victory, but Alex opted for a quiet night at a friend's house instead. This was nothing out of character for Alex, because he usually preferred laying low as opposed to going out and partying, but there was no doubt that he was avoiding the frat house revelry.

Although he was thrilled that the team dominated the Hoyas and got the year off to a robust start, it had been a puzzling afternoon for Alex. All off-season, preseason, and even deep into the practice week for this game, he thought he was the number one running back on the depth chart. But when the game started, junior Mordecai Cargill was in the starting backfield. Alex didn't even get on the field until the second quarter, and in the end he played a scant role in the victory.

"It was the game plan that we were going to come out and run some power scheme offense, and they wanted a bigger back in for that at the beginning of the game," Alex said. "He had a lot of success early so he got a lot of the reps."

Cargill, a six-foot-one, 221-pound bruiser from Cleveland, rushed fifteen times for ninety-two yards and scored Yale's first touchdown, and the first of his college career, 1:27 into the game after Chris Smith had returned the opening kickoff eighty-two yards. Cargill then caught an eighteen-yard TD pass from Patrick Witt late in the first quarter that tied the score at 14–14.

Alex made his season debut midway through the second period with a six-yard run, finished the game with twenty-five yards on eight carries, and was going to have a whole lot of questions for the coaching staff when the team reconvened Sunday morning.

"I wasn't really sure how it was going to work, but you want to be carrying the ball as much as possible," he said. "It was not something I'm used to throughout my football career. I'm definitely a high-rep back; the more reps I get the better rhythm I can get into."

The hardest part for Alex was that he wasn't used on special teams, so he was standing there in dry dock for a long time, and he remarked, "I'm usually a semi-slow starter, and that was true trying to find the rhythm and the flow of game. It's challenging to stay focused. Mentally it's tough to stay into it while you're not really contributing. You have to make your personal adjustments, and you have to be ready when your number is called."

The Hoyas took a 17–14 lead early in the second quarter, but even then, Alex said the Bulldogs never really felt like they were in trouble. They felt like they could score at any time, and they also knew their defense would eventually settle in and stop Georgetown's offense. And that's what happened.

Witt hit Chris Smith with a thirty-one-yard touchdown pass to give Yale the lead for good, and the Bulldogs extended a 21–20 halftime advantage to 37–20 by midway through the fourth quarter.

A great start, for sure, but Alex showered and dressed quietly, made a brief appearance at the post-game tailgate party to be with his family, then headed off for a quiet night of reflection. "It's a little uncertain right now," he said of his role. "I hope I get more reps this coming weekend early on and get a chance to get going, and hopefully the rotation is more defined."

BACK IN THE GROOVE

It could have been a frustrating week for Alex, filled with uncertainty about his status in the Yale backfield. Instead, running backs coach Rod Plummer put the senior's mind at ease right away on the morning after the Georgetown victory.

"Coach Plummer saw that I was a little frustrated, and he kind of approached me on it," Alex said. "He pulled me aside after our meeting and he said he knew I was disappointed about the rotation and he said he'd work on getting a better rotation this week. My biggest issue was not knowing when to be ready and when I was going in. Part of that is he's also the special teams coordinator, so he splits his time with them, and that's a big part of the game, so I know it's a struggle to do both jobs."

As the practice week began and preparations were made for the Ivy League opener against Cornell, Alex could see that he was going to be more involved in the game plan, and in front of an announced crowd of 14,435 at the Yale Bowl and a national cable television audience on the VERSUS network, he certainly was.

Cargill still drew the start, and he ended up with fifteen carries as opposed to the eight that Alex received, but Alex out-rushed his junior understudy, 84–57, thanks to an explosive fifty-eight-yard touchdown run in the fourth quarter that sewed up Yale's 37–17 rout of the Big Red.

"Coach said he'd be more definitive about the reps I would get, and I definitely got more opportunities to be in the game than I did last week," said Alex. "The coaches are good about talking things out. They're honest with you, and during the week we talked about it and they said they would try to get me more reps early in the game, and they did."

Before the game was eleven minutes old Yale had a 17–0 lead, as the Yale defense produced an interception and two three-and-outs which resulted in Patrick Witt's five-yard touchdown pass to Allen Harris on a pretty fade route to the back left corner of the end zone, Cargill's one-yard touchdown plunge, and Philippe Panico's thirty-two-yard field goal.

Alex was on the field during the first possession, and on the fifth play, from the eleven-yard line, he had a three-yard run wiped out by a holding penalty. His first extended time came on a series that bridged the first and second quarters as he carried three times and caught a short pass, though the drive ended with Panico missing a field goal.

Cornell kicked a field goal on the final play of the first half, then marched ninety-six yards to make it 17–10 early in the third on a touchdown reception by Luke Tasker, the son of former Buffalo Bills standout Steve Tasker.

Here, Big Red coach Kent Austin, sensing a momentum shift, tried to surprise Yale with an onside kick, but Cliff Foreman alertly recovered for the Bulldogs, and with a short field to work with, it didn't take Yale long to pounce. Alex busted an eighteen-yard run on first down behind a great block by Gabe Fernandez, and three plays later, Witt threw a thirteen-yard touchdown pass to Cameron Sandquist. After an exchange of touchdowns, Yale took possession early in the fourth quarter and Alex blew through the Cornell defense and sailed untouched to the end zone for the clinching score.

"You try not to think, just react, but I do remember seeing a gaping hole and I remember Eli (Thomas) taking out the Sam 'backer and making a cut off that and seeing a lot of green grass, which was set up by Allen's block," Alex said of his career-long touchdown run. "Being able to get into stride and have no one near you is an incredible feeling. It brings me back to the high school days. I had a few of those back then."

PREP STAR

It was not his personality to do a silly celebratory dance, or pound his chest and self-orchestrate adulation from the crowd, or go all Terrell Owens and grab a cheerleader's pom-poms and wave them at the fawning fans. When Alex used to score touchdowns at Ansonia High he'd flip the ball to the nearest official and jog to the sidelines so the Chargers could get lined up for the extra point.

"It's just something I don't do," Alex once said when asked by an inquiring reporter about his business-like approach to glory, which he continued to practice at Yale. "We're a respectful program. It's like our job. You do what you have to do, give it back to the ref, and do it again."

And Alex did it again and again and again during a magnificent career where he set Connecticut state high school records for career rushing yards (8,279), touchdowns (114) and total points (747), while playing for a program that owns a record nineteen state championships and has had more than forty-eight seasons where the team lost one or zero games, defining what a dynasty truly is.

If the directors and producers of the now-defunct television show *Friday Night Lights* hadn't decided to shine their Hollywood spotlight on Texas high school football, Ansonia would have been the perfect replacement for the fictional town of Dillon.

It is a small rural burgh of about eighteen thousand located in southern Connecticut where, for decades and decades dating back to the Great Depression, the high school football team has been the blood that courses through the town's veins, giving it life, and purpose, and as its most prized civic asset, a certain mythic stature. To this day, generations of boys remain inexorably linked by the uniform they wore so proudly—lavender-colored until the 1960s, navy blue since. That link is evident by the scene each fall day during practice. As the kids are put through their paces by iron-fisted coach Tom Brockett, men in their sixties and seventies—retired from places such as American Brass and Farrel Corporation, whose mostly boarded-up brick plants are now downtown blights that employ a small fraction of the work force they once did—stand outside the fence that rings the field at Jarvis Stadium sizing up the latest squad.

"Ansonia has a great tradition, great coaches, and great kids considering how small of a town we have," Alex said. "Somehow we always field a great team, and everybody is really passionate about football in the town. It's one of the smaller schools in the state, but I think we can compete with some of the best of the bigger schools."

To be a football player at Ansonia is a privilege that is not to be taken lightly, and if you are fortunate enough to be a Charger, you are part of a lifelong brotherhood and thus maintain celebrity around town long after you've graduated.

And there was no bigger celebrity in the mid-2000s, or any era for that matter, than Alex. During his final two years at Ansonia, the team won all twenty-six of its games by an average margin of victory of more than thirty-five points. The Chargers won back-to-back Class S state crowns, and were the top-ranked team in Connecticut covering all classes both years, a feat never before accomplished in the school's storied history.

Coach Tom Brockett was still in diapers when the legendary Woody Hayes was forced to retire as head coach at Ohio State in 1978, but you'd swear he grew up in the 1960s and '70s at the elbow of Hayes, whose three-yards-and-a-cloud-of-dust power running game bludgeoned Big Ten opponents. Brockett, Ansonia's offensive coordinator for five years before taking over as head coach for retiring Jack Hunt in 2006 when he was just thirty years old, installed a simple I-formation offense and basically told the team, "We're going to give the ball to Alex on just about every play, and we're not going to stop until the other team stops him." Nobody ever did.

Alex closed out his junior year with 264 yards and three touchdowns in a 34–12 rout of Bloomfield in the state championship game, setting the stage for a senior season that was beyond compare. Early in 2007, Alex lined up against conference foe Woodland-Beacon Falls in that deep tailback spot and carried the ball forty-four times for a state-record 518 yards and seven touchdowns. He then capped his career by carrying the ball on fifty-four of Ansonia's sixty-three plays, gaining 249 yards and scoring three touchdowns to lead the Chargers to a 35–0 state championship game victory over New London. He finished that year with 3,596 yards and forty-seven touchdowns, both single-season state records that may never be surpassed.

If you ask Laura Thomas, she'll tell you the youngest of her six children from two marriages was going to be a running back, because that's all he ever wanted to be. He played some baseball, a little basketball, and he really took a shine to soccer, but when his brother Ryan started playing football, that's the game Alex wanted to play.

"I just thought it was awesome, and because I was faster than most of the kids at the time, I always wanted to be a running back," Alex said. "My mother wouldn't let me play that year, but she let me play the next year, and we had Pop Warner, the junior pee-wees. I started off playing running back, but the coach wanted me to play quarterback at times, and all I would do is run around the end. I think I threw it a few times, but when you're that young throwing really isn't that big a part of the game. When he wanted me at quarterback I was miserable, and one day I went crying off the field to my mother because I didn't want to play quarterback, and she always tells the story that I said they were wasting my talent."

Once he reached the high school he was a starter on the junior varsity, as a linebacker rather than a running back, but his background in soccer enabled him to be the varsity kicker. "I was doing both because soccer gave me a capable leg, but I was frustrated because I wanted to play running back and follow in my brothers' footsteps. He was the fullback at the high school before I got there, he graduated when I was in eighth grade, he'd won two state championships, was all-state for two years, and he held all the rushing and touchdown records at Ansonia. They ran a triple option offense so he was carrying the ball all the time."

Alex was a scrawny 140 pounds, so he hit the weight room and bulked up over the summer, easily won the starting running back job as a sophomore, and within three years his brother Ryan's name was erased from the Ansonia record book.

LEHIGH LOW

The one thing the Yale football team did not lack was leadership. With a roster that included eight former high school class presidents, nine valedictorians, seventy-seven high school team captains, and sixty-two National Honor Society members, coach Tom Williams didn't have to worry about his Bulldogs straying off the path.

Linebacker Jordan Haynes was selected captain at the annual end-of-season banquet back in November 2010, and Williams said that the senior from Folsom, California, was clearly deserving of the honor. But it's not a one-man job, and Williams has typically called on the entire senior class to help guide the squad. As Williams said, "Alex is one of the leaders of our offense, he's one of the lieutenants."

So, with the Bulldogs on the road for the first time this year, Williams decided it was time to speak to the seniors. Following a Chick-fil-A dinner with the entire team at the hotel that included last-minute discussions about what the Bulldogs would be facing in their game against a very good Lehigh team that was ranked thirteenth in the Football Championship Series top twenty-five poll, Williams dismissed the underclassmen and addressed the seniors.

"Coach held the seniors to encourage us and tell us that we control our own destiny; this is our time and our team, so don't let it slip away, and lead the team in whatever way we can," Alex said. "I was extremely fired up after that. We have the best team we've had since any of us has been here; we have potential at every position, and even though it was stuff we already knew, I definitely took the talk seriously. As an underclassman you look at it as the seniors' team, and if it doesn't happen this year you can do it next year. But as a senior it's definitely a different feeling, and it's like reality sets in and you realize this is your last shot and I can't let it go to waste because I'll never have this opportunity again."

Unfortunately, the bonding session didn't matter much on the field on the first Saturday of October. The Mountain Hawks took advantage of a terribly sloppy Yale performance that included five turnovers and numerous dropped passes and blown assignments, rolling to a 37–7 victory in front of about six thousand fans at Goodman Stadium.

"It was not a good day," said Alex, one of the few Elis who had a decent game. He carried seventeen times for eighty-nine yards and clearly reestablished himself as the number one back on the team. "Lehigh was a good team, but we made a lot of mistakes, kept shooting ourselves in the foot, and put our defense in some pretty bad spots. There wasn't any execution of our key plays; people weren't making plays and that was the biggest issue."

Three of the turnovers came in the first nine minutes of play and helped set up Lehigh's first ten points. As if that wasn't bad enough, Yale also lost seven points when a holding penalty wiped out a thirteen-yard touchdown run by Alex. The Bulldogs got back into the game with a sixty-six-yard touchdown drive that ended early in the second quarter on Patrick Witt's third-down pass from the five-yard line to Deon Randall.

When junior linebacker Will McHale intercepted Lehigh's Chris Lum at the Mountain Hawks twenty-nine, the Bulldogs had a chance to seize momentum. Instead, the offense stalled, Philippe Panico missed a forty-six-yard field goal, and Lehigh drove the other way to a touchdown for a 16–7 halftime lead.

In the second half Yale managed only six first downs, its deepest penetration was the Lehigh twenty-seven following Alex's twenty-five-yard scamper, and the defense allowed Mountain Hawk touchdowns on three consecutive possessions, which turned the game into a rout.

Alex did not start the game, but his chance came right away in the first quarter, and he was ready for it. "I think I impressed them, I was running hard, it was the best game I've had so far this year, so it sucks that we lost, but individually I think I showed the coaches something and hopefully I'll get more touches moving forward."

KEYSTONE KOPS

They stunk. Coach Tom Williams was never one to mince words, and there was no reason to start doing so after his Bulldogs had been blown out by Lehigh. They stunk, Williams made sure they knew it, and there wasn't a single player who didn't wholeheartedly agree with that characterization of their play.

"Coach Williams talked about coming back and getting the stench off us from last week," Alex said after Dartmouth played the role of Dial soap during Yale's supremely cleansing 30–0 victory the following week at the Yale Bowl. "That team that played last week wasn't us, and I think we wanted to come back and make a statement in the League and that's what we did."

Well, that team was back again on its second visit to the Keystone state. The Bulldogs traveled a little further west on Route 22 to try their luck at Lafayette, and the result was another loss to a Patriot League team, this time 28–19. "I don't know what it is," Alex said of the double-flop in Pennsylvania. "We were ten minutes down the road and the same thing happened."

In the victory over Dartmouth, Alex rushed for 130 yards, 74 coming on the fourth play from scrimmage when he set the tone for the day with an explosive touchdown jaunt, the longest of his Yale career. Mordecai Cargill tacked on 83 yards, 40 coming on a dazzling touchdown run, as the Bulldogs totaled a whopping 269 yards on the ground. Patrick Witt threw for 203 yards and a 44-yard touchdown to Chris Smith. The special teams got into the act when Gio Christodoulou returned a punt 53 yards for a score and in the process became Yale's all-time leading punt returner. And the defense pitched a shutout in holding Dartmouth to 178 yards including just 39 rushing by the 2010 Ivy League co-MVP, Nick Schwieger.

"We were an angry football team," Williams said after watching the Elis improve to 3–1 overall and more importantly, 2–0 in the League. "We had a lot to prove. We were tired of walking around all week with people looking at us strangely because we didn't play very well last weekend. We could have played this game last Sunday, truth be told. It's a measure of a strong football team to come back the way we did."

And then the Bulldogs were brutal against Lafayette.

They fell into an early 14–2 hole, their only points coming when an errant long snap on a punt from the end zone forced the Leopards to take a safety. They were still down 21–9 at the half when Witt's ten-yard touchdown pass to Elijah Thomas was matched by Lafayette quarterback Andrew Shoop's twenty-yard TD to Mark Ross with 1:19 left in the opening half.

Yale seemed ready to turn the game in its favor in the third quarter as the defense did its job by forcing Lafayette to punt on its first three possessions, and the offense produced a pair of scores to make the score 21–19. With momentum clearly on the Bulldogs' side, Williams decided to call for a surprise onside kick. Unfortunately, Lafayette recovered and eight plays later Ryan O'Neil plunged into the end zone from the six-yard line and that was the game's last score.

Alex thought Williams was making the right call because Lafayette was reeling, and it seemed like a perfect time for a trick play because they couldn't have been expecting it.

"It was there, but the kick wasn't executed properly," Alex said. "That type of thing is tough to be precise on, we practiced it a bunch of times this week, but it didn't work out. That was a situation where if we'd gotten that ball, it would have been a critical swing of momentum, and we probably would have gone down and scored again and that would have been a huge change in the game. [But] it turned into a key momentum swing for them."

HAVING FAITH

With a student body made up of men and women from all fifty states and numerous foreign countries, the Yale campus is a cultural melting pot where just about every perspective on just about any socioeconomic topic is represented.

For Alex, studying the strengths and weaknesses of a 3–4 defense—which is what he had been spending plenty of time doing in advance of playing powerhouse Penn—was only a sliver of who he was as an individual. As prominent as football had been for him ever since he discovered the game in grammar school, the most important aspect of his life, was his Christianity.

Never was that more apparent to him than his first semester at Yale when things were unraveling academically and athletically. Having grown up in a household where his mother, Laura, taught him and his siblings that the Lord would always be their guiding light, Alex knew exactly where to turn. "I'm a religious person, so my faith really helped me get through that time in my life," he said.

Three years later he was on the brink of graduating, and his unrelenting faith had played a distinct part in his collegiate experience through his involvement with Yale's chapter of Athletes in Action, a Christian ministry group that helps its members strike a balance between academics, athletics, and their spiritual beliefs.

"It's an opportunity for Christian athletes to fellowship together," Alex said. "Yale can be a hostile environment for Christians; there's some anti-Christian sentiment on campus, in my opinion, so it's a good place to hang out with nice people who are all athletes and it's a way to meet other people on campus."

Through AIA meetings and Bible study sessions, Alex found solace from the difficult days that the combination of football and his course load often produced. "You're with people you have things in common with, and we hang out together, talk, listen to worship music, play games for bonding, and there's usually a short message from our pastor."

The week of the Penn game, the main topic of the meeting was Yale's upcoming hosting of Paul Byrd, a Major League Baseball pitcher who spends a good part of his offseason speaking to Christian-based organizations such as AIA. As part of the leadership team, Alex would be involved with some of the publicity and hospitality for Byrd's appearance. "I'm really looking forward to it," he said. "He's a Christian with a great message, and I'll get to hang around with him after."

Though he was excited about Byrd's speech and his involvement in the event, the timing wasn't exactly great for Alex. School is always a grind, but it had been a bit more so this week, particularly in his product seminar class where his group had decided to change its project. Instead of trying to find a way to decrease the condensation that builds up on water bottles—"We felt it was something that's already been done, so we decided to go in a different direction rather than try to reinvent the wheel"—they were going to work on a device that Alex referred to as a shower timer. The premise was that people waste far too much water taking interminable showers, so this product would be installed in the shower and would measure the gallons used per minute, and calculate the amount of energy needed to heat the water, and when certain thresholds are reached it would sound an alarm to inform the showering person that it's time to rinse off and wrap it up.

If only figuring out the Penn defense could be that simple. The Quakers had been the dominant team in the Ivy League for three years and they were bringing a seventeen-game Ivy winning streak into the contest at historic Franklin Field, the longest active conference winning streak in the NCAA Division I Football Championship Subdivision, second-longest in all of Division I, and tied for the second-longest in League history.

"Penn is the two-time defending Ivy champion and I have a lot of respect for them as a program," Alex said of the Quakers, who had beaten the Elis in fifteen of the last nineteen meetings. "They've been a great program and still are. They're one of the most physical teams in the League, and I think that's part of their mentality. They pride themselves on their physicality and they try to bully the other teams in the League, and they've been successful. We're looking to change that around this year."

WOUNDED KNEE

As the teams changed ends at Franklin Field to begin the fourth quarter, Alex and his Yale teammates couldn't have been in a much better situation.

For three quarters the Bulldogs had punched the rough-and-tumble Quakers right in the mouth, which was the only way to succeed against them, and they were clearly dazed and confused. Yale was leading 20–10, Alex had already rushed for 119 yards and a touchdown, and the announced crowd of 11,413 was sitting passively, wondering if a changing of the guard in the League standings was about to take place.

About forty real-time minutes later, the Bulldogs trudged off to the Spartan visiting locker room wondering what the hell had just happened.

"It sucked, that's the best way to put it," Alex said of Yale's fourth-quarter collapse that saw the Bulldogs give up four touchdowns in less than eight minutes to lose, 37–25. "The worst part is having the feeling going into the fourth quarter that we were getting ready to put away the game, and then we made some mistakes that changed the momentum."

As if the sting of the defeat wasn't painful enough, Alex ended the greatest game of his college career—204 yards, the sixth-best total ever recorded by a Bulldog—by limping off the field with a knee injury that would force him to miss a couple games at the minimum.

"It was a little scary," Alex said of the injury, which he suffered on a 17-yard run that put him over the 200-yard barrier, the first back to do that against Penn since 1997. "I don't really know what to do with it because I've been very blessed and I've never been injured before."

The teams came into the game tied with Harvard atop the standings with 2–0 records, and as Alex had said days before the kickoff, this was an opportunity for the Bulldogs to make a statement.

It looked as if they would. Yale led 7–3 at the half thanks to Patrick Witt's twelve-yard touchdown pass to Chris Smith, and the lead ballooned to 20–10 in the third. Alex capped a seventy-two-yard drive with a one-yard plunge, and after Penn answered less than two minutes later on a twenty-two-yard touchdown pass from Billy Ragone to Joe Holder, Yale did not blink as 1:03 later Witt hit Smith down the right sideline with a sixty-yard touchdown pass.

And then it all fell apart. With Alex carrying six times for thirty-four yards, the Bulldogs penetrated Penn territory and seemed on their way to perhaps putting the game out of reach late in the third quarter. They reached the Quaker thirty and were facing third-and-two when Witt, a Rhodes Scholar candidate, made an unusually poor decision. Under siege from the Penn defense, he intentionally grounded the ball, and that not only killed the drive, it pushed the Bulldogs well out of field goal range and they had to punt. They didn't know it at the time, but the game turned right there.

"That was huge," Alex said. "Had we gotten a first down there I think it would have been an entirely different game because we would have kept the drive going. We were wearing the defense down at that point and we probably would have gone down and scored."

Penn pulled within four points two minutes into the fourth period when Ragone capped an eighty-eight-yard drive with a sixteen-yard touchdown pass to Luke Nawrocki. Kicker Connor Loftus missed the extra point, but he redeemed himself on the kickoff, purposely popping it up to make one of the Yale wedge men field it. When no one did, Penn was able to recover the live ball, and three plays later Ragone scooted into the end zone from eleven yards out to give Penn a 23–20 lead.

On the ensuing possession, Alex ran like a man possessed, carrying on five straight plays for a total of forty-four yards which helped set up Philippe Panico's tying thirty-five-yard field goal with 8:31 left to play. However, it was a momentary reprieve. Penn promptly marched eighty yards in five plays with Ragone finding Ryan Calvert for a twenty-yard go-ahead touchdown, and then the Quakers forced another special teams gaffe when Yale's Deon Randall coughed up the ball on the kickoff. Starting from the Bulldogs thirty-four, it took the Quakers fifty seconds to score again when Brandon Colavita broke free for a twenty-five-yard touchdown run that made it 37–23.

"It's frustrating," said Witt, who passed for 258 of Yale's 466 total yards of offense. "You're up by ten going into the fourth quarter, you'd like to think that two scores going into one quarter would last a little longer than it did."

Penn took a deliberate safety in the final minute to give Yale its final two points, but the issue was decided by then. As Alex wondered how serious his knee injury was, he tried to assess how difficult it was going to be for the Bulldogs to win the Ivy championship now.

"It's not so much a mountain to climb, but we know we have to win the rest of our games, do what we can do, and when we're no longer in control of our fate just hope for a Penn loss," he said. "We have to take care of our business."

BAGGED BY BROWN

Unfortunately, they didn't. This was supposed to be the year, Alex thought. With so much talent up and down the roster, clearly the most during his four years at Yale, this was supposed to be the year the Bulldogs were not only going to contend for the elusive Ivy League championship, they were going to win it.

Well, this was not going to be the year because their 34–28 loss on November 5 to Brown—which wasn't as close as the score might indicate—officially eliminated the Bulldogs from contention.

"I'm actually shocked," said Alex, who was forced to sit out due to his knee injury, just like he had the week before when the Bulldogs defeated Columbia, 16–13, in a freakish late October New York City snowstorm. "I always have high expectations, and I actually had expectations of going undefeated this year, so losing one game was a surprise enough for me. To be sitting here with a 4–4 record, if you told me we'd be in this situation at the beginning of the season I would have laughed at you."

No one wearing the *Y* on their helmet was laughing after this one, as Brown's defense held Yale to an embarrassing seven yards net rushing, opened a 27–7 lead in the third quarter, and then held off a late Bulldog surge in the fourth quarter to improve to 4–1 in the League, 7–1 overall, and keep its own Ivy title aspirations intact.

A week earlier, Yale had shaken off its collapse against Penn and defeated the Lions with snow cascading down on the artificial turf at Wien Stadium, turning it into a slushy hundred-yard skating rink. The conditions were apparently perfect for Mordecai Cargill, as he took advantage of Alex's absence and enjoyed one of the greatest days a running back has ever had at Yale. Cargill ran for 230 yards, the fourth-best total in school history.

And no one was more pleased for the junior from Cleveland than Alex. "I would love to have had those carries and yards, but at the same time you're a teammate, you see him working hard and you're happy for him," Alex said. "Sure I was frustrated because I know I would have had a big day, but I have the reassurance that God has a plan for my life."

With word coming from Providence that Brown had upset Penn, Yale vaulted into a tie with Penn and Brown at 3–1, one game behind 4–0 Harvard in the standings. "Huge for us," Alex had said. "Now we have a chance."

Alex thought he would have a chance to play against Brown, too. For three rehab sessions a day—pre- and post-practice and then again later in the afternoon following class, about an hour for each—he rode the stationary bike, did deep squats to gain flexion, and endured the pain of having the trainers bend his knee with the goal of getting his heel to touch his butt. "I was feeling a lot better and it was night and day compared to where it was early in the week, but after the Friday walk-through I still wasn't there. In my mind I wanted to try to suit up and play, but I knew I wasn't ready and the coaches agreed."

So he stood on the sidelines again and watched in dismay as the Bears throttled the Bulldogs in the early going, taking advantage of numerous miscues in all phases.

"It's frustrating to watch," Alex said. "Seeing how inconsistent we can be in big games like this. It has continued to haunt us since I've been here, running into those situations in big games where we just don't show up until it's too late and that's exactly what happened. It's not like guys aren't playing hard, but some key mistakes are being made in key situations and we aren't executing like we're capable. If you look at the tape, I think in most of the games, we've dominated. Brown's defense did a good job against our offensive line, but in the rest of the games, we've been the more physical team, in my opinion."

The problem all season was that Yale just hadn't won as much as Alex, or anyone involved with the program, thought it would.

RAMBLING RETURN AMID CONTROVERSY

With Yale's chances of gaining at least a share of the Ivy League championship having been blown to smithereens, the safe thing for Alex to have done was sit out the game at Princeton Stadium to make sure, absolutely sure, he was ready to go for the season-ending Harvard game the following week. Are you kidding? With two games left on the schedule, most likely the last two of Alex's football career, did anyone seriously expect him to sit out if his knee was healthy enough to give it a go?

"We don't have a chance at winning the Ivy League anymore, so it's pretty easy to give up on a season at that point for a lot of teams, but not for us," Alex said. "We know that Princeton is a rivalry game; we're their biggest rival, and we knew they would be eager to play us. We know that to salvage our season it's very important to take care of business and come out and show the team what we're capable of these last two games, and we did that."

Alex made sure he was a part of that proving, and if anyone wondered whether he'd made the prudent decision on playing, he quelled all doubt midway through the third quarter when he ripped off a sixty-two-yard touchdown run to boost the Bulldogs' lead to 31–17 in a game they would ultimately win, 33–24.

There was still pain in Alex's knee at the start of the week, but it began to go away as the days and the rehab sessions passed. He took a good deal of practice repetitions on Thursday, took the bulk of them in Friday's walk-through before the bus trip down to New Jersey, and by Saturday morning he knew he was going to be fine. "That was my issue last week, getting confidence and trusting my knee, and I was able to get that trust back by Thursday," he said.

Mordecai Cargill started, but Alex was on the field during the first series, and he wound up getting the lion's share of the work with twenty carries for ninety yards. Of all the plays in a game where the Bulldogs piled up five-hundred yards of total offense, Alex's TD jaunt was quarterback Patrick Witt's favorite. "He's been battling to get back on the field; it was almost as if he limped all the way to the end zone," said Witt. "We were so happy that he was able to play."

After the game the Bulldogs officially found out that they would be able to say the same thing about Witt when Harvard came to the Yale Bowl for the 128th playing of The Game.

All season Witt had known that if he was going to interview for the prestigious Rhodes Scholarship for which he was a candidate, he was going to have to miss the Harvard game. His district's interview sessions were scheduled for November 19 at Emory University in Atlanta, and there was almost no chance that it could be moved. This came to light in the media prior to the Princeton game, and Witt was deluged with interview requests, many of which he granted. His story wound up in the pages of the *New York Times*, the *Wall Street Journal, USA Today*, and *Sports Illustrated*, among others.

After the Princeton game, Witt publicly revealed that he would pass up the Rhodes Scholarship interview to play against Harvard, something he had known all along but was waiting to announce in case he came out of the Princeton game injured, in which case he might as well try for the Rhodes.

"We didn't talk about it much," Alex said. "We knew he was playing (against Princeton) so we had to take care of business there and that was our main focus. But the press was going crazy about it, so there were a lot of interviews. People were calling him and some of us about it. I was joking around with him because the *Wall Street Journal* called me so I was thanking him for giving me the chance to be quoted in the *Wall Street Journal*. I know he was sick of the attention. I had a feeling he would play because if he wasn't going to play he would have told us earlier so we could start preparing for that and giving our backup quarterback more reps. I gained a lot of respect for him, I can't imagine how difficult a decision it must have been. It's a testament to his character, a selfless act, definitely."

As it turned out, though, maybe not. Witt's character came into serious question a couple weeks after the Harvard game when it was reported that, unbeknownst to Alex and the rest of the Yale team, Witt really didn't have a choice to make at all between the interview and the game. It was revealed that back in September a female student had gone to Yale's Sexual Assault Harassment and Response and Education Center and filed an informal report that Witt had assaulted her in her dorm room. Citing confidentiality policies, Yale never released this information, and it didn't have to because the woman never filed a formal complaint with the school or went to New Haven police with her accusation. Further, Connecticut law does not require colleges or universities to report suspected sex offenses.

In early November, the Rhodes Trust learned of the allegation through unnamed sources, contacted Yale and Witt, and opted to suspend Witt's candidacy. The Trust said the only way Witt could regain his status as a candidate would be if Yale re-endorsed Witt for the honor in writing by November 15, which the school did not. Three days before that deadline, Witt, apparently knowing Yale would not re-endorse him, announced that he was going to play against Harvard.

Witt, who wanted to pursue a career in the NFL, completed his class work in December with a 3.91 GPA and a degree in history and left school to begin working out for the NFL combine scheduled for February. He hired Atlas Strategies as his representative in that endeavor, and the president and CEO of the company, Mark Magazu, released a statement indicating that Witt believed the informal complaint regarding the assault had been dismissed and would not affect his Rhodes interview. "While the committee can refer an informal complaint into a formal process if more substantial disciplinary action may be warranted, it did not do so in Patrick's case," Magazu said. "At that time, all parties, including the university and Patrick, considered the matter ended."

But before any of that unpleasantness was revealed, there was the matter of The Game. Yale's season hadn't gone the way anyone connected with the program thought it would, but for the next week, there was an opportunity to erase the disappointment of what had transpired on the field. Beating Harvard would cure a lot of those ills. And for Alex, Witt, and the twenty-two other Yale seniors, this would be their last chance to achieve a victory over the Crimson.

The week of The Game is unlike any other week at Yale. There is an un-mistakable pulse pounding through the campus every day, but that vi-brancy mushrooms when the men from Harvard are scheduled to be in town.

It's sometimes difficult to get two groups of people, or even two people, to agree on anything being discussed at Yale, whether it's Barack Obama's foreign policy, or which of the twelve residential colleges has the best looking coeds, or whether Toad's Place is still the place to be on Saturday nights now that an influx of New Haven townies and Quinnipiac students seems to have altered the demographic of the once all-Yale establishment on York Street.

But there is one thing every son and daughter of Eli agrees on: Harvard sucks, and it must be defeated in The Game.

However, the problem, and the reality, is that Harvard did not suck. Yalies may hate everything that Harvard is, but no one could deny that the Crimson had been better than the Bulldogs in football for the last decade, as their nine victories in the last ten meetings would attest.

"It has gotten ridiculous," said Yale senior offensive guard Gabe Fernandez, who not only had school pride but family pride on the line, as his older brother, Frank, was an all–Ivy League center for Harvard a few years earlier. "It's embarrassing. Even my brother's Harvard friends, who I've come to know and like ask me, 'When are you guys ever going to beat us?'"

Alex, and Fernandez, and the rest of the Bulldogs were hoping it would be November 19, but it was going to be a tall order. When the Crimson took the field at the Yale Bowl, they would do so as the already-crowned Ivy League champions, a team that had won eight games in a row since an opening day 30–22 loss at Holy Cross, and a team that had won its six Ivy games by an average of seventeen points including a 37–20 victory over two-time defending League champion Penn, which clinched the title the previous Saturday.

"They have a great program this year," said Alex, who was trying to avoid being part of just the sixth Yale senior class to not have tasted victory against Harvard. "We're going to have to play our best game of the year to beat them."

For the Bulldogs, The Game was a chance to salvage what had been a desultory season. There were high expectations for this Yale team, but there were too many lapses at inopportune times, and four losses later, all that was left was Harvard. And thank God for that.

"We're disappointed with how our season went, but we still have the Harvard game," said Alex. "We could go 0–9 and then win the Harvard game and everyone on campus would think we're the greatest team. That's the only game that really matters in people's eyes, at least in the Yale community. That's what you sign up for when you come here, and it's an awesome experience for the one week that football mania does last around here. It's something I have been hoping to get for the past four years now, a win over Harvard. If we could do it, that could basically redeem all the disappointment we had this season and make up for the past three losses. It would be a great way to end my college career."

THE GAME

Imagine that you are twenty-two years old, and the one activity you have loved more than anything in your life has just been taken away from you, and you know you will never be able to enjoy it again. You are twenty-two years old, just beginning what will likely be, God-willing, the greatest four or five decades of your life, but something you have been doing since you were a little kid, something you have poured every ounce of skill and passion and blood and sweat and tears you had into doing it to the best of your ability, is gone forever.

That's what Alex was left to face, because when the final gun sounded on this sour Saturday, there was no more football to play. It was like the game died for him, and the crushing and demoralizing 45–7 loss to archrival Harvard in the 128th playing of The Game served as the funeral for Alex's now extinguished football career.

"It's surreal that it's here," Alex said, his brown eyes glazing at the thought as he sat outside the equipment storage room at the Smilow Field Center, adjacent to the Yale Bowl where the carnage inflicted by Harvard had ended about an hour earlier.

This is how it is for college football players across the country, about 95 percent of whom will never play football again once their last year of eligibility is complete. The best of the best of the best will get to play in the National Football League, and everyone else—including all but a mere handful of Ivy

League players through the years—will move on with their lives due to the finality of football. Golfers can play their sport until they are octogenarians; baseball players can always turn to softball when their reflexes won't allow them to hit a ninety-mile-per-hour fastball; basketball players can play ultra-competitive pickup at the YMCA or on the playground; same with hockey players at the local rink. But where can you find twenty-two men, outfitted in full pads, willing to replicate and play a game as physically demanding and sometimes dangerous as tackle football? You can't, so when that gun echoed throughout the mostly emptied-out Yale Bowl, Alex knew it was truly over, and he would never again don shoulder pads and a helmet and play football the way he'd always played it.

"We have all the time in the world to prepare for it, and when it comes you're still not prepared for it to end," Alex said, the raw emotion of that realization splashed across his unshaven face. "I was aware that this was going to be the last time that I was going to walk onto the field, and I tried to take everything in today. I was really emotional after the game, and that's when it really hit home. It's going to be very weird for the next couple of days and weeks."

There wasn't a lot at stake for either team in terms of the Ivy League standings. Harvard was the champ and its goal was to finish with an undefeated Ivy record; Yale had a chance to finish alone as the runner-up if Penn and Brown lost their games, which, by the way, both did. However, this being The Game, everything was at stake in what is undeniably the preeminent athletic competition in the Ivy League. One of the most overused clichés in sports is that you throw out the records when certain teams play each other. Well, it is absolutely the truth when Harvard and Yale are staring across from each other on a football field.

The team with the better record won this game, and Tom Williams's guys may have been ready to play, but they didn't play well. In fact, the Bulldogs saved one of their worst performances of the season for The Game that they wanted to win more than any other.

"We got beat by a better football team today; they looked really good on video, and they looked even better in person," Williams said in a solemn postgame press conference that was further subdued when school officials shared details regarding a tragic pregame accident in one of the Yale Bowl parking lots. A U-Haul truck driven by a Yale student careened into a group of people, killing a thirty-year-old Massachusetts woman, an incident the players did not hear about until after The Game.

With a bright sun helping to take some of the chill out of the November New Haven air, Yale opened the scoring midway through the first quarter when Patrick Witt threw an eighteen-yard touchdown pass to Jackson Liguori. It was a play that brought a huge roar from about half of the announced crowd of 55,137. The other half—only a handful of whom were aware of the accident—was still out in the parking lots partying at various organized tailgating events. It's an oddity that is unique to this ultimate rivalry game when it is played at the Yale Bowl. "They'll come into the stadium when they feel like it," said Sam Rubin, a 1995 Yale grad who works in the sports information office. By the time the masses got around to checking out The Game, they probably wished they'd stayed right where they were. Soon after Liguori's touchdown, things took a drastic turn for the Bulldogs, and it ended up being a long, miserable day as Harvard scored the game's final forty-five points without a Yale response.

Harvard senior quarterback Collier Winters, looking rather un-Harvard-like with his long, unruly blond hair flowing out of his helmet, began shredding the Bulldog defense. He wound up passing for 355 yards and two touchdowns, plus he rushed for another 62 yards and one touchdown, capping his Crimson career in high style. Harvard also scored a touchdown on a fake field goal as kicker David Mothander took an option pitch on a beautifully designed play and scooted untouched around the left side to give the Crimson a 21–7 lead early in the second quarter. And late in the fourth quarter, the Harvard defense joined the scoring parade when Crimson captain Alex Gedeon, a senior linebacker, intercepted a poorly thrown Witt pass and raced 32 yards for the touchdown that produced the 45–7 final, Yale's worst loss to Harvard since the 1982 match at Harvard Stadium that ended with the same count.

Alex never got going, finishing with only forty-five yards on nineteen carries and four pass receptions for twenty-eight yards. "They flew fast to the ball, and I'm still not as healthy as I'd like to be. I felt like my speed was a little slower, and they definitely took advantage of that," he said. "I remember one of the screens, it was wide open and they caught me from behind. But no excuses, we didn't play well."

That would include the normally unflappable Witt, who lost his way after the touchdown pass to Liguori and threw three costly interceptions. The defense had no answers for Harvard's skillful players, allowing 506 total yards, and in addition to being fooled on the fake field goal touchdown, the special teams also had a field goal blocked when the score was only 14–7, a moment that Harvard coach Tim Murphy felt turned the tide for good in his team's favor. No doubt, this was a total team loss.

"The biggest thing for us was eliminating the stupid mistakes and executing our offense," Alex said. "We felt all season that our biggest threat is ourselves, and if we beat ourselves we can't win. We didn't play well enough today to give us an opportunity. But no discredit to Harvard, they played a heck of a game and they stuck it to us when they had the chance."

Following Yale's Friday walk-through, Alex and the rest of the seniors had begun cleaning out their stalls in the Smilow locker room, leaving only the things they would need on game day. Now, Alex stood in front of what had been his personal space for four years, and he silently emptied the rest of his belongings into a black plastic trash bag, then slung that bag over his shoulder and walked out of the room and down the stairs for the last time as a Bulldog football player.

FAREWELL TO FOOTBALL

Like the members of the four senior classes before him, Alex came to understand the fortuitous timing of Thanksgiving break falling the week after the Harvard game.

Those seniors had all lost their final game to the Crimson as well, but with school not in session, they weren't faced with the deluge of, "Hey, what happened the other day?" questions.

"We have the week off, so I've been able to avoid seeing people at school who would ask a million things about the game," Alex said after finishing his part-time work duties in a business office at Science Park, where he split time working on Excel projects and doing grunt manual labor. Now that the season was over, he would be able to earn a little extra cash because he'd be able to pull a few more hours in between writing papers and studying for exams without football taking so much of his time.

The sting of what happened three days ago at the Yale Bowl was still there, and Alex knew it would be for a while. "I'm better than I was, but it's tough to get over," he said.

The night of The Game, the parents of the twenty-four seniors hosted a banquet to honor their sons at the downtown Omni Hotel, and they were all introduced, feted, and given commemorative plaques. Both of Alex's parents were there, as were his brothers and sisters, his paternal grandmother, and a couple aunts and uncles, and while the mood was anything but celebratory, "It was actually pretty cool. It was nice to be honored like that."

He spent the rest of the evening wandering around campus where his fellow students, seemingly oblivious to what had happened earlier in the day—not only the disappointment in the stadium but the tragic accident outside—were partying their asses off because that's what you do at Yale on the weekend of The Game. "There was a bunch of stuff going on," Alex said. "All the frat houses have parties and it's pretty chaotic, so I kind of floated around and saw a bunch of people."

The memory of the singular loss—even one as horrific as 45–7 to Harvard—would eventually fade, but his reflections on his football career would continue to linger. Outside of his family and his faith, football had defined who Alex had been for much of his life. Those remarkable nights at Ansonia, where he became the most prolific ballcarrier in Connecticut high school football history, have forever elevated him to legendary status in his small hometown. And while his career at Yale may not have played out exactly the way he envisioned it, he wouldn't alter one moment of his time in the Ivy League.

"There definitely has been pressure I have felt being here, especially living twenty minutes from where I played high school ball," he said. "You look back on the past and the success you had in high school, it's not really comparable to what I'm doing now. Some people see that as a fall-off, but college football is a different game, and that is something I understand. Early on it was something I struggled with, just trying to live up to those expectations. You always want more for yourself, but it's over now and you can't look back; you can't change anything that's happened. I've had success, formed some great friendships, and played with some great guys, and I was doing it here at Yale, so those are things that you will never forget."

Now, he knew, it was time to move on. For the first time since he enrolled at Yale in the fall of 2008, Alex was no longer a football player; he was a full-time student, and in a few short months, he wouldn't even be that. He would graduate with a degree in history, though he had no idea what his future held.

"I guess I just have to figure out what the next step in life is going to be, start thinking about jobs and what I'm going to do. I'm still uncertain, I don't know what's out there, I haven't done much investigation. But I'll have a liberal arts degree, and it's from Yale, so I could do a lot of things."

Which is exactly why he came to Yale in the first place: to be a student, and an athlete.

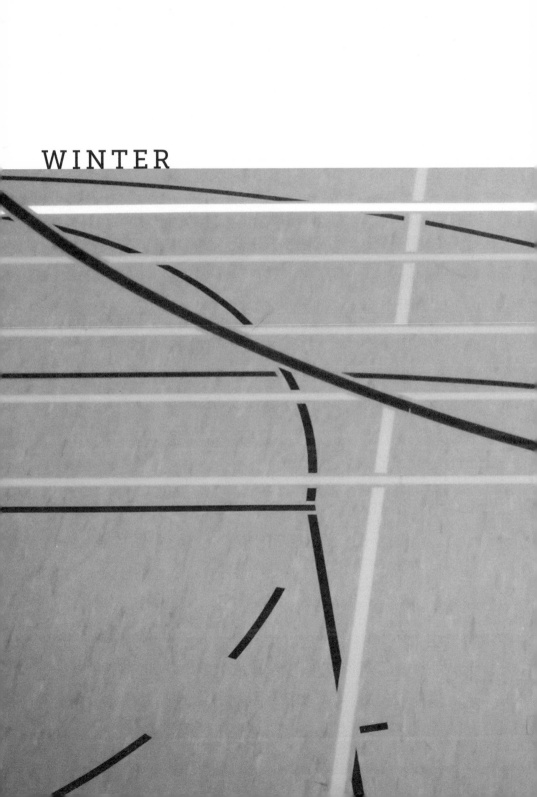

WINTER

SHEILA DIXON

BROWN WOMEN'S BASKETBALL

During her sophomore year at Brown, Sheila was asked by *Brown Bear Magazine* to share the story of her upbringing for the Spring 2011 edition of the alumni publication, and Sheila happily and proudly agreed to do so. She wasted no time getting right to it as she started her piece this way:

"I was born in St. Clare's Hospital in Schenectady, New York. My biological mother was a drug user and abandoned me at the hospital. Because of my mother's drug use during the pregnancy, the doctors found traces of cocaine in my blood when I was born. Luckily, at twelve days old a foster parent in the Department of Social Services started looking after me. Four years later, Phyllis Dixon officially adopted me, and I became the youngest of fifteen Dixon children, eleven of whom were adopted, four of whom were my mom's biological children."

Yeah, that caught the attention of a few people because that's not a story you hear too frequently pertaining to Ivy League students. "People were pretty shocked," Sheila recalled. "They were shocked that I had fourteen siblings and came from a pretty unique background. I got e-mails from a lot of Brown alums and they're all glad that I was able to come here and be part of the Brown community."

One afternoon, more than thirty years ago now, Phyllis was sitting in her Schenectady home watching a local public television program called *Thursday's Child*—a show whose mission was to find people willing to adopt abandoned or orphaned children—when, to her astonishment, her great niece, Shirley, appeared on the screen.

"She was being featured for an adoption, and I saw her on TV," said Phyllis of the little eight-year-old girl who was the granddaughter of her sister, also named Shirley. "I had had some contact with her mother (Phyllis's niece, whose name was Rhonda), before. She had asked me to take Shirley because she was going to go to California, and I said, 'You only have one child, why don't you bring her?' The next thing I knew, about a year later, she left and she gave her up."

At that time Phyllis had three teenage children (a fourth had passed away) of her own from her first husband, Robert, and was the stepmother to the six children of her second husband, Lloyd. Still, she knew she needed to do something, so she called the number on the TV screen to inquire about what was going to happen to Shirley. When told that unless adoptive parents could be found Shirley would remain in a foster home, Phyllis started the process of legally adopting the little girl left behind by a drug-addicted mother who never came back to Schenectady and years later was found stabbed to death.

"I didn't have any thoughts about doing it; I went through everything to get her, and then after she came into my life, that was going to be it," Phyllis said. "But what happened is once I did that the county started calling me about other children."

And Phyllis couldn't say no.

After Shirley, there was Clifton, who was one of Lloyd's six children whom Phyllis legally adopted as her own. Then came two sisters, Comeka and Galinda, and when their mother lost all her parental rights, her other two children, Tara and Malcolm, were reunited with their younger sisters in Phyllis's home. Later, there was another brood of three from the same family, Nayla and twins Antonio and Nadia. Then came Damise, Rasheen (who is Sheila's biological brother), and, finally, Sheila.

Had it not been for Phyllis, many of them, maybe all of them, would have remained in the child welfare system, an unrelentingly harsh place where the hopes and dreams of innocent children often get crushed by the reality of their abandonment and absence of a family structure. Even though Phyllis had separated from Lloyd right around the time she adopted Shirley, and she knew in every instance that she would be undertaking the caregiving on her own, Phyllis believed she could provide these kids, her kids, enough love and support and guidance to at least give them a chance at somewhat normal lives.

"These children were supposed to be emergency, or short-term care, but they never went home," said Phyllis. "It just never worked out, so I ended up adopting them. Each one of these kids, they became a part of my life. It was hard, and there were a lot of tough times, but I felt that's what I had to do; I had to say yes. I don't know what I would do without them in my life, being the way it is. I don't see it."

The story of how Sheila wound up in Phyllis's life actually predates her 1991 birth by more than a year. Phyllis had taken in Damise when he was five days old, raised him until he was three, and was beginning the adoption process when his birth mother decided she wanted to take him back. Phyllis and the rest of the children were devastated to lose the little boy, so when Social Services called shortly thereafter to ask if she would take another infant boy, she agreed, partly because Rasheen would help fill the void left by the departure of Damise.

"We were all heartbroken when we lost Damise and we didn't know what to do, so we had to work through that," Phyllis said. "When they called me about this little boy up at the hospital, Rasheen, I went up and looked at him and decided to take him."

As it turned out, the following year, Damise's mother decided to permanently relinquish her parenting rights to him, so he was returned to Phyllis (who made his adoption official two years later). Around that same time, there was another phone call from the agency; Rasheen's mother had given birth to another child that she did not want. This one's name was Sheila, and the hope was that Phyllis would be willing to keep the siblings together. Not surprisingly, she was.

"Sheila was very sickly because her mother was on drugs and Sheila had cocaine in her body at that time, so she had to stay in the hospital a little while," Phyllis explained.

But soon the cocaine was expunged, Phyllis nursed her back to health, and so began a life that Sheila knows she would never have had if not for this caring woman.

For the majority of her formative years, Sheila and her siblings coexisted happily, though Sheila had a naturally closer bond with her biological brother, Rasheen. Her memories of that period in her life are happy ones, of Christmases when the house in the Woodlawn section of Schenectady was jam-packed with family; of playing sports with her siblings, particularly Little League baseball, basketball, and football; of swimming in the community pool; of excursions to local eateries where strangers would remark to Phyllis how well-behaved her children were—"Be seen, not heard."

However, as some of her older brothers and sisters reached their teenage years, problems began to arise. Some of it had to do with their interest in reuniting with their birth parents and the tension that created. Some of it was associating with the wrong school mates and the resulting juvenile delinquency that produced. And some of it was just kids being kids and thinking they knew better.

"It started falling apart, and it was horrible for a while," said Phyllis, who saw some of her adopted children run away, and a few of them never returned. "Some of the kids left for a time because they didn't want what I had to offer; they wanted the street and that's what they chose."

This crushed Sheila, and to this day it saddens her that she has lost touch with several of the children she grew up in the same house with.

"It was difficult to see how this great family came apart," she said. "I struggled with the fact that this woman had given her life to raising us and taking care of us as her own children and when my siblings got to the point where they'd find out where their biological families were in some cases, then she didn't mean anything to them. That hurt me, and I had a hard time dealing with it. I was just a baby when I came, so I knew nothing else, but I knew the quality of life I had, and would have, far exceeded what I would have had."

CROSS-TRAINING

If you didn't know better, you might think that Brown assistant strength and conditioning coach Brett Crossland is a little crazy. But the thing is, Sheila did know better, and she still thought this guy was a little crazy—maybe even a lot crazy—and she loved it.

"He's the best strength coach I've ever had, just an amazing coach to work with," Sheila said of Crossland, the energetic purveyor of all things fitness who took great pleasure in whipping all the Bears into the best shape possible so that they could perform at their peak level, be it on the field, the court, the ice, wherever. "He came in my freshman year and killed us. He's so hard on us, but it's rewarding to see how we've progressed. Every day he tries to bring something new, always changing it up to keep it fresh. Sometimes we'll come in in the morning and he'll say, 'This is what I thought about last night at the dinner table.' And we're like, 'Coach Cross, why are you thinking about us at the dinner table?' I just love how much he gets into our program and wants to work with us continuously."

On a Monday afternoon, with the regular season only a few weeks away from starting, Crossland put the women through one of his typical sessions where he worked them like a lobbyist up on Capitol Hill, pushing, pushing, pushing. His primary emphasis with the men's and women's basketball teams was sprints because that's what basketball players do—they sprint up and down the court for forty minutes. Longtime women's coach Jean Marie Burr wanted to play an up-tempo style this season, so stamina would be vital. It wouldn't be an issue on Crossland's watch.

"Our starting five averaged about thirty minutes a game last year, which was an improvement over the year before," Sheila said, recalling her sophomore season when the Bears continued their climb up the Ivy League ladder with a fourth-place finish, better than their sixth-place standing when Sheila was a freshman, and vastly better than the three consecutive last-place finishes prior to Sheila's arrival from Schenectady, when Brown won just five of forty-two League games and ten of eighty-four overall. "We were able to go harder and longer and a lot of that had to do with the conditioning we did in the preseason."

Sheila loved Crossland and his fanatical workouts, like the one last year when Jordin Juker turned twenty and Crossland "honored" her by putting the team through a workout that featured twenty-second sprints, prompting Juker to warn everyone to not broadcast their birthday. Not surprisingly, though, Sheila was ready to start playing games, and part of that was the different vibe resonating inside the Pizzitola Sports Center, fueled by the genuine hope that the Bears could compete for the League title this year.

When Sheila arrived in the fall of 2009, the program was at its lowest point since coach Burr took over in 1988 as it endured a three-year stretch that included records of 5–23, 2–26, and 3–25. But there had been incremental improvement since, and after an 8–20 record when Sheila was a non-starting freshman, Brown improved to 10–18 in 2010–11. As a full-time starting sophomore (save for two games when she had swine flu and one when Burr decided she deserved a benching), Sheila led the team in scoring (11.0 points per game) and rebounding (6.3 per game), was voted the team MVP, and was a second-team All-Ivy selection.

"I think I can do really well again," she said. "I have a lot to work on and improve on, but I think I can continue to get stronger and develop. I've never had the fundamentals of basketball, but I've always been athletic and that's helped me out the most. My coaches think I can make first-team all-Ivy."

To get there, and to get the Bears back onto the radar screen in Ivy League women's basketball, Sheila would need help, and she thought she was going to get it with the entire roster back and an influx of impressive freshmen.

"We have a lot of positives coming back," she said. "We've had some negativity and emotion on the team, but this year everyone is gung ho for what we have to do. We're going to lose some strong seniors (at the end of 2012) with Aileen Daniels and Hannah Passafuime, real motivators and leaders, so this is the year we need to do it. I'm excited to see how well we can do."

TAKE A SEAT

There were six minutes left to play, the twenty-point lead Brown had enjoyed early in the second half against Albany was down to one, the player Sheila was responsible for guarding, Ebone Henry, had just knocked down her fifth three-point basket, and Bears coach Jean Marie Burr called for a timeout.

"We were falling apart, our defense was breaking down, this girl was making every three-point shot, and I got frustrated," Sheila said, explaining the outburst she had in the huddle which earned her a seat on the bench. "At the timeout I was upset and I said, 'Come on everybody, get it together' and coach Burr pulled me aside and said, 'We don't need you to get mad, we need you to stay composed.' I said, 'I don't care right now.' And she said, 'Oh, you don't care? Then I'll see if someone else cares and we'll take you out.'"

So, even with the Bears collapsing and perhaps on their way to their third consecutive loss to start the season, Burr sent in sophomore Maggie Smith and sat Sheila, her most dynamic player who'd scored a team-high seventeen and nineteen points in the first two games.

Reflecting about the brief time she sat simmering on the bench, Sheila realized she deserved it. "I've never spoken to a coach like that," she said. "I was out for a couple minutes and she asked me if I was composed yet and I said 'yes' so she put me back in the game and we finished it out. It ended well. That was rough because I didn't mean to make an outburst, she knows I respect her and that was not intentional."

Albany took the lead at 48–46 when Burr sent Sheila back in, but Sheila helped to restore order and she contributed three free throws while Lauren Clarke and Hannah Passafuime made some big baskets and the Bears outscored Albany, 19–5, the rest of the way to earn their first victory, 65–53, one that Sheila said, "We really needed."

That's because the season hadn't gotten off to a very good start. The Bears dropped a 72–67 decision to New Hampshire and then lost, 70–66, to New Jersey Institute of Technology, and Sheila and her teammates felt the unusual nature of the practices leading up to those games played a major factor in the disappointing results.

"Coach Burr was very aggressive in relaying her message and the feelings weren't all positive going into the first two games just because of how practice had gone," Sheila explained. "People weren't as confident. She doesn't yell often in practice, and if she does she'll apologize. But that week it was yell, yell, yell, and yell some more and everybody was a head case. I don't know if she was trying something new to get us fired up, but it didn't leave us feeling too high-spirited going into our first game."

Naturally, Phyllis Dixon heard all about this. She heard about everything because Sheila called her practically every day. Sheila is the baby of Phyllis's brood, and with several of the adopted children out of Phyllis's life, and with the ones who are still in touch now grown and on their own, there was a special bond she had with Sheila. More than two years after Sheila enrolled at Brown, mother and daughter still struggled with the separation.

So Sheila tried to call Phyllis every day, regardless of how busy her practice or class schedule was, and after every game there was always a rehashing of what went on, and how Sheila played. This conversation, though, was a little more involved because of the benching, and Phyllis reiterated what she had always told her children: "Be seen, not heard." Sheila broke that tenet, and as Phyllis told her, she got what she deserved. "Coach Burr benched me, and I learned my lesson," Sheila said.

BIG EAST BEATDOWN

Sheila was trying to get her head around what the Bears were up against in the championship game of the Brown Bear Classic the first weekend of December. Cross-town rival Providence College was the opponent, a team Brown had not defeated since 2002, a team that, the day before in the first round of the tournament had blown out Fairfield, 75–43, the same Fairfield team that had defeated Brown, 63–55, earlier in the week.

"So I was thinking, 'OK, this is going to be a challenge; we might get our butts kicked.' That was the thought in my head, but I didn't share that with anybody," Sheila said, laughing at herself.

Cue up the cliché: This is why you play the games. Sheila pumped in sixteen points as Brown played its best basketball of the season in running out to a 36–13 halftime lead. And while Providence made a run to get within striking distance in the second half, it wasn't enough and the Bears wound up with a 70–57 victory. Sheila finished with a career-high twenty-six points on nine of thirteen shooting from the floor, including five of six from beyond the three-point arc, and was named the tournament's most valuable player.

"Everything just felt right," Sheila said. "I was composed and I was just feeling it. I made five of six three-pointers, which is ridiculous. Two of them were prayers, I had to shoot them up because the shot clock was running out, and they went in. It was just one of those games that I was feeling really good about. We knew they were very athletic, they jump, they're fast, and in my first two years playing against them they pretty much wiped the floor with us. But we came out amazing, we were so fired up."

Sheila talked to her mother after the game to share the big news, and she told Phyllis what was so gratifying about the victory is that it came against a profile Division I school.

"Providence is a Big East school, so these are girls who have been heavily recruited; they're supposed to be part of the top of the nation. They're probably looking at an Ivy League team, and even though we're Division I, we're not always given the same respect. So I told my mom I went into it trying to show that we're still Division I, we're playing at the same level as you guys, and we're going to bring it to you. That was my mind-set. I wanted to show that we could play them, and we could beat them."

After losing three of their first four games, the Bears had now won four of their last five, two victories coming over Thanksgiving break when Brown went up to the University of Maine and won the Dead River Company Classic. The Bears defeated the University of Evansville, 55–47, and then host Maine in the title game, 61–59, in overtime, even though Sheila didn't think she played up to her standards.

"I struggled against Evansville and kind of struggled against Maine, so it's nice to know we have a team of players who can carry the weight when someone is struggling," she said. "We've been to that tournament six times and coach said that was the first time we've won it."

With one more game to go, against Vermont, before a three-week break for finals and Christmas, Sheila was thrilled with where the Bears stood.

"We're playing well, so now we want to win this last game and then finish off the semester because we're all going a little crazy right now with school, finishing up papers and studying for finals," she said. "I've got so much work to do, but we all have a lot of work to do.

HELP ALONG THE WAY

What happened in this final game before Brown's exam/holiday break was a perfect example of why Sheila believed the Bears had a real chance to make some noise when the Ivy League games started in January. Sheila was the best all-around player on the team, the Bears' leader in scoring, rebounding and steals. However, if Sheila wasn't having a good night—and she wasn't against Vermont at the Pizzitola Center—this Brown team could pick her up, and that was the case as the Bears pulled out a 61–57 victory over the Catamounts.

"I always put pressure on myself to top what I've done, but knowing that we have a team that can score, and I'm part of a team that doesn't need one strong player because we have four or five, is a great thing," Sheila said.

Sheila just wasn't stroking it against Vermont. Coming off her MVP performance in the Brown Bear Classic, she made only three of twelve shots from the field, but it didn't matter. Senior cocaptains Aileen Daniels and Hannah Passafuime combined for thirty-four points, nine rebounds, six assists, and three steals which lifted the Bears to their third straight win and sent them to the break with a record of 6–4.

Yet even on an off night, Sheila was still a key contributor because after Vermont tied the game at 57–57 on a three-pointer with twelve seconds to play, Sheila drew a foul and calmly sank two free throws with nine ticks to go to provide the winning points.

This was nothing new for Sheila, because for almost as long as she had been playing the game, she had typically been the player who has risen up and made the big shots when they needed to be made. "I've always had a desire to be successful at whatever I do, and I'm very competitive, so I like being in that situation," she said.

As a kid Sheila had no particular affinity for basketball; all she wanted to do was play, and it didn't matter what the sport. "I was such a big-time tomboy," she said with a laugh, recalling her interest in football, the game she loved most and was told that she couldn't play because she was a girl. But when one of her brothers erected a couple of makeshift hoops at their home—one in the backyard, one on the driveway—the seed began to germinate, and Sheila spent hours out there dribbling and shooting.

One day during recess at Page Elementary, the school principal, Paul Scampini, saw Sheila holding her own with the boys on the playground and he approached and asked if she'd be interested in attending an overnight basketball camp at nearby Siena College. The little fourth-grader with the motor that never stopped sure was.

"That was the first time I did anything organized with basketball," she said. "I enjoyed the atmosphere of basketball, and the experience of being able to go away and play at a camp for the first time, that really sparked my interest."

And then when she reached seventh grade, "I really got interested, and I tried out for the modified team (at Central Park Middle School). I'd been at the Siena camp a few summers and I was being recognized and getting better and it made me want to improve and to make basketball my thing."

By eighth grade she was asked to try out for the freshman team at Schenectady High School, and she made it, and when she enrolled there the following year, Sheila skipped junior varsity and went straight to the varsity as a freshman. During her four years she averaged fourteen points per game, and as a senior she led the Patriots to their first regular-season league title and a semifinal berth in the sectional tournament. All the while, she was excelling in the school's rigorous International Baccalaureate academic program.

It was away from school, though, where Sheila really made a name for herself. In the spring of her freshman year she began playing AAU ball, first for the Saratoga Sparks team and later for the higher-profile Albany City Rocks squad coached by Keith Danzy.

"When I went with coach Danzy I got the coaching and the training and practicing that helped me improve," she said. "He recruited girls and had a lot of strong players on the team and we all got better. That's when I knew

I might be able to play Division I basketball in college, and that was one of my aspirations."

With the Rocks, Sheila played in several elite tournaments, traveling as far away as North Carolina and Georgia, and the exposure she and her teammates received was tremendously beneficial. "Coach Danzy was very passionate about helping get the girls into good schools, and just about all the girls I played with went D-I or D-II. Once he knew I wanted to go to the Ivy League, he got the word out, and that's how I got recruited by Brown."

At first, Phyllis was skeptical of Danzy, a man who rubbed some people the wrong way, including Sheila's high school coach, Carol Lupo. "There were people that were involved who didn't have anything good to say about him, so we had to make up our minds that this was something good for her," said Phyllis. "We didn't know that he was going to follow through, but he did."

FINAL EXAMS

Sheila was lying in her dorm room bed in the wee hours of a Friday morning, giving serious thought to how much she really cared about the take-home exam for her Legal and Constitutional History class.

"We had twenty-four hours to do it, and by the time I started I was mentally checked out," she said. "I almost didn't think I could do it, and at one point I was contemplating what my grade would end up being if I handed in a paper with just my name on it. It was a pass/fail class, but I realized I had to do it. It was my last one, so I pulled an all-nighter and finished it."

When she turned that test in, she was done for the semester, and when she arrived at the Pizzitola Sports Complex for practice a couple hours later, her body was limp and fatigued, her brain was like mush, but her spirits were soaring. As she said, "I don't have anything due for the next six weeks! It was such a relief; I felt a weight off my shoulders. Just being out there and not having to worry about school was an amazingly good feeling. I was on like two hours of sleep, but who cares, I was done."

Sheila's last day of fall classes had been December 9, and after she finished final papers in her Legal and Constitutional History class and her criminal justice and engineering courses, in addition to taking finals in the history and engineering classes, and Social Changes in the 1960s, she was gassed.

"Everything was kind of like one right after the other," she said. "The papers that were due, and the exams, and it seemed like it was going on forever. Just chaotic and stressful."

The week of finals is a stressful period for all college students, but it's a little more difficult for the kids at the Ivies, as well it should be given the academic reputation of the eight schools. The good news for the athletes is that while the League boasts over and over that they are treated no differently than the rest of the student body, that is also the case during finals week. Typically, there are no athletic contests scheduled during this period, which affords athletes—like everyone else—the proper time to study for exams and finish term papers.

Even practice schedules are curtailed, and in Sheila's case, coach Jean Marie Burr—understanding that the Bears weren't playing again until the weekend of New Years'—even canceled a workout when captains Hannah Passafuime and Aileen Daniels expressed concerns about some of their younger teammates struggling to get their work done.

"Coach Burr was very aware of our exam schedules and they worked it out where we could have some days off from practice," Sheila said. "They took into account what we had to do and they gave us days off and some short practices. Not having games allowed us to focus and we needed to focus."

When she returned home to Schenectady, there was no basketball to be played, no term papers to work on, no tests to study for, and she reveled in the opportunity to walk around a Schenectady grocery store with her mother, stocking up for the big Christmas dinner that Phyllis would be preparing and serving in a few days.

"I'm so glad to be home," Sheila said. "This was my most stressful semester thus far. People say that third year always hits you hard. It was definitely the hardest so far. My brain was kind of fried finishing up the semester, so it has been nice to not have to worry about deadlines, getting things in, reading—and just being able to hang out and chill, and catch up on sleep I don't normally get during the semester."

When she wasn't sleeping, she would spend almost every waking moment with Phyllis, because even now, into her junior year at Brown, Sheila still missed being home and cherished every opportunity to be in Schenectady with the only parent she has ever known, or needed.

Sheila had never met her biological mother, nor did she ever want to. There was a time in high school when the woman contacted Phyllis to ask if

Sheila would like to meet her, but when Phyllis relayed that message, Sheila wanted nothing to do with a reunion.

"I never really wanted to know who she was," Sheila said. "Me and my brother, Rasheen, don't know anything about our mother, and I haven't had any interest in following up with that. From the time I was a baby till now [Phyllis] has always taken care of me, and my real mother didn't want me."

As for her father, she and Rasheen would occasionally visit him when he still retained parental rights, but there was little satisfaction derived from it. "At one point, I think we were eleven or twelve (after he had relinquished his rights and Phyllis had officially adopted both children), we went up to Central Park, which is in Schenectady, and he asked us if we wanted to do visits with him again, and we both said we didn't," Sheila remembered. "He had his opportunity to be our father and he lost it, and this woman had been taking care of us since we were both pretty much straight out of the hospital."

Phyllis loved all of the children she adopted, and tried her best to give them a good life, but her care and generosity wasn't always appreciated, and through the years the family splintered. Sheila was the one constant, the one child who never gave Phyllis trouble, never questioned her authority or parenting methods, and unconditionally loved and respected the woman who literally rescued her.

"Sheila listened to me, she went along with me, and we've always been very close," said Phyllis. "She was always a good student, not a child that gave me any problems, just had a smile and was a very loving, happy kid."

Which is why it was so hard for Phyllis to sign off and allow Sheila to go away to school at Brown.

"One thing Sheila had to deal with was me," Phyllis said. "I did not want her to go; I spent a lot of time going to her games, and I knew it would be hard for me. I wanted her around here, and I couldn't see why she didn't go to Union or Skidmore. But I'm very proud of her. I feel fortunate to have been able to raise her, and having someone like her in my life."

So Christmas would be a wonderful time for mother and daughter to reconnect, but then Phyllis would have to say goodbye again, much sooner than she would prefer, because Sheila and her teammates had an abbreviated holiday break due to their much-anticipated trip to Northern California to play two games against Dominican College and San Jose State during New Years' weekend.

Sheila would be on the other side of the country for about five days, but Phyllis would be on her mind and in her heart the whole time.

"I am so grateful that I was given to my mom and she took me in," Sheila said. "The quality of life I would have had couldn't even compare to what I've been given. The moral support, the love that I've been given, never mind material-wise. I knew she'd always have my back and be there for me no matter what I would be going through."

CALIFORNIA DREAMIN'

The Facebook pages of some of the women on the Brown basketball team were lighting up because coach Burr was lost at Pier 39, the famous tourist attraction on the edge of historic Fisherman's Wharf in San Francisco.

"It gets very foggy there in the early evening," Sheila explained. "We were just walking around and we went one way and coach Burr went the other and we couldn't find her for about fifteen minutes. The assistant coaches had to go find her, and everyone was posting it to their Facebook as it was happening. She said, 'I didn't see anybody, but it was foggy and I thought you were up ahead, and then it started getting quiet.' She wanted to go out to the end to see the sea lions and otters; she was kind of fascinated by all that, so she just kept going. It was so funny."

Burr laughed about the whole thing after and said, "They thought they were going to find me in the ocean. But they did come looking; they didn't just leave me out there, so that's a good thing, right? They're such a fun group of kids, I can't say enough about this team."

Sheila had only flown on an airplane a few times in her life, and she'd never been to the West Coast, so the trip to San Francisco to play a pair of nonconference games qualified as a thrill.

"It was really exciting, really a great time," she said after the Bears wrapped up their cross-country excursion and got a jump on their New Years' Eve celebration with a 61–47 victory over San Jose State, which came on the heels of their 66–45 blowout over Dominican two days earlier.

Outside of a possible Ivy League championship and a berth in the NCAA tournament, the road trip to San Francisco was the highlight of Brown's season, an adventure the players and coaches had been looking forward to ever since the schedule was announced several months earlier.

"I've never been to the West Coast, and four of the girls on the team are from California, so it was good to see them around their family. They just accepted us and the hospitality was awesome," Sheila said. "We're a very close team, more than any other team I've been on, and the trip just made it even stronger and tighter. We took so many pictures and just had a blast hanging out."

The team had dinner one night at the home of Lindsay Gottleib, a 1999 Brown grad who played for Burr and is now the head coach at the University of California. They spent a day touring San Francisco, highlighted by trolley car rides, shopping, and time spent at Pier 39 gazing out at gorgeous San Francisco Bay, the Golden Gate and Bay bridges, Alcatraz, and yes, all those sea lions and otters lounging on floating docks. And the family of senior Hannah Passafuime hosted the team for a dinner at their home in Santa Cruz.

As for the basketball, the Bears had little trouble winning either game, and this served as a perfect tune-up for the start of the Ivy schedule after the Bears had been off for nearly four weeks.

Against Dominican, Brown scored the first fourteen points, led 41–15 at the half, and Burr played her bench players most of the rest of the way. Sheila struggled with her shooting after the long layoff and made only four of fifteen for nine points. In the San Jose game she shot a little better (five of ten) and finished with eleven points, four coming in a critical span of eighteen seconds midway through the second half. San Jose had tied the game at 34–34, but baskets by Lauren Clarke and Lindsay Nickel gave the Bears a four-point lead. Sheila then drove for a layup, and followed that with a clean steal and layup. Just like that Bears were in charge at 42–34 and they steadily pulled away to an easy victory.

It was back to reality New Years Day as the team flew back to Providence to a campus that was mostly vacated, except for the athletes. But that was OK because classes didn't start until the last week in January, so Sheila and her teammates would have plenty of time to focus on basketball, enjoy some rare free time, and recount the bonding experience they all shared out West.

SHOOTING SLUMP

The one thing that Sheila feared when the Bears opened the Ivy League portion of their schedule at home against Yale was that the team wouldn't be ready for what it was about to face. And that fear was realized during a 75–65 loss to the Bulldogs.

Brown had little trouble beating Dominican and San Jose State on its trip to California, it extended its winning streak to six games by rolling past woeful 1–14 Rhode Island, 53–40, and then had eight days without a game before taking on Yale. So Sheila took the court wondering how the team would respond to its first true test since early December when it defeated a plucky Vermont squad in the last game before the break.

"The California trip was good for us, but the competition we faced there doesn't measure up to Yale," she said. "The games in California were confidence-boosters, but we went into the Yale game and just didn't work hard enough to win. They went on a couple runs during the game and we weren't able to answer."

Sheila's return to competition had been difficult. After a spotty showing out West, she had another tough game at Rhode Island as she made only two of ten from the floor and scored a mere six points. A couple days before the Yale game she acknowledged her struggles, saying, "I don't think I've been as much of an offensive threat; my touch has been off. I think the break affected me. I was playing pretty well and I wasn't ready to end our game play, but the break cooled me off a little too much. This week has given me a chance to evaluate my game, shake it off, and not think so much or be so hard on myself about how I played the last three games. I've had enough time to recoup and I think I can get back to where I was before the California trip. I'm just really ready to go."

And she was. Against Yale she made six of ten from the floor, seven of eight from the free-throw line, and finished with twenty points and six rebounds, pretty impressive considering she played only twenty-two minutes because of foul trouble, and ultimately fouled out.

Despite that hardship, Brown was up 47–42 midway through the second half and looking like it was taking control of the game before a sudden ten-point run thrust Yale into a five-point lead. Sheila ended that with a three-pointer, and after Yale did a little more damage, Sheila hit a jump shot and then drove for a layup that cut Brown's deficit to 58–57 with 4:08 remaining, but that was as close as the Bears would get.

"I think it was eye-opening to know that we still have to work hard every day and the Ivy League is going to be very competitive," Sheila said. "The teams are very similar and it usually comes down to who's going to show up each night. Yale outplayed us. There are a lot of expectations and new standards that coach Burr is looking for, and we have a lot to work on."

TRACKING THE BEARS

On their way to winning nine of their first thirteen games in the non-League portion of their schedule, Brown's defense was the best among the eight Ivy League teams, as it allowed an average of just 55.2 points and gave up more than 60 points just three times.

So when she was asked how she felt heading into the start of the League schedule, coach Jean Marie Burr was oozing with confidence. "We've had a great start to the year, and as we go into Ivy play, I think we're feeling good about the challenge in front of us."

And then the Bears went out and gave up a season-high seventy-five points in the home-court loss to Yale, and a few days later, in their final non-League game, they were torched for a season-worst eighty-one in a loss to Holy Cross. Not at all what Burr was expecting.

"Coming off those two losses, we went into practice focused on repairing our defense," Sheila said, referring to the three days of work between the loss to Holy Cross and a rematch with Yale down in New Haven. "We knew that if we were going to beat them, we had to play defense the way we know how. Coach Burr preached to us to stay steady and consistent and have confidence in our back line and to communicate."

The Bears responded to Burr's requests and turned in a solid effort to pull off a 60–55 victory, a game in which they held Yale to 36 percent shooting and created thirteen turnovers.

Because of foul trouble, Sheila had a minimized role in the outcome, as she scored only seven points in seventeen minutes of action, but since becoming a starter at the beginning of her sophomore year there hadn't been too many games where she hadn't been a key contributor.

Landing Sheila was a nice coup for Brown. After a decorated high school career, and the success she enjoyed at the AAU level playing for coach Keith Danzy's Albany City Rocks team, Sheila attracted interest from a number of Division I schools, most prominently the local Albany-area colleges like Union, Siena, and Skidmore.

But Sheila—despite the protestations of her mother who preferred she stay close to home—was aiming higher. "I knew I could play Division I and if I could have played at a big school I would have gone there, but I didn't get as many offers from the big schools as I wanted," Sheila said. "So when it came down to Skidmore or Siena compared to the Ivy League, obviously it was the Ivy League."

Brown was always in the mix because of Sheila's tremendous academic record, but she wanted the recruiting process to play out before she gave the school serious consideration. Paul Scampini, who had helped Sheila get her start in basketball back in the fourth grade and was the principal at Schenectady High during Sheila's time there, had been in her ear from the start, making sure she was aware that the Ivy League was not out of her reach. And when she finally decided to see what Brown was all about, Danzy took the lead.

"Coach Danzy is actually the one who contacted Brown and got them to recruit me," Sheila said. "It was amazing having a coach so involved, and it wasn't just with me. He helped all of the seniors on our team get to great schools."

At the time Brown was one of the worst women's basketball programs in the country, having won just ten of eighty-four games over the previous three years. Burr knew Sheila was the kind of player who could help get the Bears headed back in the right direction, but the trick was to get her.

"I first saw her play in AAU and she was explosive, attacked the basket, was very quick, and I thought she could be the type of player that could help us build the program back to a championship level," said Burr. "We were able to sell the point that she could make that kind of impact on our program and help us get back to the top. She has a charisma that compels you toward her; she's so bright and ambitious. As I learned about her, it was more of, 'Was she going to be able to leave the nest?' Her mother was very proud of her and Sheila was an important part of their family chemistry, so for her to go away to school, I thought it would be tough. I remember there was quite a discussion between Sheila, her AAU coach, and her mother to really reinforce that Brown would be a great opportunity for her to spread her wings a little bit and challenge herself to play in the Ivy League and learn in the Ivy League."

Sheila got the message, and when she came for her recruiting visit, "I watched an early-morning practice and I knew I could play with these girls. They were struggling and I knew for us to turn it around it would take a lot and it would be up to my recruiting class and the next one before we'd see some change."

In the end, Sheila also recognized that the Ivy League's policy of not awarding athletic scholarships didn't really impact her. Given her family financial situation, she knew she would get all the aid she would need to cover the cost of attendance, and not having a scholarship took some of the pressure off. "There were no barriers," she said. "If you have a scholarship and the coach decides to cut you because you're not good enough, or something happens like an injury, you're out of a scholarship, and then what? At Brown, I could still go to school if, God forbid, something happened, and even if I didn't have basketball, I knew that I would be getting an Ivy League education."

NOT-SO-SUPER SUNDAY

As Sheila relaxed in her dorm on Super Bowl Sunday, she wasn't all that interested in the electricity buzzing throughout the New England region as the Patriots were getting ready to play the New York Giants for NFL supremacy later in the evening.

Back from a weekend roadie to Penn and Princeton, between basketball and school Sheila had plenty on her mind, and not a lot of it was very good.

With classes having started back up, she went through a little turmoil with her schedule and was shopping her classes harder than a socialite on Fifth Avenue before she settled on a course in ethnic writing, two in political science, and an American studies seminar.

"This semester was difficult choosing my classes," she said before launching into an explanation of what she had to go through. "I'm done with my requirements for my concentration, so the next twelve classes I have to take don't have to be within my concentration. I'm supposed to be taking classes that I'm interested in, but that has been a big challenge for me because I'm not interested in about 95 percent of what Brown has to offer. I've added and dropped classes about six times within the first two weeks of shopping."

Basketball had always been her escape from the rigors of academia, but all she wanted to do was escape after the last two games when she shot four for sixteen from the floor both nights.

The Bears gave Ivy League powerhouse Princeton a good run before falling, 57–45, but Sheila just couldn't find the range (she even missed both her free throw attempts) and scored only nine points. The next night against Penn, Brown overcame Sheila's continued inaccuracy and defeated the Quakers, 59–55, in overtime. At least in this game Sheila made four of her five free throws and finished with twelve points and ten rebounds.

"I really struggled," Sheila said. "I'm a very mental player, I get inside my own head and cause myself problems with what I think I should be doing, and what I do end up doing. I felt myself rushing my shot, attacking and forcing things I wasn't supposed to. These are the times when I confide in my former coach, coach Buckley."

Buckley, who was instrumental in recruiting Sheila to Brown, quit the coaching staff at the end of the previous season because she had a baby, but she has remained close to the program. In fact, when the Bears beat Dartmouth the previous weekend for coach Jean Marie Burr's 300th career victory—all at Brown—Burr returned to campus to find her office extravagantly decorated for the occasion, courtesy of Buckley.

"She's kind of my mom away from home, and I talk to her about anything," Sheila said. "She was always very open and responsive and supportive of what I was going through scholastically or with my family. And in basketball I would work out with her, watch film with her nonstop and she would pull me out of practice and tell me to work on things. She's been a very big supporter and helped me out a lot."

Given that close relationship, Sheila called Buckley to talk things out, and as she usually did, Buckley gave Sheila some tough love. "She was blunt and she said, 'You're sucking, and I expect something a lot better this weekend.' She knows what I can create on my own, so she was just saying don't force it and go up stronger, get to the line more, and have confidence in what I'm doing and don't be a head case about it. I needed to hear that."

SURPRISE VISITORS

Burr had no doubt that Sheila would emerge from her shooting slump because if there was one thing Sheila excelled at, it was working hard.

"For Sheila it's getting in the gym and getting some shots up," Burr said a few days after Sheila had helped the Bears sweep a home weekend against

Columbia and Cornell, compiling twenty points, nine rebounds, and six assists in a 72–63 overtime triumph over the Lions, and then chipping in sixteen points and five steals in a 60–49 conquest of the Big Red.

"Even if you're a great shooter," Burr continued, "you have to be able to miss to make. But it isn't all about shooting because she gives us so much more; she's an explosive defender, her energy is contagious, she'll defend the perimeter and the post, and her defensive rebounding has helped us be in the position we're in right now."

These were traits Burr recognized the first time she saw Sheila play in AAU during the recruiting phase, and once she was on campus as a freshman in 2009, Sheila's willingness to hone her craft immediately endeared her to Brown's all-time winningest basketball coach.

"The toughest thing to teach as a coach is patience," Burr said. "Obviously you have to be extremely successful at the high school level to have a Division I program knock on your door and there's a tremendous amount of commitment that those players make in order to have those opportunities. As a head coach you recruit players that you know are going to develop. But you have to teach them patience. Now they're freshmen in college, they have to make adjustments academically and athletically, with your strength program, and learning the system. She had some pretty high standards for her own performance, so there was a transition for Sheila. You had to help her adjust to maybe a role that wasn't her ideal role, but she was always willing to do what was best for the team."

However, as a freshman she didn't do much of anything very well. Coming off the bench in all twenty-eight games she shot the ball terribly—26 percent from the floor, 43 percent from the free-throw line, and a gruesome three for forty-five (.067) from three-point territory. She also had fifty-three turnovers.

"I was one of the best players in New York State and you go to college where everybody's the best from their area and you're playing against the best in the country," said Sheila, who also battled injuries that first year in addition to the transition to college. "I really struggled. Freshman year was a slap in the face."

Heading into her sophomore year she worked on every aspect of her game, including conditioning, and she made a quantum leap and forged her way into Burr's starting lineup. "I worked out a lot, lifting, running back at home that summer, just trying to become better," she said.

Her workouts were derailed in July 2010 when her mother suffered a stroke that kept her hospitalized for a week, and Sheila dropped everything to help care for Phyllis until it was time to get back to school. She resumed her regimen that fall with the help of hard-driving strength and conditioning coach Brett Crossland, and the difference in her play was eye-opening. By season's end she led Brown in points, rebounds, and steals and had only three fewer assists than team leader Lauren Clarke.

"What she did in that off-season, that's what we all saw in her and were looking for her to bring to Brown basketball," said Burr. "She has an ability to listen, to be coached. You have someone in Sheila who, in pureness, just loves the game. She has high goals and she was willing to work for them with the enthusiasm that you need to make it contagious to other people."

This year she had continued to build on her foundation and had become an even more complete player, but the shooting woes that had hounded her off and on were back again at a most inopportune time. Locked in a battle for second place in the League with Harvard and Yale behind undefeated Princeton, the Bears earned a workmanlike 58–55 victory against Harvard on February 17, but suffered a backbreaking 57–52 loss the next night to lowly Dartmouth, just the fourth win in twenty-three games for the Big Green this season.

Sheila was a combined nine for thirty from the field and scored only twenty-one points in the two games. Clearly the more frustrating of the two was the loss to a Dartmouth team that Brown had throttled by twenty-four points just a few weeks before, and because it happened in front of Sheila's mom, who made a surprise trip to Providence to watch Sheila play for the first time in her college career.

"It was about five minutes into the game and I didn't know because she didn't tell me she was coming," Sheila said. "So I'm playing and I see my mom out of the corner of my eye. I couldn't believe it, and I did a double take and then I fumbled the ball out of bounds so of course coach Burr takes me out. I'm over there on the bench crying."

Sheila's oldest sister, Stephanie, drove Phyllis, her son Julian, and the two young children Phyllis now cares for, Nallelie and Victor Lopez, and after the game the family checked into a hotel and enjoyed a wonderful night together.

"I only expected my mom to maybe come to my last senior game and then graduation because it's tough for her, and I knew that was something I would have to give up by coming to Brown, her being able to come to my games," said Sheila. "So to see her and the twins and my nephew and sister, it was great. I always talk about my mom, she's the topic of conversation a lot, and my teammates all wanted to meet her so they were excited. I've never been more surprised in my life."

NO "CELEBRATION"

More than twenty minutes had passed since the final horn had sounded, but in recounting what had happened in the dying seconds at Cornell's Newman Arena, Sheila could not stop the tears from welling in her eyes.

In a game that Brown desperately needed to win if it hoped to entertain any thoughts of receiving a bid to the women's National Invitation Tournament— the ugly step-sister to the beautifully magnificent NCAA tournament, but a postseason opportunity nonetheless—Sheila made two unfortunate last-second mistakes that helped cost the Bears the victory.

Aileen Daniels made a jumper from the lane with seventeen seconds remaining to give Brown a 50–49 lead, and Cornell raced up court intent on attempting a potential winning shot before the Bears were set on defense. Sheila and her mates were back in plenty of time, and Cornell's Clare Fitzpatrick missed a shot from the right side, and the ball trickled out of bounds off the Bears with four ticks left.

The Big Red called time out to set up an inbounds play from under the Brown basket, and during the break, Bears coach Jean Marie Burr switched her man-to-man defense and put Sheila on Fitzpatrick, while the taller Daniels would be on the ball in an effort to make the pass for Shelby Lyman more difficult.

The moves did not work. Fitzpatrick was able to escape Sheila only a few feet from the basket, Lyman found her, and Fitzpatrick laid the ball in with three seconds remaining to put Cornell ahead, 51–50.

"I should have fouled her before she got the ball," Sheila said, lamenting the fact that Brown still had a foul to give without sending the Big Red to the free throw line. "She just bodied me under the basket and I was out of place and she got an open layup. I thought I had her underneath the basket, but apparently not. It was a nice little forearm, and it got her open. I can stop that play, but I didn't."

Brown called a timeout to set up its version of a Hail Mary play which it called "Celebration." But there would be no celebrating. Sheila came free near midcourt on the right sideline, but she tried to turn and dribble before she caught the ball, and the pass bounced off her hands and went out of bounds, sealing the Bears second straight loss to a below-five-hundred team.

"Just trying to get it and go," she said. "I got it, and I went before I had full control. "With three seconds you just want to get up and get as close a shot as you can, maybe get a foul or if not, at least get a decent shot off. I would have had a chance, I had the lane up the sideline, but I went too fast."

Now with five League losses the Bears were officially eliminated from the race, though no one was going to overtake unbeaten Princeton anyway. With ten losses overall, it was hard to imagine a scenario that would include Brown playing beyond its regular-season finale in two weeks.

"We probably don't have any chance at the (NCAA) tournament, or the NIT," Sheila said. "Beating Dartmouth would have given us some momentum because we would have been in second place and if we had won these two we might have had an opportunity to go to the NIT, but now we're probably done."

COMING UP SHORT

When Sheila arrived on the Brown campus in the fall of 2009, the women's basketball program was in shambles, and she was considered one of the new recruits who was going to help turn the Bears' fortunes around.

She had done her part. There was gradual progress in her first two years as Brown won eight games in 2009–10, and ten in 2010–11, and when practice started for this season back in October, Sheila had a firm belief that the Bears could shock the Ivy League and compete with Princeton for the title. That did not happen, and while on paper winning sixteen games and producing the first winning record since 2005–06, was a successful campaign, it wasn't good enough for Sheila.

"I thought this was our chance at an Ivy League championship," she said. "I don't think we'll have the same amount of success next year. Hannah (Passafuime) is an amazing leader and so is Aileen (Daniels) and they're both graduating. It's going to be really difficult to lose those two integral pieces."

The Bears closed out their season with back-to-back home losses to Penn and Ivy League champ Princeton to finish 16–12, including 7–7 in the League which placed them fourth. With Princeton going undefeated in the League, Brown had no realistic chance of winning the crown, nor did any other team. However, while the NCAA tournament was out of reach, an NIT berth—which the second-place Ivy team gets automatically—was there for the taking if the Bears could have won a few more games. Instead it went to Harvard, which finished 17–11 overall, but 10–4 in the League.

"It was frustrating knowing that we kind of blew our chance by not playing the way we should have," Sheila lamented. "We were in good position after the Harvard win, and then we lost to Dartmouth and we lost to Cornell, and that made it difficult to keep our heads in it."

Sheila finished the season as Brown's leader in points (366), rebounds (172), and steals (60), her 13-point scoring average was sixth in the League, her 6 rebounds per game ranked seventh, and she was named second-team All-Ivy for the second year in a row. She established a new career scoring high with 26 points in the great victory over cross-town rival Providence, she started all twenty-eight games, had three double-doubles, and was the Ivy player of the week once.

Yet Sheila, as competitive as she is, felt she could have done more. "I think I improved a lot from last year. I was more controlled in my game play. I'm aggressive, and I still have strides to make and that was evident in my stats (she was second only to Lauren Clarke in turnovers with seventy-seven, and she had a team-high eighty-seven fouls and four disqualifications). I believe I showed what I need to work on."

She was already doing that. Only days after the season ended, the Bears were back in the gym for the start of their post-season work with strength and conditioning coach Brett Crossland, putting the women through agility tests that would help set their base-lines for next season.

The players weren't exactly thrilled by this because they would have preferred a little more time to recuperate after the season. Still, there's less time on the floor, and that would leave more time for studying and enjoying other aspects of campus life, something the players miss out on during the season.

"It is nice to be able to come home after class, not being in the gym four or five hours," Sheila said. "I miss basketball, I miss the games, especially now that March Madness will be starting and you see all these teams still playing, you regret the games that you lost and not being the better team in crucial games. But I do enjoy having the extra time."

Sheila was going to go home to Schenectady soon for a visit, because she could. She would attend the upcoming appearance on campus of *Saturday Night Live* star Seth Meyers, because she could. She would hit the books and make sure she finished out her junior year on a strong academic note, because she had to. What she couldn't do was change anything about the now completed season, and she would be thinking about the lost opportunities this year and hoping to apply the valuable lessons she learned in her first three years toward next season when she would be one of the senior leaders.

"I've tried to make a positive impact on the program and I feel like I have," she said. "My teammates mean the world to me and this program means the world to me. I try to be positive about where it's going, and I'm glad to have been a part of the strides we've made."

KEITH WRIGHT

HARVARD MEN'S BASKETBALL

Keith will never forget the moment when an entire year's worth of work—a career's worth of work, really—went splat in the blink of an eye. Or, in this case, the splash of a last-second jump shot.

As October 2011 neared its end and basketball practice was in full bloom at Harvard and everywhere else across the nation, many Ivy League followers believed the Crimson would win the outright League title for the first time in the eleven decades the men from Cambridge had been playing basketball; that in turn would mean the Crimson would make their inaugural appearance in the modern-day NCAA tournament and their first since 1946; hey, they might even win the national championship. But as magnificent as all that would have been, nothing would ever quell the throbbing pain of what happened on the afternoon of March 12, 2011.

"You never file it away, you never forget it," Keith said of the devastating 62–61 defeat he and his Crimson teammates suffered that day at Yale in the special one-game playoff between Harvard and Princeton that decided who would win the Ivy title and earn the League's automatic bid to March Madness. "It's not like I broke down and cried in the locker room, but it was a tough day, for sure. It's always in the back of my mind that we were 2.8 seconds away from going to the Big Dance. Those 2.8 seconds, we're going to use that as motivation for the whole year."

A new season was upon coach Tommy Amaker's team, and the expectations for long-awaited Crimson glory were soaring. As Amaker put his team through practice in preparation for the opening game just over two weeks away against traditional local rival MIT, Amaker hadn't forgotten what happened in 2011, either.

"It was a God-awful ending to a fun year overall," he said. "If you ask me would I wish we would have won the game that would have put us into the tournament last year, I would say yes, and then look at different types of motivation for this season. It's in the back of our minds constantly; it has to be. When you get that close to something, it's gut-wrenching if you don't get there and don't finish."

Earning a share of its first regular-season Ivy title wasn't enough because Princeton matched Harvard's 12–2 League mark, and then won the showdown when the Tigers' Doug Davis took an inbounds pass on the left wing, dribbled toward the key, pump-faked Crimson guard Oliver McNally into the air, then went up and released his twelve-foot jumper as gravity was pulling a defenseless McNally back to the ground. As the breathless sellout crowd— equal parts Crimson and Tiger faithful—stood fixated on the ball, it passed through the rim as time expired, crushing what had been Harvard's greatest season.

The Crimson had lost at Princeton a month earlier, and that really wasn't anything new. For the Tigers—who had won twenty-six League men's basketball championships, tied for number one all-time with Penn—that was their 126th victory over Harvard in 164 meetings dating back to Princeton's 19–12 victory in 1901. That was the Crimson's only Ivy loss until a shocking 70–69 setback at Yale two weeks before the playoff game. They bounced back with a vengeance to beat Penn and Princeton on back-to-back nights at home in raucous Lavietes Pavilion to clinch at least a tie for the title, but when Princeton defeated Penn in the regular-season finale, the one-game winner-take-all playoff was necessary, and Yale—of all places—was selected as the neutral site.

The week of the playoff, Keith remembered it being "nerve-wracking. Everybody was on edge because we knew this was the next step. It's our goal, every year at the start of practice, making it to the tournament. On campus the atmosphere was awesome, but everybody was like, 'Oh my goodness, you guys have a chance to make it to the dance, this is going to be great for Harvard basketball.' It was very intense. There was so much pressure that was put on us. We felt it."

Having to go to Yale was a bit unsettling, too. Not only is Yale Harvard's rival in everything from basketball to biology, the Crimson had just lost that 70–69 game at the buzzer to the Bulldogs at the John J. Lee Amphitheatre. "It's hard not to think back and say if we hadn't lost to Yale we wouldn't have to be here," Keith said. "So we had just lost there and now we had to go back.

I could see if we had gone there and blown them out, we could say 'Yeah, this is our gym.' So it was tough going in there with that in the back of our head."

The playoff game was a thriller from start to finish. Harvard led by seven at the half and was up, 48–42, with eleven minutes to go, but Princeton rallied to take a 51–50 lead and over the final six minutes the largest lead was three, that by the Tigers. Down 61–60, the Crimson regained the edge when Brandyn Curry drove the lane and hit a runner with eleven seconds left, and after Princeton rushed down court only to have a Davis layup swatted out of play by Harvard's Kyle Casey, the Tigers called timeout with 2.8 seconds to go.

"I was down on the right block and I saw Doug Davis catch the ball," Keith recalled, wincing at the thought. "He gave Oliver an up fake and Oliver went. So I said, 'OK, he's shooting so I have to get ready for the rebound so they don't get a tip in.' I saw the ball leave his hands and it was like no way. I swear it went by so slow. It was like the ball was in the air five minutes, and it was 2.8 seconds, and then it went in."

More than seven months had passed. The wound was still open, and as McNally said, "This thing really doesn't go away. You'd like to say it does, but until we do something this year, it's not going to go away."

The time had come for the Crimson, led by Keith, who was a senior cocaptain (along with McNally) and the reigning Ivy League Player of the Year, to start doing something.

HARVARD'S ON THE PHONE

Keith's mother, Sabrena Tabron, can recall as if it were today the summer evening in 2007 when she received the call that changed her son's life forever. Keith was lying in bed, feeling under the weather, and not even basketball practice for the AAU team he was playing for in Norfolk, Virginia, was going to get him up. And then the phone rang, and Sabrena knocked on his door and said, "Harvard's on the phone." That got Keith up, and he's really never come down from that high.

"I was so over the calls coming in, I was ready to throw the phone against the wall," Sabrena recalled of that spring and summer when Keith was a hotshot high school recruit thanks to his stellar work as a forward at Norfolk Collegiate School. But this time it was Will Wade, who at that time was Harvard's recruiting coordinator as well as an assistant coach under Tommy

Amaker. "He said, 'Hello, I'm calling from Harvard, I'd like to speak to Keith Wright.' So I sat up, paused, and then went to his room. He looked at me and said, 'Harvard's on the phone?' He spoke to coach Wade and then he went to the workout and after he left, I was thinking 'It's freakin' Harvard on the phone!'"

That night when Keith returned from practice, he'd already made up his mind that if he qualified academically to attend Harvard, that's where he was going to school. It didn't matter that Princeton—the longtime co-kingpins of Ivy League basketball along with Penn—had already come to see him play. It didn't matter that Illinois of the Big Ten and Virginia Tech of the ACC had made contact or that several mid-major programs including Davidson and George Mason had called. Harvard called. Freakin' Harvard.

"A lot of the kids I meet here, they're bred Ivy League," Keith said. "From when they were young, they were going to Harvard. To me, Harvard was something you only saw in the movies. The brand itself—Harvard. Everybody knows Harvard. That was really the selling point for me. So when they called, I knew from then on I wanted to go to Harvard, and it wasn't because of Tommy Amaker. Even though he's a great coach, and I'm blessed to have him here as well, it's Harvard, man."

To borrow a phrase from the Tom Cruise movie *Jerry Maguire*, Harvard had Keith "at hello." Had it known then how easy it was going to be to reel him in, perhaps it could have avoided some unpleasantness that arose concerning its recruitment of him and another player, Max Kenyi, from the Washington, D.C., area, during the summer of 2007.

In March of 2008, after it had been revealed that Amaker's first recruiting class, scheduled to enroll that fall, had earned recognition as one of the top twenty-five in the nation—an unprecedented feat for an Ivy League school—Pete Thamel of the *New York Times* wrote a story questioning the ethics of Harvard's recruiting tactics, and Keith was in the middle of the controversy.

At issue was alleged improper contact with Keith and Kenyi that had been made by Kenny Blakeney, who had played pickup hoops with both players during a period when the NCAA does not allow contact with prospective recruits. When interviewed by Thamel, Blakeney explained that because he was not an employee at Harvard—he was officially hired on July 2, 2007, weeks after the contact—that no rules violations were possible. "I was unemployed," said Blakeney, who played at Duke when Amaker was an assistant coach there in the mid-1990s. "I don't know if it's a gray area or anything like that.

I hadn't signed a contract. I didn't have any type of agreement with anybody. How could I recruit them to Harvard if I'm not employed?"

Keith and Kenyi signed with Harvard a few months after Blakeney was hired, and Thamel reached both for comment regarding Blakeney, who worked at Harvard through the end of the 2011 season. Keith told the reporter, "[Blakeney] actually got to play with us (at an AAU practice), because he wasn't on Harvard's staff. He didn't sign anything yet. We talked and exchanged numbers."

The article also insinuated that Harvard had made a conscious decision to lower its academic standards so that Amaker could recruit from a wider pool of athletes. Thamel contacted members of previous coach Frank Sullivan's staff who said some of the players Harvard was recruiting would have been untouchables for them based on the school's stringent adherence to the Academic Index measure.

The Academic Index is a formula based on standardized test scores and high school grade point average to determine the recruitability of potential incoming Ivy League athletes. Basically, a student's SAT score is divided by ten to produce one part of the number, and the other number is derived from their Converted Rank Score, calculated on class rank and class size with the scale providing more points for larger schools. Adding these two figures gives you the AI score. For example, a student who graduates fifth in a class of 200 with an SAT score of 1,300 would receive 130 points for the SAT and 71 points for the CRS for a score of 201. This same student from a class of 1,000 would get 78 CRS points for an AI of 208.

The minimum AI allowed for an athlete is 176, but the AI for any new member of a class of recruited athletes across all sports (except football, which uses a different system) has to be within one standard deviation of the mean AI of all students at a particular institution, as calculated when they entered as freshmen. For instance, if Harvard's mean AI for a given year was 220, it would have a deviation of about 13 points, so in order for an incoming athlete to be eligible to be recruited, he or she would have to have an AI of at least 207. Historically, the approximate AI average of Ivy applicants has been around 200 while the average AI of accepted students has been closer to 210. Because Harvard typically has the Ivy League's highest mean AI across its student body, its athletic recruits must therefore meet a standard higher than the other seven institutions.

Keith was an outstanding student and a member of the National Honor

Society, but his AI was slightly below the previously acceptable level for Harvard, yet he was allowed to enroll. "I knew I was smart, but not Harvard smart," Keith said. "If it wasn't for basketball I probably wouldn't have come here."

Harvard athletic director Robert Scalise admitted that Amaker and his staff had been allowed to go after some players whose academic profiles would not have been considered for enrollment in the past because he wanted to give Amaker every opportunity to "change the culture of the program." In other words, Scalise wanted to contend for Ivy League championships in the only sport Harvard had never won one.

"What has happened is very simple," said retired *Boston Globe* columnist Bob Ryan, who covered the Hub's sporting scene for more than four decades. "Harvard has made a commitment to win that they never gave a previous coach since the early 1970s. They tried to win in the early '70s, and they couldn't win then because they were up against Penn and Princeton when those teams were top ten teams. They were never good enough to beat them, so they went back to being Harvard again and never gave another coach the resources to seriously challenge Penn and Princeton until Bob Scalise didn't renew Frank Sullivan and hired Tommy Amaker.

"Tommy is a dynamic guy," Ryan continued, "and there's no question they're getting guys they weren't getting before. Right away there were questions about pushing the envelope with the workout charges and all that. They're getting kids that Frank Sullivan couldn't get; there's not any doubt in my mind, and that's fine. If those kids that qualify can hang in academically, then fine, I want Harvard to be good. What the ramification will be, I don't know."

University officials vehemently denied that Harvard had softened its admission policies, and ultimately, a five-month Ivy League investigation into the allegations in the *Times* article cleared Harvard of any wrongdoing as it pertained to admitting academically undeserving students and Blakeney's role in Keith and Kenyi signing with Harvard.

By that time, Keith was already on campus, ready to help Harvard do what Scalise was hoping for.

"Princeton was pitching its great basketball tradition, but I didn't want to be a part of someone's tradition and history, I wanted to come to Harvard and make history and do something that's never been done," Keith said.

"Win an Ivy League championship and go to the NCAA tournament, that's something that's never been done here."

JUMP BALL

A few days before Harvard's season opener against MIT, Keith was sitting at a pub in Harvard Square enjoying twenty-five-cent wing night with a few of his Crimson teammates, and he was surprised by the roiling in his stomach. No, it wasn't the wings because they were great. The unsettling feeling was rooted in the fact that the season was about to begin, his last at Harvard, a season where expectations of greatness were soaring. National attention had descended on the program, and the reigning Ivy League player of the year knew that he would need to be great if glory was to be achieved by this team.

"I was talking to my mom and I was telling her that I'm anxious to get it going, but also nervous because everyone is looking at us and me being a senior, it's my last year and it's going to be a really big year and I've never felt this nervous in my life."

Coach Tommy Amaker knew what Keith was feeling. He played at Duke, for Mike Krzyzewski, on Tobacco Road, where playing in the NCAA tournament was a foregone conclusion, and anything short of a national championship was a disappointment. The proverbial bull's eye was always on Duke's chest when Amaker played and coached there, and it has remained long after he left Durham, North Carolina. He understood that you have to overcome the pressure of knowing that night after night you're going to get the opposition's best shot, and now he had to teach the Crimson how to handle that.

This had never been an issue for Harvard hoops, a program that had finished above .500 in just eleven of the previous forty years and had never won an Ivy League title until the one it shared with Princeton in 2010–11. But with every player on the 2010–11 squad back, the team that was 2.8 seconds away from earning the Ivy League's automatic bid to the NCAA tournament had that bull's eye emblazoned on its Crimson uniform.

"We return everyone, we have great leadership in the program right now," said Amaker. "We're optimistic, we're excited, and we have a lot of pride about the journey we've been on. We've wanted to create something, we wanted to put ourselves in position to be thought of as a basketball program. We're doing the things we have to do, and now we have to continue."

Well, things certainly got off to a good start when the Crimson rather easily dispatched spunky but overmatched MIT, 76–49, behind thirteen points by Keith and sixteen off the bench from sharp-shooting guard Laurent Rivard. And then a few nights later at Holy Cross, the Crimson went on a 16–4 run during a four-minute stretch in the second half to break open a tight game and escape Worcester with a 73–64 victory.

"We're confident, but we're working extremely hard," Keith said. "Coach Amaker doesn't want us to get complacent, or reading articles about where we're supposed to be. We have a saying that 'expectation' is an external word, so our internal word is 'standard' and we have a standard to live up to every day."

The standard would now be put to the test as the Crimson would travel out to Southern California to take on Loyola Marymount, and then head to the Bahamas over Thanksgiving to play in the inaugural Battle 4 Atlantis tournament where they would face Utah in their first game, and could run into Florida State and/or defending national champion Connecticut before the three-day event concluded.

CHAMPIONS OF PARADISE

One of Keith's fall 2011 term classes explored the history of R&B and soul music, and he was involved in a group project that was acting in and producing a film about the Temptations, one of the iconic Motown groups of the 1960s and '70s.

One of the Temptations' most popular songs was "Just My Imagination (Running Away with Me)," which reached number one on the *Billboard* chart in 1971, was voted in 2004 by *Rolling Stone* magazine as one of the five hundred greatest songs of all time, and now was unwittingly serving as a theme song for the Harvard basketball squad.

Seriously, was it just their imagination that the Crimson won the Battle 4 Atlantis tournament in the Bahamas? "We did the unexpected," Keith said following Harvard's 59–49 victory over Central Florida in the no-one-could-have-predicted championship game. "The mind-set going down there was to win, and we did."

A week earlier the Crimson had flown out to Los Angeles and rallied from an early thirteen-point deficit to defeat Loyola Marymount, 77–67 behind Oliver McNally's sixteen points, Keith's fifteen, and Kyle Casey's fourteen. That trip paled in comparison to what happened in the Bahamas. In the first-year Atlantis tournament, where the host Atlantis Resort paid each of the eight teams $2 million to come down and play, no one expected the Ivy Leaguers to be hoisting the hardware, not with fourth-ranked defending national champion Connecticut, and twenty-second-ranked Florida State in the field. But the Crimson embarrassed Utah, 75–47, in the first round, out-uglied Florida State in the semifinals, 46–41, and then watched in amazement as Central Florida upset UConn, 68–63, to set up a most-unlikely championship game which Harvard had little trouble winning.

"People are starting to see that we are for real," said guard Brandyn Curry.

Such as Seth Davis, *Sports Illustrated*'s senior college basketball writer and studio analyst at CBS, who was in the Bahamas for the tournament. When asked by the *Harvard Crimson* what he thought of Harvard's performance, Davis said, "It's not a surprise that they're a good team, but it was a surprise that they could beat Florida State, and beat Central Florida as convincingly as they did. We had a lot of expectations for Harvard, and what they did here this week is going to serve some notice."

After arriving on the island a couple days before the start of the event, Keith and his teammates appreciated the warm weather and the spectacular resort, but it was clear right from the opening tip against Utah that the Crimson weren't in town to frolic on the beach. "We were down here on a business trip and once we accomplished what we wanted to accomplish, we could enjoy the beach and the water slides," said Keith, who was named the tournament's most valuable player as he scored thirty points and pulled down twenty-two rebounds in the three games.

The Utah game was a joke. Now playing in the Pac-12, the Utes were rebuilding, and they fell behind, 21–4, in the first eight minutes and never challenged thereafter. "It was a statement for us," said Keith.

The next day Harvard was confronted with a talented and athletic Florida State team that had advanced to the Sweet Sixteen of the 2011 NCAA tournament. However, the Seminoles were simply brutal as they missed their first fourteen shots from the field and did not score until more than eleven minutes had been played. Fortunately for Florida State, Harvard was nearly as cold and the teams went to the break tied at 14–14. Both teams picked it up in the second half, and Keith's three-point play off a resounding slam dunk with 8:53 left to play gave the Crimson the lead for good at 26–24. Laurent Rivard's two three-pointers in the next two minutes stretched the margin to 34–26. When it was over, Florida State's forty-one points were the fewest Harvard had allowed in a game since Dartmouth scored only forty in a 1996 game.

Having seen Central Florida upset UConn, the Crimson knew they'd be tested in the championship game, but they aced the exam as Casey had fifteen points and nine rebounds, and the defense limited the Knights to 33 percent shooting, which included a four-for-fifteen performance by Marcus Jordan, the youngest son of Michael Jordan.

"We've been building towards something like this," coach Tommy Amaker said. "We've talked about it and worked toward it, but we certainly needed to see it happen, and it certainly happened for us here."

ANGRY YOUNG MAN

Smiling comes easy to Keith, though it wasn't always that way. To watch Keith interact at Harvard with his teammates, his coaches, his classmates, and his professors, you'd never guess that this happy-go-lucky kid with the calm demeanor, the boisterous personality, and the innate ability to be everybody's buddy and personal relationship counselor, spent much of his childhood being pissed off at the world.

"That's definitely fair," Keith said of that assessment of his formative years, which were filled with upheaval and heartache. "I went through a stage before I found basketball where I didn't know what I was doing. I wasn't doing anything crazy, but I was getting into fights all the time. I was very unhappy, my parents were divorced, and my mom sent me and my sister (Morgan) away to live with our grandparents, and I was just angry all the time."

Keith's father, Keith Wright Sr., a military man who spent time in Afghanistan during the Gulf War and was now incarcerated in Texas, cheated on his mother, Sabrena Tabron, when Keith was in early grade school and living in Jacksonville, North Carolina, about an hour northeast of Wilmington. That set off a chain reaction of events that had a profound effect on both mother and son.

While Sabrena was settling the divorce proceedings and trying to figure out how she was going to make ends meet, she sent her two children all the way to her hometown of San Francisco to live with her parents.

"When I put them on the plane, it was with the idea that we weren't going to be a family for a little while," Sabrena recalled, tears coming to her eyes as she revisited the pain. "It was very hard to send them away."

Just like that, Keith, who was in fourth grade, had his world turned upside down, and not surprisingly, he didn't know how to deal with it. A self-proclaimed "nerd" who favored reading and listening to music over playing sports, Keith was picked on constantly, and he spent much of his youth in detention at the various schools he attended.

"I was always getting into fights," he remembered, "because I took out my aggression that way. I'm telling you, I was angry until I was in the ninth grade. My mom, being the protective person that she is, really didn't fill me in on everything that was going on in the divorce. She didn't tell me my dad was cheating on her, so I had this vision in my head of, 'Why are you doing this to my dad, he didn't do anything wrong?' She was just trying to not tarnish the image we had of him."

In San Francisco, Keith would board a bus each morning for school and he'd spend all day in the heart of the big city, and then come home to an ever-present feeling of abandonment. "I kind of felt alone," he said. "My mom wasn't there and my sister was so young, so she didn't understand. I had all this anger and I had nowhere to vent it, so I would get into fights."

When Sabrena joined her children a little more than a year after she'd sent them out west, they all shared a single bedroom in her parents' tiny house, and she knew that was an untenable arrangement. "I decided that wasn't the life I wanted for them," she said. "So I started on the Internet and looked at places where I could afford to live and where the kids would get a good education."

Virginia Beach, Virginia, was the place. By now Sabrena had a third child, conceived out of wedlock with a man she had started a relationship with after her divorce was final, but whom she did not marry. Elijah was born in San Francisco and was just an infant when Sabrena packed the kids into her Jeep Cherokee and trekked back across the country to what she hoped would be a better life.

"I was nursing and driving and the kids were changing diapers in the back, but we did it," she said.

Keith, who was now in the middle of sixth grade, remembered the trip as being "fun" because they were a family again, and along the way they stopped at motels that had pools so he and Morgan could swim after being cooped up in a car all day.

While in Virginia Beach, Sabrena married another military man, Anthony Tabron, and the couple had a child, Keith's youngest sister, Olivia. The family moved to the Fredericksburg, Virginia, area for a while when Keith was in eighth and ninth grade, but when Sabrena and Anthony split, she returned to the Virginia Beach/Norfolk area, and it was there that Keith took an interest in basketball and began to chart his course to, of all places, Harvard.

"After they separated we went to live with my mom's friend, and she was sleeping on the floor and I was in the bunk bed with her son," said Keith. "It was a period of struggle, but that's how we'd always been my whole life so it was something I was used to. You don't really think about it until the struggle is over, so when you're going through it, you're just living life. That period really humbled me and it's a big part of who I am today."

PROGRESS IN A LOSS

Last year when Keith and his teammates walked out of the Hartford Civic Center following a gruesome 81–52 defeat at the hands of then undefeated and soon-to-be national champion UConn, they did so with their heads humbly hanging.

"They ran us out of the gym a year ago," coach Tommy Amaker said, recalling Harvard's second-worst loss since Keith joined the program in 2008. "We had no chance in that game, it seemed, from the opening tip."

That wasn't the case this time when the Crimson traveled to UConn's campus to play at Gampel Pavilion and gave the ninth-ranked Huskies all they wanted for most of the game before eventually falling to the Big East powerhouse, 67–53.

"This was obviously different," said Amaker, who saw his team's eight-game season-opening unbeaten streak come to an end, meaning it did not become the first Ivy team since Columbia in 1969–70 to begin a year 9–0. "I'm very pleased with our ball club. We have a ways to go, but I think we have some bright things in front of us."

Keith had scored thirteen points and grabbed eight rebounds in Harvard's hard-earned 55–48 victory over Vermont, and after beating Seattle, 80–70, to improve to 8–0—the best start by an Ivy League team since Princeton in 1997–98—the Crimson made school history when they were voted into the Associated Press top twenty-five poll for the first time, landing at twenty-five. They also cracked the ESPN/USA Today poll at number twenty-four, and those feathers in their caps were blowing in the wind as they bused to UConn fully confident in their ability to not only stay with the Huskies, but beat them.

It did not happen, mainly because UConn held the Crimson to 36 percent shooting from the floor (Keith was three-for-ten), and put together a killing 17–3 run in the first eight minutes of the second half to break away from a narrow 30–28 intermission lead. Harvard did not fold and it trimmed the deficit to 61–53 with 2:57 left to play, but did not score another point thereafter as the Huskies won their 102nd consecutive pre-New Years on-campus home game, an amazing streak that dated back to December 5, 1973.

A few nights later when Amaker brought his team across the Charles River to neighboring Boston University to take on the Terriers at Agannis Arena in the final game before a nearly two-week exam break, the mission was simple: Forget UConn, and get back on track. And it did.

"We responded really well," Keith said following a 76–52 blowout during which Kyle Casey scored twenty points, Laurent Rivard had sixteen on six-of-seven shooting from beyond the arc, and Keith had eight points and a game-high nine rebounds. "We moved on and played a great game. We knew we could have played better at UConn, and it was time to show that we were a better team than we showed at UConn. Coach stressed at the start of this season that this team can go places that we've never dreamed of, but we have to believe that as well."

TOGETHER FOR THE LONG HAUL

Exams went fine for Keith because as a senior, he had much of his heavy lifting behind him. Still, when he closed the books for the semester, he admitted, "It feels good. I think it went really well, I was really confident about the semester and I really enjoyed the classes that I took. Before, I was taking classes that I had to take, but these were classes that were a lot more interesting."

If basketball didn't work out for Keith, he wanted to go into family or marriage counseling, and his schedule was filled with courses in that discipline—three psychology courses in the areas of close relationships, social development, and decision making and probability. And then there was his history of rhythm and blues and soul music course which, for a music aficionado like Keith, was an absolute joy. For the final class project, the students were separated into groups and were tasked with putting on skits featuring some of the artists they had learned about throughout the semester. In his group, the always fun-loving and jocular Keith played several roles.

"They had me dressed up as Diana Ross and Michael Jackson, and I was one of the Temptations," he said. "I was the young Michael so I wore a glove and I had this wig and had to make my voice really high. I think the teacher really liked it, and we got some laughs in the class. We incorporated a lot of the material that we learned in the course, so I think we're gonna get a really good grade."

With school done for a month, it was back to basketball for Keith and the Crimson, and like she was for every home game at Lavietes Pavilion, Sabrena Tabron sat in her customary seat a few rows behind the Crimson bench, cheering on her boy during Harvard's 63–51 victory over Florida Atlantic. And like always, the former college basketball player from San Francisco State couldn't resist imparting instructions as she watched Keith work the low post on his way to scoring twelve points and grabbing a game-high eleven rebounds. "He listens to me as I'm yelling from the stands, but he plays so much better than me," she said with a laugh.

Just the fact that this scenario was playing out on a chilly night in Massachusetts a few days before Christmas stopped Sabrena in her tracks when she thought about it because while she was thrilled by the way things had worked out for Keith, this wasn't what she envisioned for her oldest son. At least not the basketball part.

"When Keith was young," Sabrena recalled, "I told him, 'You have three strikes against you; you're black, you're a male, and you will be raised by a single mom.'"

So Sabrena's wish for Keith was to be able to rise above that perceived adversity, and she thought the best way for him to do so was to not waste his time playing sports and, rather, concentrate on his studies. "Basketball defined me as a person, and academics never did, and I wanted him to be an academic person," she said. "So when we came to Virginia I didn't allow him to play sports. I wanted him to be different than what the world saw him to be, which was a big black kid who must be a basketball star, or running track, or playing football."

For a long time Keith was fine with the path his mother steered him down, one that led to outstanding grades, and a keen interest in reading books, writing stories, and listening to music. But eventually the basketball bug started to beckon, and Keith decided he wanted to give the game a try. When he was in ninth grade and living in northern Virginia he announced to Sabrena that he was going to try out for the junior varsity, and she reluctantly was going to allow it, until he brought home his report card which contained a "C" and that was the end of that. No hoops.

The next year, after he had moved back to Virginia Beach and was enrolled at Princess Anne High School, the school's basketball coach spotted Keith in the gym during physical education class and he sidled up to the sophomore who was already well on his way to the six feet, eight inches he has risen to today.

"He said, 'I want you to come to our open gym.' I was a new kid, I was tall, and he said, 'Maybe you could try out for the team.' I was going to do it, but to have someone ask me to do it gave me a little more motivation and confidence."

What it did not give Keith was the skill set he was going to need to become a player worthy of being on the floor, and Sabrena recognized this immediately. "I didn't want to be hard on him, but when he said, 'I want to play basketball,' he wasn't very good, and I needed to get him a trainer," Sabrena said. "He didn't grow up dribbling a ball or playing AAU and all that, he was carrying books, so he needed to learn how to play."

Sabrena did not have much money, but whatever she could afford she put toward Keith's basketball sessions at Velocity Sports Performance, where he was able to learn skills, hone them, and get into better shape, which was definitely an issue that needed tending.

"I was a heavy kid, and I needed to work on my body because it wasn't as mature as the other guys who had been playing for a long time," Keith said. "But I picked it up extremely quickly and I felt like I was at an advantage even though I started out late, because people pick up bad habits, and I didn't have those."

And one of the reasons was Sabrena. Keith had coaching in high school, he had it at Velocity, he had it when he finally played AAU later in high school, and he had it when he went home at night as Sabrena would break down his performances.

"My mom taught me my post moves, and that's been the basis and foundation of my game, those moves that my mom taught me," he said. "She's very knowledgeable about the game. My mother turned my life around, not a coach. When she realized I was serious about basketball, she got serious about it. We were in this thing together."

HAPPY NEW YEAR

Two nights earlier when Harvard went over to the Conte Forum and beat the snot out of Boston College for the fourth year in a row, this time by the lopsided score of 67–46, the victory was even more impressive given the fact that both Keith and Kyle Casey endured sloppy offensive performances.

Harvard's two main inside threats combined for just ten points on four-of-fifteen shooting, and the Crimson had to rely on the three-point bombing of reserve guards Laurent Rivard and Corbin Miller, who teamed for thirty points including a scorching eight-for-thirteen from behind the arc.

"Coach pulled me and Kyle aside after practice and told us we really had to step up," Keith said, referring to the conversation Tommy Amaker had with them before they took the court for a New Year's Eve matinee at Lavietes Pavilion against St. Joseph's.

The two kids took the talk to heart and had monster games as the Crimson rallied from a fourteen-point first-half deficit, and an eleven-point hole with 10:50 left to play, and overcame the rugged Hawks, 74–69, to stretch their home-court winning streak to twenty-one games. Casey had a season-high twenty-six points, while Keith went for sixteen as Harvard improved to 12–1.

If anyone was still wondering whether it was time to start taking the Crimson seriously, these two games should have quelled the doubt. Boston College was down this year with a roster that included nine freshmen, but a trend had developed in this neighborhood series, as the Eagles hadn't beaten Harvard since Keith arrived in Cambridge, and their average margin of defeat in the four games was twelve points. Prior to 2008, Harvard had played Boston College fourteen times going back to 1977 and had won only once, in 1992. Some of the losses were by thirty- and forty-plus points.

Boston College coach Steve Donahue, who before coming to Chestnut

Hill coached at Cornell for several years and guided the Big Red to the Sweet Sixteen of the NCAA tournament in 2010, was really impressed by the Crimson.

"I grew up on Ivy League basketball in Philadelphia," he told the *Boston Globe*. "I saw the 1979 Penn team that went to the Final Four. The '98 Princeton team was ranked seventh in the country. The runs that Penn made and our (Cornell) team. When you can get it going at those places, the intelligence and the unselfishness on those teams is what separates them. I think Harvard has that same formula."

St. Joseph's came into Lavietes riding a five-game winning streak that included a thorough 74–58 pounding of Big East power Villanova, and a solid win over a very good Creighton team. As tests go, this was a big one for the Crimson, and they knew it.

"Facing a team that blew out Villanova and knocked off some really good teams, we knew this would be a tournament-type team; that's how we saw it," Keith said. And what the Crimson saw in the first half was an otherworldly shooting performance as the Hawks made 79 percent of their shots from the floor in opening a 48–38 halftime lead.

Harvard picked it up at the defensive end in holding the Hawks to twenty-one second-half points, and Casey went wild on offense as he made eight of his last nine attempts and scored twenty points after the break, nearly outscoring St. Joseph's all by himself. With the Crimson still down eleven, Casey made two free throws, then Keith scored inside on back-to-back possessions to cut the deficit to 61–56. Keith scored his final basket to get Harvard within 66–63, and after Brandyn Curry gave Harvard the lead at 69–68, Casey nailed a three-pointer from the right wing with forty-one seconds remaining and Rivard's two free throws iced it.

"It was a gutsy win by our team against an outstanding basketball team," Amaker said. "I told our team that this is a preview that we might see a lot, teams that will be ready for us. We showed a little grit that's necessary to have a special year, and we're hopeful that this can end up being something like that for us."

FORDHAM FLOP

Every once in a while Keith looks at his iPhone and finds a text from his former Harvard teammate, Jeremy Lin, and there was one when he powered it on during the bus ride back to Cambridge following the Crimson's surprising 60–54 early-January loss to Fordham.

"We stay in touch, probably talk once a week and we exchange texts," Keith said of Lin, who in 2010 became the first Harvard basketball player to make an NBA roster in more than half a century when he signed a free agent contract with the Golden State Warriors. "He's there for us; he's still interested in the program and how we're doing, and it's good to know he has my back and he's supporting us all the way."

Keith needed a little pick-me-up after the twenty-first-ranked Crimson suffered their second defeat in fourteen games and became the first ranked opponent Fordham had beaten in its last fifty-four tries dating back to a victory over number eighteen Georgetown in 1978. The loss also spoiled the occasion of Keith scoring the 1,000th point of his college career, the twenty-seventh player in school history to achieve that milestone.

Riding home from the Bronx, Keith had time to mull over what Lin had texted. "He basically said, 'You're a senior, you were the player of the year in the League and you need to play like that,'" Keith said. "Getting that text and receiving calls from him really means a lot and it boosts my confidence. I think I needed that. It was big-time to have him text and let me know that."

Lin was in basketball limbo, which is where he had seemed to be for much of his career. He was an all-state player in California during his high school days in Palo Alto, but he couldn't convince anyone to offer him a scholarship, not even his beloved Stanford right in his hometown. Harvard took a look because of his tremendous transcript, but at first assistant coach Bill Holden thought Lin was nothing more than a Division III player.

However, Lin eventually won Holden over, and when no one else recruited him, Lin headed across the country to Cambridge and became one of the most decorated players in school history. By the time he graduated in 2010 he was Harvard's fifth-leading career scorer (one-1,483 points), and his play, the arrival of Amaker as coach, and Amaker's first two recruiting classes, which included the likes of Keith, Kyle Casey, and Oliver McNally, combined to lift the Crimson out of the ashes and chart the course upon which the program was now traveling.

Once he left Harvard, though, Lin sank right back into basketball's netherworld. None of the thirty NBA teams drafted him, and he seemed destined to play professionally in Europe, but he caught a break when he impressed scouts at a 2010 summer league game where he outplayed 2010 number one overall draft pick John Wall of the Washington Wizards. Four teams offered him a contract, and Lin went with hometown Golden State, though many felt it was more of a PR move for the Warriors to bring in the NBA's first American player of Taiwanese or Chinese descent.

He saw very little playing time in 2010–11 bouncing between the Warriors and the NBA Developmental League—basically the NBA's version of triple-A—and then was cut by new Warriors coach Mark Jackson on the first day of the lockout-delayed 2011–12 training camp. The Houston Rockets picked him up in mid-December, cut him on Christmas Eve to clear salary cap room to sign another player, and Lin landed in New York a few days later, though he told Keith he was the last man on the Knicks' bench and fully expected to be reassigned to the D-League at any time.

Still, Lin was someone Keith respected mightily, and regarded him as a role model. "His work ethic, how hard he worked at the game and his craft," Keith said when asked what he learned from Lin during their two years together at Harvard. "It got him to where he is now in the NBA. He's not getting the playing time, but he's still there and I'm learning off that, following his example."

PLAYER OF THE WEEK

The one thing that losing to Fordham reinforced for the Crimson was they were no longer considered the plastic-pocket-protector nerds from the Ivy League. Harvard—that's right, Harvard—was now a legitimate basketball program, led by a big-name coach with a roster full of players that, believe it or not, other Division I schools recruited.

As the Rams proved a couple weeks earlier, Harvard was going to get everyone's best game now, and Tommy Amaker's boys had to be ready for that. "I think we noticed that after winning the Battle 4 Atlantis tournament," Keith said. "We're starting to sell out every venue that we're at; we expect it, and we expect to take teams' best punches, so we have to play accordingly."

In the three games since Fordham, that's what the Crimson did. They waxed Dartmouth at Lavietes a week ago in their League opener, 63–47, and then closed out the non-League portion of their regular-season schedule with a two-game sweep, winning 70–61 at Monmouth, and then by a 69–48 count at home against George Washington, pushing their record to 15–2.

In the three games, Keith totaled thirty-nine points and twenty-eight rebounds, including a monstrous eighteen-point, fifteen-board effort against Monmouth, and the League took notice and named him its Player of the Week for the second time this season.

At Monmouth, Keith was a man among boys. He had twelve points and thirteen rebounds in fourteen first-half minutes as the Crimson built a 36–25 lead. Monmouth made a nice second-half adjustment by double-teaming Keith and making it almost impossible for him to get involved in the offense, and the Hawks pulled within 57–56 with 6:27 to go. But once again, the balance of this Harvard squad proved vital and the starting guards closed the victory out in style as Brandyn Curry drove for a layup and nailed a three-pointer to make it 62–56, and Oliver McNally scored Harvard's last eight points on free throws.

George Washington was no match as Harvard ran out to a 33–13 halftime lead and coasted to its twenty-third straight home-court victory. The star of this game was freshman Steve Moundou-Missi from the soccer-loving nation of Cameroon, who made all seven of his field goal attempts and scored a career-high sixteen points, while Keith scored eleven points and grabbed eight rebounds.

It had been a nice few weeks for Keith and his teammates, living the life of basketball players with no school in session. "Peaceful, not much stress right now, I can relax, hop in the cold tub, watch the girls' games, check out the swim team, the hockey team, so it's cool not having work and classes and being able to see them," he said. But reality would beckon a week hence when the second semester—Keith's last at Harvard—would begin, and the basketball schedule settled into the traditional Ivy League pattern with no mid-week games, and back-to-back play on Fridays and Saturdays.

TWEET THAT

The Crimson did not need a reminder of where they were going. Tommy Amaker never had to reference the fact that twice they took the court at Yale's Lee Amphitheater last season, and twice they walked off last-second losers, once to Yale, and once to Princeton in the special one-game Ivy League-deciding playoff game.

"It was a very business-like trip," Keith said. "Coach never mentioned it, but obviously it was a thought on our mind that the last two times we've been down there we've lost by one point."

There was no buzzer-beating drama this time. No heartbreaking loss to swallow. The twenty-third-ranked Crimson, looking like a team that could run through the League schedule undefeated, embarrassed the Bulldogs on their home floor, 65–35, the most one-sided game in the eleven-decade-long, 183-game history of the rivalry.

"It's embarrassing," said Yale senior center Greg Mangano of a dreadful Bulldog performance that included twenty-two turnovers and a point total that was twenty-seven fewer than Yale's previous season-low. "You're supposed to try to win every game here and protect your court, and we didn't do that tonight."

Instead, the Crimson stormed Yale's court and by the time the final seconds were ticking off the clock, most of the first sell-out crowd at Yale since 2008 had vacated the building, leaving only the rabid and raucous Harvard cheering section, way up in the rafters, to cheer wildly when Keith pointed to them following the post-game handshakes.

"I was just showing them thanks," Keith said. "They put our students way up top and I just wanted to show appreciation for them making the trip down and supporting us. The last time they were there they left disappointed just like we did, so this win was for them, too."

The thirty-five points was Harvard's lowest allowance in twenty years, and coupled with the previous weekend's thirty-eight-point effort against Dartmouth, it was the first time since 1946–47 it had held opponents below forty points in back-to-back games.

Keith had a quiet night with just seven points and five rebounds while his rival, Mangano, scored seventeen, but the scoreboard told the only story that mattered. Although he refused to acknowledge it, it was certainly a sweet night for Keith. Last year when Keith was named the Ivy League's player of the year, Mangano was, to say the least, a little perturbed he wasn't the choice.

Mangano had a pretty strong case. His eighty-five blocks were a school record, and his fifty-one blocks in League games set a new standard. Further, he led the Ivy League in rebounding (ten per game) and was second in scoring at sixteen points per game, becoming the first Bulldog since Chris Dudley in 1986–87 to average a double-double for the season.

Keith had a solid resume as well, as he led the League in field goal percentage at 58.3 percent, trailed only Mangano in double-doubles with twelve, he was third in scoring at 14.9 points per game, and second in rebounds with 8.3 rebounds to go with fifty-four blocks.

In the end, the Ancient Eight coaches determined that Keith meant a little more to his team, as he helped lead the Crimson to a share of the League title for the first time in school history and an appearance in the NIT. Mangano's reaction to the vote was regrettable, as he used his Twitter account to bash the process as well as Keith's candidacy.

"He said some things on Twitter last year after I won the player of the year," Keith remembered. "He thought he should have won it based on his numbers, and he used some profanity. I didn't say anything back."

Keith said nothing then, and he said nothing after the game. Then again, winning by thirty said more than enough. "I'm not one to talk in the games," he said. "The only people I talk to on the court are my teammates. I have no problems with him or any player. He was mad at the Ivy League committee for getting the pick wrong. It was probably stuff a player shouldn't say, but everyone is entitled to their own opinion and they can say whatever they want."

Keith's way was to be mild-mannered. His co-captain, Oliver McNally, was a little more feisty, and he let it be known that he didn't appreciate Mangano's attack. "He's a punk, an absolute punk," McNally said. "I'm not taking anything away from him as a player, he's a very good offensive player, but teammate-wise, the fact that he put so much into that, he probably could put more focus into his team. I have no time for people like that."

JADWIN JINX

Superman had kryptonite. Elizabeth Taylor had marriage. Harvard basketball had Princeton's Jadwin Gymnasium.

That old barn was a very bad place for the Crimson, a house of horrors, really. They hadn't won a game in the building since 1989, and that futility continued, the losing streak reaching twenty-three games as the Tigers broke free from a 46–46 tie with 5:37 left and outscored the Crimson 24–16 the rest of the way to secure a 70–62 victory. It was Harvard's first Ivy League loss of the season after seven victories, and just its third setback in twenty-four games.

"Of course we wanted to end it," Keith said. "That was our mind-set and of course people brought up the fact that we lost to them last year, all the usual stuff you would expect. That's always on our mind. We talked about it, but they were playing really hard, and we didn't step up the way we wanted to. They wanted it more."

That's what was so disappointing for coach Tommy Amaker. Rarely had this been the case in the long, one-sided series with Princeton, but Harvard had the better team this year, and it may have last year, too. But last March the Tigers were one point better at Yale in the one-game playoff, so they went to the NCAA tournament as League champs, and Harvard headed to the lesser, almost unnoticeable National Invitation Tournament.

The Crimson couldn't wait to get to Princeton because this was supposed to be the night the Jadwin jinx was going to end. And why would anyone doubt it was going to happen? Since the blowout victory at Yale, the Crimson had extended their winning streak to nine with victories over Brown, Cornell, Columbia, and then the night before the Princeton game, they went into the fabled Palestra and left with a gritty 56–50 conquest of Penn.

Instead of Harvard completing its first sweep of the annual Penn-Princeton road trip since 1985, the Tigers—as they almost always seemed to do, at least against Harvard in this place—made all the big plays when they needed them, particularly forward Ian Hummer. The junior, who is the nephew of former NBA player John Hummer, scored twenty points, grabbed nine boards, and dished six assists, one night after he'd gone zero for eleven from the field in a victory over Dartmouth.

"This was a tough loss for us," said Amaker, whose team became the first ranked opponent Princeton had beaten at home since the Tigers knocked off Notre Dame in 1977. "I was disappointed in our ability to make the plays defensively in the second half. I told our kids Princeton deserved to win. They played an exceptional second half, did an outstanding job of getting the ball into the post, and shot tremendously."

With their confidence soaring after the win at Penn, where Keith scored only four points but pulled down thirteen boards, the Crimson walked onto the Jadwin floor prepared to end the drought. Two hours later, they were trying to comprehend how they'd lost there. Again.

"We started off well, it was kind of the same thing that happened to us last year (at Yale)," said Keith, who despite the loss had a terrific night with sixteen points and twelve rebounds. "We were ahead and then they started hitting some shots; we broke down defensively, and this game was definitely on our defense. I've beaten them once in four years. We wanted to win every (League) game, but that's not the case now. We just have to move on."

LINSANITY!

On a weekend when the Crimson bounced back from the Princeton disappointment and played two textbook-perfect games at Lavietes Pavilion, dismantling overmatched Brown, 69–42, and then hammering archrival Yale, 66–51, to improve to 9–1 in the League and 23–3 overall, the only thing pertaining to Harvard basketball that anyone was interested in was a player who left the program two years ago.

Jeremy Lin.

Yes, Jeremy Lin, erstwhile Harvard graduate and barely employable NBA player who in two weeks' time had become a worldwide phenomenon, his remarkable story of perseverance and achievement transcending basketball and sports and vaulting him into the rarefied air of the 24/7 news cycle usually reserved for the LeBrons and Tigers and Obamas of the world.

Linsanity!

Every pun seemed to work—Linspiration, Super Lintendo, Linvincible, Linconceivable, Lincredible, Linderella—but none more so than Linsanity because that's exactly what it had been for the NBA's first American-born player of Chinese or Taiwanese descent.

One month ago he was biding his time as the last man on the New York Knicks' bench, waiting for an inevitable demotion to the NBA Developmental League, which came on January 17. Now he was a rock star, a basketball god, the most talked-about athlete on the planet. Truly Linsane.

"It's really exciting," said Keith, who watched on TV as Lin scored twenty-eight points and dished out a career-high fourteen assists, leading the Knicks to a victory over the defending NBA champion Dallas Mavericks, their eighth win in the nine games since New York coach Mike D'Antoni made Lin the starting point guard. "We're proud of him. He works extremely hard, and he did when he was here. It's extremely inspirational to see what he's doing and seeing all the hard work he's doing pay off. We're getting interviewed a lot and asked if we still talk to him, all that stuff. I don't get tired of the questions. It's exciting to see a friend do well."

When Lin was sent down to Erie, Pennsylvania, in the D-League, he seriously considered taking off for Europe, so tired was he of banging his head against the wall trying to break into the NBA. However, he was summoned back to New York within a week, and when D'Antoni became irritated by the Knicks' lethargic play in a loss to the Boston Celtics on February 3, he decided to start Lin the next night against New Jersey.

After racking up twenty-five points and seven assists in a victory over the Nets, Lin started again against Utah. This time he had twenty-eight points and eight assists in another victory. So he started again, and again, and before you knew it he had six straight games of at least twenty points, topped by an eye-popping thirty-eight-point explosion where he outscored Kobe Bryant by four and the Knicks beat the Los Angeles Lakers at electrified Madison Square Garden.

Linsanity was born. Scalpers at the Garden were rejoicing, Lin's number seventeen jersey became a worldwide sell-out, and the NBA marketing mavens were beside themselves with joy. A month earlier he was sleeping on the couch in the apartment of his brother, Joshua, a dental student at New York University, texting with some of his former Crimson teammates and wondering where his life was going. Now he was larger than life, his and just about anyone else's, and back in Cambridge, Keith and the Crimson were reveling in his success.

Before Lin, only three other Harvard men had ever played in the NBA, and no one had done it for nearly sixty years. Watching Lin had given Keith renewed motivation to become the fifth.

"It really solidifies in my head that if he can do it, so can I. There are athletes in the Ivy League who are trying to make it as professionals, and if anything he's opening that door a little wider for us. It's huge for what he's doing for Harvard, it's exciting that people are becoming even more aware of the program, and seeing the talent that we have in the Ivy League."

BUMP IN THE ROAD

A few days before Keith was going to play his last two games at Lavietes Pavilion, he didn't want to consider the emotional gymnastics that would entail.

"It'll be like every other game and it probably won't hit me until later," he said. "It's a big weekend for us, and what we're trying to do here is bigger than my last game at home. When the season is over and I reevaluate everything and realize I'm not playing here anymore, maybe it will hit me then. We just want to walk out of here with a couple wins."

Well, the Crimson walked out of Lavietes with a wonderful win over Princeton, a hard-fought 67–64 decision that gave this special Crimson team a program-record twenty-fourth victory this season, avenged the loss to the Tigers two weeks ago, and gave Keith just his second victory in nine career games against Princeton.

However, the next night, Senior Night, with a chance to clinch at least a share of the Ivy League championship for the second year in a row, the Crimson lost in shocking fashion to Penn, 55–54, blowing a nine-point lead in the final eight minutes. Gone was Harvard's twenty-eight-game home-court winning streak, second-longest in the country behind only Kentucky, and so, too, was the stranglehold grip Harvard had on its destiny.

"It's tough to hear that buzzer go off when we're down at the end," said Kyle Casey, who scored a team-high twelve points, but who also committed the foul on Penn senior guard Zack Rosen, the likely League player of the year, with twenty-three seconds remaining, which resulted in the two free throws that decided the game.

Against Princeton the Crimson fell behind by ten in the first half and were still down seven with eleven minutes to go in the second half before a strong defensive stand turned the tide. The Tigers went nearly seven minutes without a field goal and made only five shots the rest of the way. During that drought, Keith scored six points in a row to give the Crimson the lead, and Oliver McNally made six consecutive free throws in the last eighteen seconds to ice it.

For much of the Penn game it looked like the momentum of that rally would carry the Crimson as they opened an eleven-point lead early in the second half. But Rosen, who had been terrific all season, scored fourteen of his twenty points thereafter, including Penn's last nine.

After his two free throws made it 55–54, the Crimson had two chances to win, but Corbin Miller missed a three-pointer, and after the ball went out of bounds off a Penn player, Casey took the inbounds pass, drove to the hoop and scored what appeared to be the winning basket, but he was whistled for a charge and the hoop was nullified, stunning the sell-out crowd.

Like Harvard, Penn had only two Ivy losses. Thus, if the Crimson hoped to capture the elusive outright Ivy title and the accompanying automatic bid to the NCAA tournament, the first thing they were going to have to do was win at Columbia and at Cornell. Then, they would need help because if Penn swept its home games against Dartmouth and Yale, and its season-finale at Princeton, another one-game playoff would be necessary to decide the crown.

"It's a devastating loss, it's a disappointing loss and we should feel those things," said Amaker. "It's a normal reaction and feeling to have. The good thing is if we can channel it the right way, maybe it can help us. That's what we're hoping for next week."

MAKING HISTORY

Midway through the first half of Harvard's regular-season finale Saturday at Cornell, its most important game of the year because a share of the Ivy League championship was on the line, Keith stepped to the free-throw line after getting hacked in the lane.

The voluble Big Red student section in Newman Arena was giving him the customary business, trying to distract him from the task at hand. Meanwhile, a couple rows behind the Crimson bench, Keith's little brother and sister, Elijah and Olivia, were completely oblivious to the vitriol being spewed at their oldest sibling because they were playing a video game on Elijah's Nintendo DS XLS.

"They like the hotels and the restaurants," said their smiling mother, Sabrena Tabron, who drives to just about all of Harvard's road games with her little ones in tow. "They usually don't know what's going on in the games."

Oh, if only Sabrena could enjoy that blissful and innocent disconnect as opposed to the tension that only a parent can feel when her child is in a highly energized and pressure-filled situation, as Keith and his Crimson teammates were.

The Crimson survived a major scare from Columbia before pulling away to a 77–70 overtime victory in front of a full house at Levien Gymnasium that included film director and New York basketball junkie Spike Lee, and his new best friend, Knicks point guard/phenomenon/Harvard grad Jeremy Lin. Then they bused five hours through the night to upstate New York to serve as the opponent for Cornell's emotional Senior Night, where they had to withstand a furious push from Big Red senior guard Chris Wroblewski before finally subduing the upstart Cornellians, 67–63.

"Oh my God," Sabrena said with her eyes wide open about a half hour after Harvard had held off Cornell to secure at least a share of the Ivy League title for the second year in a row, and the second time in school history.

Of course nothing had come easy for the Crimson, so naturally, the postgame celebration was tempered because nothing had been decided. Penn won its two weekend games at the Palestra, blowing out Dartmouth and Yale, meaning that if the Quakers could go into Princeton's Jadwin Gymnasium and defeat the Tigers in the Ivy League finale three days hence, Harvard would have to play Penn in a one-game League-deciding playoff. But that was a discussion for another day. Outside the visiting locker room one floor beneath the Newman Arena court, all Keith wanted to think about was, "The history we keep making. That's why we came here. This win is a huge one for us and our program, to be two-time Ivy League champs is tremendous. If someone told me coming into Harvard you'd be Ivy League champions twice, I'd take that any day of the week."

And if you had told Keith that someday he'd be playing a game for Harvard in which Spike Lee was in attendance, he would have called you insane.

"That was crazy," he said of the game at Columbia. "I actually didn't notice at first. He got there in the second half, but when I'm in the game I don't hear anything except the coach and my mom sometimes. Then I got a traveling call or something and I looked in the stands and Spike Lee was standing there doing the traveling call like he does at the Knicks games and I was like, 'oh.' I was surprised by how small he is."

Then there was the presence of Lin, a player Columbia fans were booing two years ago, but now were bowing to because of his sudden rise to fame playing with the Knicks.

"He's still the same kid, man, he's the same guy," Keith said. "But it's crazy what's going on. After the game security said, 'We'll take you to the elevator and then out the back door so nobody bothers you' and we were like, 'That's crazy.' This is Jeremy Lin, somebody I was sitting with on the bus joking and talking and practicing with. He's a really good friend and I'm just tremendously happy for him."

Putting the Columbia excitement behind them, the Crimson went into Cornell knowing the Big Red were going to be pumped, and they were.

However, as had been the case all year, someone needed to step up and do what was needed to earn a victory, and in Ithaca, that player was Brandyn Curry. Harvard led by as much as twelve in the first half, but Cornell tied the game two minutes into the second half and had all the momentum. However, Curry knocked down four consecutive three-pointers in a span of three-and-a-half minutes to get Harvard back on track. And then down the stretch, with the Big Red giving it all they had to keep the game close, it was Oliver McNally who delivered the knockout as he scored Harvard's last nine points, the final four on clutch free throws.

"These kids were picked to be in this position before the season started, and for us to remain where we are right now is an incredible compliment to these kids," said Tommy Amaker.

PUNCHING THEIR TICKET

When Keith walked out of his Psychology of Human Sexuality midterm, he had a good feeling about how it had gone. Considering what had transpired the night before, his performance on the exam was as impressive as anything he'd done on the basketball court this season.

Keith, his roommate and teammate, Andrew Van Nest, and Keith's girlfriend, Jessica Ferry, were in Keith's room in Leverett House trying to study and watch the Internet live stream of the Penn-Princeton game at the same time. Obviously, it was somewhat difficult to concentrate, given that a Penn victory meant Harvard would have to play the Quakers in a one-game playoff to decide the Ivy League title, while a Princeton victory meant the Crimson could skip that exercise and advance directly to the NCAA tournament for the first time since 1946.

"It was a very cool and exciting night," Keith said. "We had the game on the Xbox while we were studying, but as it got down towards the end in the second half, the books kind of went to the wayside and me and Andrew were focusing on the game. I felt bad because we were keeping my girlfriend from studying, but we were really excited."

As soon as Princeton's victory was complete, and the reality hit that the Crimson were going to the Big Dance, Keith and Andrew ran outside and were "running up and down the street screaming. We had people yelling out their windows congratulating us, so it was pretty cool."

So imagine how cool it was for Keith and the Crimson when they arrived in Albuquerque, New Mexico, a little less than a week later for their first-round NCAA tournament game against Vanderbilt.

"It's a dream come true," Keith said. "All the hard work that we put in during these four years here is paying off. We're part of the first team in sixty-some years to do this, so it's awesome. Our names will go down in history as the first team under Tommy Amaker to go to the NCAA."

The day before the game, Sabrena Tabron was sitting near courtside at The Pit on the campus of the University of New Mexico watching Harvard go through its open practice in full view of fans and media. Sabrena, a self-proclaimed hoops junkie, also stuck around to observe the other teams that had been placed in this pod of the tournament's East Regional—Wisconsin and Montana were the others—go through their open practices, and one thing struck her.

"My mom commented that we were the only group that went and got water, meaning we were the only ones working hard enough to warrant water," Keith said. "The other teams were just shooting the breeze and doing light workouts. We were out there for about forty minutes and we just went through a pretty normal practice. We did our drills pretty hard."

Forgive Harvard for not understanding the protocol for these dog-and-pony-show on-site practices. Remember, this was the first time in sixty-six years the Crimson had earned an invitation to the Big Dance. It was practice time, so they practiced.

When last a Crimson basketball team participated in the NCAA tournament in 1946, the Ivy League as we know it today hadn't even been formed. Only eight schools were invited to play in the NCAA, and even though the winner—which that year was Oklahoma State—was considered the national champion, the NCAA wasn't the premier post-season event. That honor was held by the NIT, which typically drew more elite fields because the nugget was the possibility of playing the semifinals and finals at Madison Square Garden in New York City.

Times have changed, and today the NCAA tournament is one of the greatest spectacles in all of sport, a sixty-eight-team monstrosity contested over three weeks that is watched by hundreds of millions of people—in person at arenas all across the country, and on four different television networks. If you didn't know better, you'd think Bracketology was a college major, and come to think of it, for some people, it just might be.

Yet even though this was a completely new experience for every member of the Harvard team—except for Amaker—there was nothing about the magnitude of what was going to take place the next day that overwhelmed Keith or his teammates. The twelfth-seeded Crimson would be playing against fifth-seeded Vanderbilt, a team that only a few days earlier had knocked off the number one team in the country, Kentucky, in the championship game of the Southeastern Conference tournament. But, as Gene Hackman pointed out in the movie *Hoosiers*, the basket was still ten feet above the floor, whether it was Lavietes Pavilion in Cambridge, or twenty-two-hundred miles to the west at The Pit. There would be a lot more pomp and circumstance than Harvard had ever encountered, but when the ball was tossed up at center court, it was still a forty-minute basketball game, a game the kids from Harvard had been playing all their lives, just like the kids from Vanderbilt, Kentucky, Syracuse, or any other team.

"I don't think I'm going to be any more nervous than I am for any other game," Keith said. "We did our scouting and practicing, so there's really no need for us to be nervous."

There was a reason for Keith to be rolling his eyes, though, but he did so in a good-natured way because while the media was predictable in the questions it asked him and the other members of the smartest team in the tournament, he enjoyed the repartee.

"A lot of the buzz was Harvard vs. Vanderbilt, the battle of the brains and stuff like that, which is what you would expect," said Keith. "The corny jokes about who is smarter. I got a couple *Jeopardy!* questions and a couple Scrabble questions, and someone asked me what was the last book I read and I said, 'It was probably a textbook. I haven't had a class where I needed to read a book in quite a while.' Just goofy questions, but it was cool to have people interested in you and the program."

GOOD NIGHT CINDERELLA

As the Crimson broke their huddle following a media timeout with 3:26 remaining in the first half, electricity was coursing through The Pit, the Madness of March in full flight in this city along the banks of the Rio Grande.

The voluble Harvard cheering section, filled with parents and friends and alums, was on its collective feet hootin' and hollerin', and the contagion of excitement spread throughout the arena—save for the cadre of Vanderbilt fans in attendance. There was no doubt who the underdog was in this first-round game, and there was no doubt that most everyone in the crowd of 10,774 was rooting for that underdog.

The Ivy Leaguers had spent the first sixteen-plus minutes trading baskets with the bigger, more tournament-tested Commodores from the Southeastern Conference. Now, as play was set to resume with Harvard trailing just 22–20, there was a sense that the Crimson were capable of shocking the college basketball world and recording only the third win by an Ivy League team in the NCAA tournament since 1998.

"We were right there, playing well, right with them," Keith said.

However, in that final 3:26 of the first half, reality slapped the Crimson across the face. The Commodores' wonderfully talented guard tandem of John Jenkins and Brad Tinsley combined to outscore Harvard 11–3 to open a 33–23 halftime lead, and when Vanderbilt maintained that momentum in the second half and eventually ballooned its lead to 62–44 with eight minutes remaining, the issue was pretty much decided. Harvard would put on a spirited rally to cut the deficit to five in the late stages, but Vanderbilt ultimately held on for a 79–70 victory, ending the season for the Crimson, as well as Keith's college career.

Keith scored Harvard's first four points, and after Vandy grabbed a 12–6 lead, the Crimson went on a 14–5 surge to open a 20–17 advantage as six different Crimson players contributed points, the last three coming on a bomb from Christian Webster. But Vanderbilt's Jeffrey Taylor answered with a three-pointer of his own, and then grabbed a rebound and scored on a put-back to give the Commodores the lead for good at 22–20 right before the media timeout. Jenkins, who would finish with a game-high twenty-seven points, started the end-of-half run with a free throw, and Tinsley later made a pair of three-pointers to quiet the pro-Harvard crowd at the break.

As the second half began, Vanderbilt really started to impose its will. It made its first six field goal attempts and pushed the lead to 49–33. Only the red-hot three-point shooting of Laurent Rivard, who made six of seven in the game for a Crimson-high twenty points, kept the contest from being a blowout.

When Taylor stripped Brandyn Curry and raced down court for an emphatic dunk to make it 62–44 and forced Tommy Amaker to call a thirty-second timeout, the Crimson looked deflated and defeated. They weren't.

Kyle Casey came out of that break with a dunk, followed with a three-pointer, and Curry made a layup to make it 62–51. The Commodores were still up eleven with 3:17 to go, but Curry scored off a turnover, and Casey and Keith each made a pair of free throws following empty Vanderbilt possessions, and the crowd was alive as the Crimson were down just five points at 70–65 with 1:51 to play.

"I thought we were going to come back," said Oliver McNally. "It's well-publicized that Vandy lost in the first round the last three out of four years, so we knew if we were hanging around, we'd put that thought in their head and see what happened."

Well, the Commodores may have thought about it, but it did not hinder their finish as they coolly made nine of ten free throws to ward off the upset.

Amaker, Keith, and McNally represented Harvard at the postgame press conference, and all shared poignant thoughts about this magical season.

"It's just a dream come true," Keith said of getting a chance to play in the NCAA tournament and fulfilling the goal that was set the moment he signed his letter of intent to come to play for Amaker. "We've worked so hard, we've put a lot of time, blood, sweat, and tears into this basketball program. Unfortunately, we didn't come out with a victory, but this is something that we're going to carry with us for the rest of our lives. It's a stage where not many players get to play, and we are definitely grateful for that."

Asked about the journey he and Keith had been on, McNally said, "It's been really special. The best part of me and Keith's experience is that we were here when it wasn't that good, when no one came to the games and nobody cared about Harvard basketball when coach Amaker first got here. We were part of the transition to a really successful program. That makes it even more special for us. I came here to make history. Everything has been done at Harvard, but basketball was kind of wide open and you can leave your mark, and we did."

Amaker was then asked what it meant to him to have had those two kids sitting next to him for four years.

"It was mentioned in the locker room how special they are and how grateful we all are for their belief and certainly their performance on and off the court for us," he said. "They've been sensational to work with, to coach, and to teach. I think the example they've set for this program is an enormous footprint right now."

There were a couple more questions to be answered, and then the coach and his two cocaptains stood up and walked off the stage together, their hearts heavy, but their heads held high. After he had showered and dressed, Keith went out to meet his mother, her eyes filled with tears when they embraced. "What a journey we've been on," Sabrena said. "I couldn't have asked for a better one."

HARVARD SPEAKS FOR ITSELF

When Keith walked off the court following his final high school basketball game in the spring of 2008, he did so with a smile on his face. Yes, his Norfolk Collegiate team lost to Hargrave Military Academy in the first round of the Virginia state tournament, but what a career he'd had, and, guess what? "I was going to Harvard," he said.

As the final seconds ticked off the clock at The Pit, and the Crimson were on the wrong end of the score, a smile creased Keith's face again. Of course he was upset about the loss that brought to a close the most successful year in the previously tortured history of Harvard basketball. And sure, this was the last time he'd ever wear that Crimson uniform. But as he hugged his teammates, then shook hands with the victorious Commodores, how could he be sad, really?

"I didn't have any of those feelings like, 'Oh man, my time at Harvard is over'; I've never been like that," he said. "I've done some great things here, and this was just the end of my chapter here. It's time for me to move on and I'm happy with that."

Since the moment he stepped into Harvard Square nearly four years earlier, he had been challenged by coach Tommy Amaker to make history. And he did. Keith was instrumental in leading the Crimson to their first two Ivy League championships including the first outright title this year when the team set a school record with twenty-six victories and earned Harvard's first bid to the NCAA tournament since 1946. And in the 109 games he played for Harvard, third-most in program history, Keith scored the sixteenth-most points (1,178), grabbed the fifth-most rebounds (743), and blocked more shots (149) than any Harvard man ever had.

"We were part of the team that set the foundation. That's more than I could have asked for, but that's what we signed up for and we accomplished that goal. There's no way I can let this loss in the NCAA tournament overshadow all the great things that we've done."

Keith never looked back, only forward, and his was a busy immediate future indeed. First up was the Reese's College All-Star Game on the Friday of Final Four weekend at the Superdome in New Orleans. Two weeks later he would head down to his old stomping grounds in the Tidewater/Virginia Beach area where the prestigious Portsmouth Invitational Tournament is contested. Late in the regular season Keith learned he had been one of the sixty-four players invited to compete in the sixtieth-annual event, which is bird-dogged by scouts and general managers from every NBA team as well as professional teams from around the world.

When he returned from Virginia, he would finish off his senior year at Harvard and in late May he would gather in the Old Yard along with Melanie Baskind and the rest of the graduating senior class, the 361st at Harvard, to receive his Ivy League diploma.

He didn't know what his future held. The hope is that he would be drafted by an NBA team in the coming summer, and if not, perhaps he could sign as a free agent, get into a training camp, and try to win a roster spot. If not, maybe there would be avenues to explore overseas. And if that didn't work out, he knew with a Harvard education the world was his oyster.

"I was thinking about after basketball, after the ball stops bouncing," he said. "It was all about me making the right choice for the next four years of my life and setting myself up after I graduate and I'm done playing basketball. If you're good enough to play at the next level, people are going to find you, they'll see you no matter where you are. I still have that dream that I can make it to the NBA, that's what every basketball player's dream is. But if it doesn't work, I'll be fine. Harvard speaks for itself."

ANDY ILES

CORNELL MEN'S HOCKEY

On a glorious early autumn Saturday afternoon in upstate New York, Cornell University was bursting with activity.

Under a cloudless sky and a blazing sun, dozens upon dozens of high school students and their parents were touring the rolling landscape, many perhaps getting their first wide-eyed look at the Ivy League's largest school; at Schoellkopf Field, more than six-thousand football fans were being thoroughly entertained, though ultimately disappointed, by the Big Red's 41–31 loss to Ivy rival Harvard; a little farther up Campus Road at Berman Field, the men's and women's soccer teams were also hosting their counterparts from Harvard in a doubleheader; and in the various quads around campus, Frisbees and footballs were zipping through the air as undergrads of all ages were enjoying a welcomed break from academia on Columbus Day weekend.

But for Andy, it might as well have been the dead of winter because on this lovely day, he was encased in his goaltender equipment, standing sentry in his crease on the ice surface inside Lynah Rink, home of the Big Red hockey team, while several of his teammates peppered him with shots.

Practice didn't officially start for another week, but for a goaltender, too much practice is never enough practice, so whenever there's an opportunity to hone this specialized craft, you take it.

"Lately I've been on the ice every day, but I take Sundays off," said the sophomore who was born and raised in Ithaca, began following the Cornell hockey program as a little tike, and followed his dream and his heart when he decided to pass up scholarship offers from other Division I schools to play for the hometown Big Red. "I was taking pucks two or three days and skating on the other days, but now every time I'm on the ice I'm seeing pucks, tracking it and feeling it."

They are a unique breed, these hockey goaltenders, a band of brothers often linked by their common idiosyncrasies. Of course you'd have to be a little off-kilter to volunteer to stand in front of a chunk of vulcanized rubber traveling at speeds of eighty or ninety or one hundred miles per hour. But ever since he was a tiny tot, he knew goalie was the spot for him, and he kept asking his coaches to let him play the position.

This season he wouldn't have to ask to play. As a freshman in 2010–11, Andy split time with junior Mike Garman and helped lead the Big Red to the ECAC championship game. This year, with Garman having decided to graduate a year early and forgo his final season of college eligibility to pursue a professional career, Andy was the clear-cut No. 1 goalie for the Big Red, and the burden of expectation weighed heavily on his still-filling-out five-foot-nine, 180-pound frame.

"I'm excited to get the season going," Andy said. "I feel like I made some strides over the summer, I'm happy with where I'm at and I have a new sense of confidence. In talking to the coaches and the guys, we're all excited and confident in each other. I know the guy who's going to be between the pipes is the guy who's playing the best that week in practice, and all I can do is go out there and perform and compete every day in practice and hope everything works out."

And that's why, rather than covering his face with sunscreen, he was wearing his goalie mask. He stayed home to attend Cornell for two reasons: To get an Ivy League education, and to be the goaltender for the only college program he really ever wanted to play for, the one that's literally right in his backyard. It really wasn't that difficult of a choice.

His high school grades, achieved initially for a year at Ithaca High School, for two years at a prep school in Connecticut, and a final year at a public school in Ann Arbor, Michigan, where Team USA's National Team Development Program is based, were outstanding. So if all Andy had to offer to a prospective university was a grade point average and an SAT score, most would have welcomed him with open arms. Given the fact that he was also one of the best teenage goaltenders in the United States, needless to say Andy had options. Lots of them.

Harvard was interested, and so was Yale. Colgate and Clarkson, Boston College and New Hampshire, even some schools in the Midwest, though they were ruled out because one of the primary prerequisites Andy established in his college selection was an East Coast locale for the simple reason that, "I wanted my family to be able to get to my games."

So, imagine his glee when Cornell—situated right there in Ithaca, a program he had followed passionately from the time he was old enough to lace up his skates because that's what young hockey players in Ithaca do—was the very first school to inquire whether he'd be interested in matriculating and playing for the hometown team.

But here was the dilemma. Ivy League schools don't offer athletic scholarships, and Andy did not want to burden his parents—Dave and Amy, both CPAs in a downtown Ithaca accounting firm—with massive tuition bills.

"I remember in my junior year when I had all my offers on the table—some opportunities at a few other Ivy League schools, plus a few scholarship offers from some non-Ivies," Andy said. "I sat down with my (prep school) coach at Salisbury and I remember one thing he said which sticks with me to this day. He said, 'When it comes down to making your decision, don't let money be a factor; you can always take care of that in the long run.' I had always dreamed of getting a scholarship and helping my parents out from that end. So when coach (Andrew Will) said that, and then I sat down with my parents and they re-instilled that point that it was for me and what school I liked the most, that's when I knew what I was going to do."

Of course it was going to be Cornell. It had to be; the hometown kid playing for the hometown team.

"Growing up here and playing in Ithaca, you're surrounded by Cornell hockey and it's a big deal in this community," said Andy, who learned some of the lore of the hockey program and the university from two aunts and two uncles who are Cornell alums, and from his dad who took him and his brother, David, to games whenever the boys weren't playing for their own youth teams.

"He was mesmerized," Andy's dad said. "When the little kids come to watch the games, if you can get two periods of their interest you're doing good because they get tired. Andy was the kid who would sit on my lap and couldn't get enough, he would just watch the entire flow of the game and couldn't take his eyes off it. David was one of those kids who, after a couple periods, would get antsy and needed to do something. Andy didn't leave my lap, he wanted to watch the whole thing, and he understood it."

And as he continued to become enamored with the game, and Cornell, Andy came to understand how important Big Red hockey was to Ithaca.

"The people who live here love Cornell hockey and follow it and appreciate it, and I fell into that right away," Andy said. "I wouldn't say I was a diehard rink rat around here, but I loved coming to Lynah and it was always a goal to play here."

And not just because Cornell has one of the great hockey programs in the country; there was that whole Ivy League thing, too.

"I'd always worked hard in school; academics were always very important in my family, and I felt that the chance of playing professional hockey is so slim," he said. "I mean even if you get that opportunity, the chances of making it a career where you don't have to work another day in your life are even slimmer. So for me, it was all about going to the school where I could excel both athletically and academically. I visited the campuses and when it came down to it, I realized I had taken this place for granted because it was so close to home, but it's a place that I've fallen in love with."

ALL ABOUT PREPARATION

When Cornell coach Mike Schafer went up to Lake Placid, New York, in August 2011 to check on Andy's progress during a week-long camp where the Team USA coaching staff was evaluating prospects for the squad it would send to the World Junior Championship tournament at Calgary, Alberta, in January, he had one thing to say. "He played awesome up there."

From the time Cornell's 2010–11 season ended with a disappointing 6–0 loss to Ivy rival Yale in the ECAC championship game, Andy had been on a mission to wipe that game from his memory, and the only way he knew how was with hard work. Andy had been the starter against the Elis that March night in Atlantic City when an NCAA tournament berth was on the line, but he was smoked for five goals inside of thirty minutes and Schafer mercifully pulled him.

"He was very disappointed and I think it drove him all through the summer to become better and park it and move on," said Schafer. "He's a pretty driven kid in everything he does. He did a tremendous job in Lake Placid. And so far he's played well in practice; I think he has elevated his game and brought it to a higher level."

With a new season upon the Big Red, Schafer had enough to worry about as he tried to put together a team that would include nine freshmen, and he didn't need to add goalie to the list. He was pretty sure he wouldn't have to. Throughout the summer months and into the fall, Andy had become one of strength and conditioning coach Tom Howley's pet projects. As an undersized goalie, Andy got bounced around pretty good during his freshman season, and he knew he had to get stronger, so he and Howley really got after it.

"This summer was big for me," Andy said. "I stayed here for the most part because the thing I wanted to work on was developing my body and getting bigger and stronger so I can compete with these older kids at this level. We worked on quickness and agility and making sure that as I build strength I'm maintaining my flexibility and lateral speed."

Cornell was his priority, but Andy also used the summer sessions to get himself ready for the National Team Development Program evaluation camp. He served as the backup to Jack Campbell when Team USA won the bronze medal in the 2011 World Junior tournament in Buffalo, New York, and he had a great chance to make the squad again, especially after the way he performed in Lake Placid, where he led all the U.S. goalies in minutes played (162), goals-against average (0.34) and save percentage (.962) in four games against teams from the United States, Finland, and Sweden.

"It's an awesome experience, anytime you can put on the USA jersey and represent your country," Andy said. "That's special, and it carries a significance for the rest of your life. I had the opportunity last year, which was unbelievable, and I'm hoping to have it again, but my focus is to get this season going and have a strong year at Cornell. USA hockey will track me and the other players throughout the beginning of the year and whoever is playing best at that time, those are the guys they'll go with. All I can really do is focus on my year here. If I have a strong year here and we're having success as a team, they pretty much go hand in hand and things will work out on that end."

NOT A SNAPPY START

Andy was not superstitious, which is why he didn't consider what happened just before the October 29 season opener against Mercyhurst a bad omen, or an ominous sign of things to come.

Because he is a creature of habit, Andy has a regimented game-day schedule that he sticks to without compromise. "I like the same routine every day," he said. "It keeps you focused, and it's a preparation technique where if you know it's completed, you're ready for the game."

For Saturday home games, it's out of bed by nine, team breakfast at one of the dining halls on north campus, at the rink and stretching by 10:30, onto the ice for a skate at 11:30, a video session, lunch, an afternoon nap, a walk to get some fresh air and to start visualizing the game, and then back to the rink to get his sticks ready, a good stretch, and then on goes the goaltender equipment for the pregame warm-up.

"I've never seen a guy who gets more into the zone than him," said senior defenseman Keir Ross. "It's really impressive."

One of his roommates, sophomore Rodger Craig, agreed. "On game day he's a little hard to talk to. But goalies are always a little weird."

On this particular Saturday night, there was a little problem with the routine, though.

"I had my three sticks ready to go and I had plenty of time," Andy explained. "I like to give them a check to make sure they're good for the game and the first two I leaned on snapped in half. I've never had that happen before, so I was scrambling a little bit to get some new sticks."

The night never got much better as Andy allowed five goals and the Big Red, unable to shake their first-game rustiness, dropped a 5–4 decision to a Mercyhurst team that was playing its sixth game of the year.

"They played hard, they played a great game, and we were a little jittery at first because we haven't been on the ice much," Andy said. "We came out hard and then they weathered that initial adrenaline rush we had and they settled down and took it to us a bit."

Cornell took a quick 1–0 lead on a goal by Shawn Collins, Mercyhurst scored three in a row, and then after Cornell answered with three straight, the Lakers tallied twice in a span of 2:07 midway through the third period, the winning goal coming on a play where it appeared Mercyhurst's Nardo Nagtzaam kicked the puck past Andy.

Coach Mike Schafer said based on the postgame video he saw the goal shouldn't have counted, but what he was more upset about was the little things Cornell didn't do that cost it the game.

"We have a lot of work ahead of us," Schafer said.

There isn't a lonelier moment, or a more helpless feeling, for a goaltender than the mid-game skate to the bench. More times than not a coach will switch goalies as a way to shake up his team rather than as a form of punishment for the allowance of too many goals. Every goaltender knows this, and in general, accepts this. Still, no one who plays the most important position in hockey ever believes he should be removed from a game, so seeing the coach summoning you, in effect running the white flag of surrender up the pole, is an eyebrow-furrowing experience every time it happens.

"It's tough, but that's part of being a goalie," Andy said. "You're going to have some really glamorous moments, and you're going to have some rough moments."

Andy had his share of each as a freshman, but none was more noticeable than that night at Boardwalk Hall in Atlantic City, when he started but failed to finish against Yale in the 2011 ECAC championship game and had to make that skate to the bench midway through the second period with his team trailing, 5–0.

"As a freshman I was given the opportunity to play in that game and I wanted to play well and have an impact on the game. Obviously it was a terrible ending."

The Bulldogs were the class of the Ivy League and the ECAC that year, and their roster included several players who two years later helped lead Yale to the 2013 NCAA championship. When they faced off against Cornell they were the third-ranked team in the country, and they played like it. They scored on five of their first fifteen shots so Mike Schafer called a timeout, patted Andy on top of his goalie mask, told him it sure wasn't his fault, and sent junior Mike Garman out to finish what wound up being the last period and a half of his collegiate career.

"The only thing you want to do is hop back on the ice, but there was no opportunity to do that," Andy said. "That was it for us. And for me, it was really hard because I felt like I let my team down, and let down all the people who were watching and supporting Cornell. As a goalie that's going to happen; it happens to the guys in the NHL. It's a tough position because you're not going to be sharp every night and when you're not sharp, it's really noticeable. Other guys have great games and poor games, but for a forward, you really only notice their great games, you rarely notice their poor games. It's different for a goalie. If I make a mistake, it's in the net. Everyone notices that."

Naturally, upon the release of the 2011–12 schedule, the first thing Andy checked was when the first game with Yale was. It was November 4, at Yale's home barn, Ingalls Rink, and in front of national cable audience on CBS Sports Network, Andy and the Big Red enjoyed a night of sweet redemption as Cornell routed the ninth-ranked Bulldogs, 6–2, to end an eight-game losing streak and nine-game winless streak against their Ivy antagonist.

Cornell withstood an early surge by Yale as Andy made seven saves before the Big Red had recorded a shot on goal, but once they did that, the offense found its rhythm and John Esposito and Joel Lowry scored to give Cornell a 2–0 lead. Yale scored thirty-two seconds into the second period, then would have tied the game if not for a sturdy goal post, but that was pretty much the end of the drama. Brian Ferlin scored late in the second period and Lowry tallied again early in the third to make it 4–1, and the Big Red locked it down from there.

"I tried to flush it away as fast as I could," Andy said of the loss to Yale in the ECACs. "I knew I couldn't dwell on one performance that I had, but at the same time, whenever you have a difficult time against a team in the past, your next time against them you want to be better. For me, it wasn't so much personal redemption but as a team; that's a team we've struggled with for three or four years and it was really on our minds, and we knew if we went out there and executed we would be successful."

UNBEATABLE

One of the tenets Andy had established for himself was to make sure that every time he took up residence in his goal crease he did his job and gave his team a chance to win. Given the vagaries of his position, that's really all he could do. Well, for the last five games, specifically the last three, Andy had certainly done that.

"I'm seeing the puck pretty well right now, and when you get into a groove the puck seems to find you," Andy said in what would have to be considered a classic understatement. The Big Red stretched their winning streak to five games with a 1–0 non-conference victory over Niagara, which not only was the program's 500th all-time victory at Lynah Rink, it was Andy's third consecutive shutout.

In making twenty-four saves, Andy pushed his shutout streak to 202 minutes and 28 seconds, which was third-best in Cornell history behind a pair of runs put together by 2010 graduate and current NHL player Ben Scrivens of 206 minutes, 44 seconds, and 267 minutes, 11 seconds.

With Andy at the absolute top of his game, the Big Red climbed to seventeenth in the USCHO.com national poll and were off to a 6–2 start. Following the win over Yale, there was a loss at Brown, and they hit the road the next weekend for games at Dartmouth and Harvard and they earned 4–2 and 3–2 victories, respectively. Back in Lynah for their next three games, and there were three more victories without the allowance of a goal. Andy pitched back-to-back 4–0 shutouts over Princeton and Quinnipiac, and then the 1–0 win over Niagara. In recording the first shutout of his twenty-four-game college career, Andy needed to make only fifteen saves against Princeton. He had to work a little harder against Quinnipiac, as the Bobcats fired thirteen shots his way in the first period alone, and thirty-two by the end of the evening, but none of them found their way into Andy's net.

So now the Big Red would ride a big wave of momentum into Madison Square Garden, where on the Saturday after Thanksgiving they would take on fifteenth-ranked Boston University in the biennial Red Hot Hockey match in front of what would be a sellout crowd of more than eighteen-thousand.

"We're looking forward to it," Andy said of the game at the world's most famous arena. "It's going to be exciting, but I have to approach it like every other game. You have to prepare the same whether it's eighteen people or eighteen-thousand people. It's pretty simple in reality."

RED-HOT HOCKEY

That night proved to be tremendously exciting, but ultimately disappointing, and moments after their 2–1 overtime loss to the Terriers, Andy sat on a leather sofa in a room just down the hallway from the locker room he and his Cornell teammates had occupied wearing an expression of bemusement on his face that screamed, "What more could I do?"

In front of a sellout crowd in midtown Manhattan, three-fourths of whom were loud and proud Cornellians past and present, on the biggest stage

Andy had ever performed on, he was outstanding with twenty-five saves. Unfortunately, he had no chance when Adam Clendening, a 2011 second-round draft pick of the Chicago Blackhawks, buried a second-chance shot just inside the near post during a two-man BU power-play advantage in the first period. And then he was simply stupefied in overtime when a shot from the point deflected off the stick shaft of BU's Ross Gaudet, went between Gaudet's legs, grazed his upper thigh which altered the path of the puck a second time, and it sailed past Andy to give the Terriers the victory.

When you're going as good as Andy had been going, that's what it took for the Terriers to win—scoring while they were two men up, and with a shot that changed direction more than the conspiracy-theory JFK bullet.

The Clendening goal ended Andy's shutout streak at 213 minutes and 35 seconds, second-longest in Cornell history. Andy then blanked the Terriers for the next fifty-plus minutes, and thanks to a goal by Locke Jillson with 8:57 left in regulation, the game went into overtime, only to end at 2:48, stopping Cornell's five-game winning streak.

Despite the loss, it was an unforgettable night for Andy and the rest of the team, not to mention a clear measuring stick of where this Big Red squad was in terms of the national picture.

"It was a lot of fun and it was a great learning experience," Andy said. "Teams across the country that we see ourselves as equals to and teams that we want to compete with for a national championship, they play in rinks and environments like this all the time. They play in high-profile NHL rinks, and for us in a smaller conference in smaller rinks, we don't get that every day, so it's huge for us to have played this well here. It lets us know that we can play a team that's a high-profile team in front of a sellout crowd, and hopefully we can use that to our advantage. Our goal is to play in regionals and national championships and that's the environment that we have to get used to."

HOME-ICE HEAVEN

Andy was playing the best hockey of his life, and whether or not Kris Mayotte had anything to do with it, Cornell's first-year volunteer goaltender coach certainly wasn't taking any credit.

"I will take zero credit," said Mayotte, who watched Andy record his fifth consecutive home-ice shutout in Cornell's 0–0 tie with Clarkson at Lynah

Rink. "I was actually telling someone that what I've done over the last couple of weeks is genius on my part—I've said nothing to him. When a goalie is feeling that good and seeing the puck so well, you know he's in the groove. There isn't much you need to say to him."

Rarely in the long, illustrious history of Big Red hockey had a goalie been in a groove quite like this. The night before, Andy needed to make only thirteen saves in Cornell's 1–0 victory over St. Lawrence as the Big Red defense was superb, and Nick D'Agostino scored the only goal that was needed on a first-period power play. Against Clarkson he was a little busier, but remained perfect with twenty-three saves, which he needed to be, as Golden Knights goalie Paul Karpowich was even better with thirty-two saves.

The two shutouts gave Cornell five in a row at Lynah Rink, a program first, and Andy extended his home-ice scoreless streak to an unfathomable Cornell record 310 minutes, 58 seconds. He hadn't given up a goal at home since the third period of the regular-season opener against Mercyhurst five weeks earlier. With 267 minutes and 25 seconds of the shutout streak occurring in conference games, his last goal allowed coming in the second period of the 3–2 win at Dartmouth, Andy established a new ECAC record.

"It's a confidence thing and once you get it going the game comes pretty easy and things start to happen, all for the better," said Andy, who became the first Cornell goalie to post five shutouts in the team's first eleven games since Ken Dryden in 1967–68. Dryden, of course, went on to a legendary NHL and Hockey Hall of Fame career with the Montreal Canadiens. "You get in a rhythm where you're more confident on the ice, you get bounces here and there, and things seem to work out."

Mayotte joined the program this year when head coach Mike Schafer gave him an opportunity to jump-start his coaching career. Mayotte played four years for Union College in the early to mid-2000s, and after graduating he had been kicking around in various jobs and coaching goalies on the side.

"Anytime you have someone who can relate to your position, someone you can approach who has real game experience, it's awesome," Andy said. "He's a huge asset on the ice, I skate with him every day, we go through goalie-specific stuff and we break down film together, so from that end he's beyond helpful."

SNUBBED

On the first Monday of December, the hottest goaltender in the country found out he was not going to be on the Team USA roster when it traveled to Calgary, Alberta, to participate in the International Ice Hockey Federation World Junior Championship tournament.

"I don't want to say I was surprised, but I was disappointed, just because I thought I was playing some of the best hockey of my life," he said. "I played on the team last year, and seeing where my game is today compared to where it was last year, I just know I'm such a better goalie now than I was then, and I felt that with how I'm playing and my confidence level and the strides I've made, I thought I could really help them out."

Cornell coach Mike Schafer found it hard to believe that after the way Andy had played at the Team USA camp over the summer in Lake Placid, and how he had been playing the past month for the Big Red, that the officials at USA Hockey could bypass his goalie.

"With the way he was going, the camp he had in the summer, and playing well in a big-time atmosphere at Madison Square Garden, I thought those were all the indicators for him to claim one of those jobs, so it was a foregone conclusion in my mind that he was going," said Schafer. "But I think they had their mind set on the two guys and ultimately I don't think it would have made a difference if Andy had nine straight shutouts. You have to respect their opinion on it. It's one of those things, and it really doesn't matter what the reason was behind it. Andy knows he did everything possible to make the team and he doesn't have to hang his head thinking about the explanations as to why he wasn't named to the team."

And to his credit, Andy wasn't. Jack Campbell, a 2010 first-round draft choice of the Dallas Stars, had been the golden-haired goalie in the Team USA program. He helped lead the Americans to the gold medal in the 2010 tournament in Saskatoon, Saskatchewan, and backstopped them to a bronze medal finish in Buffalo in 2011.

As for John Gibson, a native of Pittsburgh who was picked to be Campbell's backup, he was a year younger than Andy, but he was also six inches taller and twenty pounds heavier than Andy, and that was a key factor in the decision. Plus, Andy couldn't argue with Gibson's resume. So far this year he'd played great for his Junior A team, the Kitchener Rangers of the Ontario Hockey

League, and the 2011 second-round draft pick of the Anaheim Ducks led the 2011 Under-18 team to a gold medal in the U18 World Championship in Germany, posting a 2.34 goals-against average and a .926 save percentage in six games.

"I've trained with him quite a bit because we kind of grew up in the national program, and then at some of these camps that we've gone to, so I know him well," Andy said of Gibson, who was selected by USA Hockey as its 2011 Goalie of the Year. "He's been my roommate at a few of these camps, and he's a good kid and a good goalie. He'll do a good job for them. The one thing that's good to know is that every opportunity I had, whether it was camp this past summer or my season thus far here, I haven't left anything open or out on the table. Stuff like that happens, but you have to take it and use it as fuel to make yourself better in the long run."

Andy had endured frustration with USA Hockey before. After playing so well in his second year at Salisbury Prep, he was selected to join the National Team Development Program, but in 2008 he tried out for the Under-17 team and was the last goaltender cut. "It was obviously disappointing, just because it was a dream to represent my country internationally," Andy said.

He did get the chance, though. When an off-ice disciplinary issue grounded one of the goaltenders who'd made the squad, Andy was the player picked as the replacement, and he was invited in August 2008 to join the team for a tournament in Slovakia. That led to him earning a spot on the Under-18 team.

"Andy was right down to the wire to make our team the previous year," said Joe Exter, the NTDP goaltending coach. "We tracked his progress the following year (at Salisbury). We needed a goalie on our U18 team, and we wanted to have the best available candidate in the country."

So off Andy went to Ann Arbor, Michigan, in the fall of 2009 for the most intensive hockey experience of his young life. "It was pretty demanding, but it was a perfect environment to hone your hockey skills. There were times you wanted to bury yourself and not go to the rink, but looking at the big picture, it was the most strides I've made as an athlete, ever."

All of the hockey players in the NTDP attend Ann Arbor's Pioneer High School through a partnership between the school and USA Hockey. A typical day for Andy consisted of going to class from 8 AM to 1 PM, and then it was over to the Ann Arbor Ice Cube—the program's training facility—where he'd spend the next five to six hours in goalie meetings, on-ice practice, weight-lifting sessions, film review, and team meetings.

As for the game schedule, it was a meat-grinder, for sure. "It makes the college season seem pretty short," said Andy, who shared time in the net with Campbell and compiled an impressive 20–6–1 record and a 2.16 goals-against average, which ranks third all-time for a single season in NTDP history.

Ironically enough, Andy's first game for the U18 team came against Cornell, at Lynah Rink, in October 2009, just after he'd announced that he would be attending Cornell in the fall of 2010. Andy expected to build many more memories at Cornell before it was time for him to bid farewell, but that night will always hold a special place in his heart.

"I knew I was starting, and it was exciting because I knew I would be coming to school here the next year," he said.

He received a heart-felt standing ovation pregame, but once the fans sat down and the puck was dropped, the local kid was wearing the wrong color uniform. Being a native Ithacan and soon-to-be Cornellian meant nothing for those two-plus hours, and they treated him just like any other visitor, as did his future Big Red teammates. "Yeah, I heard it during the game," said Andy, who beat the Big Red, 3–2, that night, "but at the end I got another standing ovation so that was cool. It just made me want to come here all the more."

IMPACT PLAYER

Andy couldn't quite remember what prompted him to become a human bulls eye, but he did remember that as soon as he strapped on the cumbersome pads, saw the effect he could have on games, and realized that he was the only player on the team that never had to come off the ice, he knew playing goaltender was his position.

"It was one of those things where when you're young no one really wants to be goalie, and it's goalie by committee," he said. "The coach says 'Who wants to play goalie this weekend?' and someone volunteers. I guess I volunteered, I liked all the equipment, and I enjoyed it. But that's who I am, I like to have an impact on the game, I like to be the central guy, it's my character and what I strive for, and that's what makes me tick. In baseball I was the catcher and in lacrosse I was the goalie and in football I was a quarterback.

I always liked those positions and I just loved it right away and kept asking the coach to play goalie."

And Andy played the position with uncanny skill, almost right from the start. He rapidly worked his way through the Ithaca youth program, and by the time he was ten years old and attending South Hill Elementary, it was apparent that he needed more of a challenge, so he sought a more competitive atmosphere.

He spent one year playing for a Connecticut-based travel team, and it did some serious traveling. One of its tournaments was a couple thousand miles away in Edmonton, Alberta, and in the championship game, with more than two thousand Canadians rooting against him, Andy led his team to victory and was named MVP. He then spent several years playing youth hockey for teams in Rochester, New York, he and his dad, Dave, making the three-hour round trip a few times a week for practices and games.

It was a sacrifice, but all those miles and driving through all those snowstorms, was certainly worth it. By the time he was in eighth grade he was sharing the starting duties on Ithaca High School's varsity, and he was the full-time starter as a freshman, leading the Little Red to the New York State Division 1 championship. "That was the most fun I've ever had playing hockey," he said.

Part of the reason was that he was playing with his older brother, David, a senior defenseman on that squad, which made it a special year for the Iles family. But beyond that, Andy said he'd never been on a team as close-knit as that one because almost all of those kids had grown up together playing in Ithaca's youth program, and this accomplishment truly meant something that will last a lifetime.

"For most of the guys, playing high school hockey was going to be their premier opportunity, so it was really neat," said Andy. "We'd have three or four buses going to our away games because it was such a big deal with the community and the student body. And the guys were so passionate about it and cherished that opportunity because all they had wanted to do since they were kids was play Ithaca high school hockey."

It was no different for Andy, but it was also very different for Andy because his hockey aspirations soared well above Ithaca High School. So before his sophomore year he chose to leave home and enroll at the Salisbury School, a prep school that is tucked into the extreme northwest corner of Connecticut, pretty much in the middle of nowhere. Andy spent two years at Salisbury, the second during which he backstopped the Crimson Knights to the New England Prep School Championship in 2008–09. He posted a record of 20–4–3 with a 1.72 goals-against average and .932 save percentage, which earned him the New England Prep goalie of the year award.

There were about two hundred fifty boys at Salisbury, most of them specializing in a particular sport, art, or academic endeavor. There were no girls.

"Yeah, that was interesting, but I'll say this; there were no distractions," he said. "No girls, and there wasn't even a grocery store nearby. We were out in the woods, pretty much, but it was a great experience. It really provides the perfect opportunity for having success and excelling at what you want to do. I was able to go there and succeed both academically and athletically and it opened up the opportunity to come to a university like Cornell."

ROADIE

There wasn't a whole lot of time for Andy to rue Team USA's decision because fall term exams were on the horizon, and with no hockey games for nearly four weeks due to exams and Christmas break, Andy became a resident in the library. One Sunday he spent fourteen hours there, and after taking his statistics final that Monday morning, he was holed up studying the rest of that day and most of Tuesday before closing out his schedule with two Wednesday exams in macroeconomics and African studies. He didn't have a final for the marketing course he took, nor the entrepreneurial speaker series elective, which was just a series of talks on varied topics that he was required to attend. All in all, not bad.

"I only had three exams, whereas last year I had five in the first semester and four and a take-home in the second, so it was nice to not have to take an exam every day," he said. "I enjoyed this semester, I was a lot happier than last year. Last year was such a transitioning process, figuring everything out and what course loads work for me, but I think I had a much more manageable load and I was more interested in the courses I took, and that made it easier to go to the library to study."

During Christmas week, Andy relaxed at his home, enjoyed a great holiday meal with his family, and naturally, he kept abreast of what was happening in the World Junior Championship. As much as he would have loved to don that Team USA jersey again, all things considered, maybe it was just as well that he wasn't there.

Backup goaltender John Gibson saw action in just one game, a 4–1 loss to Finland, and Jack Campbell played every minute of every other game as the Americans stumbled to a 3–3 record and did not qualify for the medal round, a hugely disappointing showing. So, spending a week sitting on the bench in the blustery Canadian province of Alberta probably wasn't as attractive as chilling—no pun intended—at home for a few days, and then spending a winter week in Florida where Andy played every second of Cornell's two games in the Florida College Classic and lounged on the beach during the down time with his teammates.

"Yeah, it wasn't the worst place to be," Andy said of the jaunt to Estero, Florida, near Fort Myers, where the Big Red lost, 5–2, to Massachusetts, and defeated Clarkson, 5–3. "I've never been to Florida, so to go down there to play a hockey tournament at the end of December and it's eighty degrees and you're wearing shorts, it's something a lot of New Yorkers could look forward to. I had a great time."

While in Florida he watched most of Team USA's loss to Canada on New Years' Eve, and caught highlights of some of the other games on NHL Network, but never did he feel vindicated regarding USA Hockey's decision to bypass him during the roster selection. Instead, he just felt bad for his friends on the team.

"I talked to some of the guys and they were pretty disappointed," he said. "I knew USA Hockey made their decision on me and I could only support them and root for my buddies who were there."

Cornell coach Mike Schafer had discussed the Team USA situation with Andy, and he told him there was no doubt he was one of the best goaltenders in the country, and by all rights, he should have been picked. However, Schafer also knew that the snub would only make Andy work harder for the Big Red when the season resumed in Florida, and that was the case.

This was quite a roadie for the Big Red. The team reconvened a couple days after Christmas and flew down south to play the two games in Florida that ended their four-week exam and holiday break, then jetted out to Colorado Springs to play a pair of games against sixth-ranked Colorado College. "It was a great trip being on the road with the guys," Andy said. "We went from

Florida to the Rocky Mountains where our hotel overlooked Pike's Peak, so we were pretty high up there in elevation, and it was pretty chilly. I had to pack a suitcase with winter coats and gloves and hats and then you had swim trunks and flip flops. Not our typical hockey trip."

Against UMass, Andy was clearly rusty, as he allowed three goals in the third period, more than he had given up in any of the eight previous games. But he was back in form the next night against Clarkson as he made nineteen saves and was touched for just one even-strength goal.

"It was tough to play and get back into it after the layoff," he said. "I'm a guy that just likes to play, and whenever I can get into a rhythm I can get some confidence. Whenever I take time off from practice or games, it feels like my body needs a little adjustment period to get caught up to speed and get my tracking back. I knew before the trip to Florida things weren't going to come as easy for me as they were in November and early December."

After spending the next several days playing mini-golf, hanging out at the beach, going out to eat with his teammates, and one night attending a party at a Cornell alum's house, the Big Red headed to Colorado and turned in two solid efforts. They won the first night, 3–1, and then settled for a 3–3 tie when the hosts scored on Andy with just 29.1 seconds left in regulation.

Still, to have gone 2–1–1 in four road games a long way from home, after not having played a game for nearly a month, was quite an accomplishment for the Big Red. Not only did it catapult them into the top ten in the national poll with a 9–4–2 record, it set the stage for the second half of the regular season when they would close with fourteen consecutive ECAC games.

NO MORE ZEROES

The great Ted Williams once said of his rival Joe DiMaggio's fifty-six-game hitting streak achieved in 1941, "I think Joe put a line in the record book and it's the one that will never be changed." So far, more than seventy years later, Williams's prediction is holding true.

This season, Andy put a line in the Cornell hockey record book that may never be changed, either. "It was a great streak, probably won't get matched," coach Mike Schafer said after Andy's remarkable home-ice shutout streak was finally snapped during the Big Red's hard-fought 4–3 overtime victory over Dartmouth. "He has done a tremendous job. He has played awesome."

Andy hadn't allowed a goal at Lynah Rink since the first game of the season in late October when Mercyhurst scored with 7:11 remaining to pull out a 5–4 victory. Since then he had recorded five consecutive shutouts in Ithaca, and blanked the Big Green for the first thirty-seven minutes, fifty-seconds before Dartmouth's Mark Goggin broke through to end the streak at 350 minutes, 6 seconds.

"It wasn't really on the forefront of my mind because it just happened to be a period of home games in a row and that was just timing," Andy said, pointing to the fact that there were plenty of road and neutral-site games mixed in where he had given up goals, so the streak never really felt active. "People ask me about the streak, but what mattered is that as a team we were playing such good hockey, I was feeling comfortable, and stuff was clicking for us as a team and for me."

Cornell grabbed a 2–0 lead on goals by Brian Ferlin and Dustin Mowrey, but in a span of thirty-six seconds late in the second period, Goggin scored, Cornell's Nick D'Agostino took a penalty, and the Big Green capitalized on the power play when Doug Jones banged in his own rebound after Andy had made a great stop on his first shot.

"I thought I was going to have another (shutout), I was feeling pretty good, but I made a little mistake on the first goal and gave them a little confidence and before you knew it, it was tied," Andy said.

Cornell regained the lead 1:01 later on Locke Jillson's slapshot, but Dartmouth tied it midway through the third, and it took Cole Bardreau's power-play goal 2:05 into overtime to rescue the victory.

There was no shutout the next night, either, nor was there a victory as the Big Red battled Harvard to a 2–2 draw. However, that kept alive Cornell's unbeaten string at seven games, and left it atop the ECAC standings with a sterling 8–1–3 record, though Schafer—being a coach—was a little concerned.

"We're not playing well, we're playing OK, we're finding ways to win, which is a great sign of a good team," said Schafer. "But we've lost that detailed attitude and performance that we had before Christmas."

The good news, in Schafer's view, was that his team hadn't peaked and there was lots of room for improvement. "I'd be a little concerned if we were playing at such a high level of hockey that we had nothing to shoot for at the end of the year," he said. "We want to be playing our best hockey at the end of the year, the way we were playing in early December."

If there's one thing, first and foremost, that sets Ivy League student-athletes apart from the rest of their Division I brethren across the country, it's this: Not only do they go to class, but they enjoy class, and want to be there. That explained why Andy was happy that school was back in session at Cornell. During the long Christmas break, he actually missed being in the classroom.

"I love playing hockey; that's what I'm all about, but it's almost tough to not have anything else to do," Andy said. "I'm a morning person, I need to get up and around and it's just easier for me to go to school and kind of have another outlet to take the stress away before we go to practice. Hockey is why I'm here, but I'm here for more than the hockey. When you come to an Ivy League school, you've thought about things beyond athletics."

Andy took his schoolwork seriously, and always had. He enrolled at Cornell thinking that he wanted to get into medicine. One of his grandfathers and one of his uncles were veterinarians, and while his passion was sports, not animals, he originally thought he could meld athletics and medicine together. "I kind of wanted to be a doctor affiliated with a professional team or maybe a university, using medicine as an avenue to stay in sports because that's what I love," he said.

He took some premed requirement courses last year, but it became quickly apparent that medicine probably wasn't going to be the path for him. He briefly explored nutritional science, but this year had discovered an interest in business and how that can be tied to sports marketing and financing for a possible career in sports management. That's what had brought him to the marketing, statistics, and macroeconomics courses, as well as the entrepreneurial speaker series last semester.

This semester he was taking courses in managerial accounting, international trade and finance, intermediate microeconomics, developmental sociology, and an online class, Environmental Sustainability. "I'm enjoying school right now, I'm a lot happier this year," he said. "I'm a lot more passionate about the classes I'm taking this year. I've never thought of having success in athletics as an excuse for not being a normal person. Being in the classroom, I just try to be a normal student, study, put the time in during class, and be like every other kid here. If I don't do well on an exam, it's not because I was at the rink and I couldn't study."

Being in class was certainly more enjoyable than being at the rink the last weekend in January 2012 for Andy and the Big Red. For the first time all season they lost back-to-back games, as regional rival Colgate swept their annual home-and-home series.

"It was obviously disappointing," Andy said. "We were on top of the ECAC standings and looking pretty good in terms of national perspective (ranked ninth in the USCHO poll). But it's so hard to be dominant every single night, and our league is so good; from top to bottom there are a lot of quality teams. So we took a step back."

In the game at Lynah, Colgate pulled out a 2–1 victory, which snapped Cornell's seven-game unbeaten streak, ended the Red Raiders' six-game winless streak, and gave Colgate its first victory over the Big Red in twelve games dating back to January 2007. Andy gave up two goals in the first period, then blanked the Red Raiders the rest of the way, but Cornell managed only one goal by Joakim Ryan in the second period, and had only one shot on goal during the third period.

The next night Cornell took a 3–1 lead into the final twenty minutes and then melted down at Starr Rink as Colgate scored four times—one even strength, one shorthanded, one on a power play, and one into an empty net—to earn a 5–3 victory, giving the Red Raiders their first sweep over Cornell since 2004.

"At some point in the season you're going to face a little bump and this was one of our first times where we faced some true adversity," Andy said.

IVY LEAGUE CHAMPS

When Andy was going through his college selection process, Dave and Amy Iles tried to stay as neutral as they could. After all, this was a decision he had to make for his own good.

"Our philosophy always has been to give him opportunities and whatever he does with it, that's up to him," Dave said. "So we took him to various schools, got a feel for what schools were interested, and then we didn't give him a whole lot of guidance."

However, truth be told, when Andy told his parents that Cornell was his choice, they could barely contain their excitement that he was staying home. "We would have been delighted no matter where he would have chosen to go, but when he decided to come here, I was like 'Oh my gosh,'" Dave said. "It wasn't like it was a dream come true for us; that wasn't what it was about, but we'd been traveling since he was eight years old and now his college experience was going to be right here."

On this night, Dave left his office in downtown Ithaca at closing time and drove to Lynah Rink to meet the dozen or so family members that are at just about every home game and watched Andy make twenty-two saves in a 5–2 victory over Brown that ended Cornell's five-game winless streak. The next night, Dave and Amy made the seven-minute ride from the family home to the campus to see a stellar performance by Andy as he made thirty-two saves in a 4–2 victory over Yale that clinched the Ivy League championship for Cornell, its first outright title since 2005.

"It's a weird setup in hockey where we play for the Ivy League within the ECAC," Andy said. "Our goal is to be atop the standings in the ECAC and to hopefully win the regular-season championship, and the main goal is to win the ECAC tournament because that gets you an automatic bid to the NCAA tournament. So most of the guys would say we weren't really thinking about the Ivy League championship, but once we realized it was right around the corner and we were having a great year, it was definitely exciting because anytime you can win a championship with a group of guys, it's special."

And it meant a little more to Andy because the clincher came against Yale. While he'd already exorcised his demons regarding the loss to Yale in the ECAC title game last spring with a victory at Yale in November, it was still sweet to beat the Bulldogs. As for Dave and Amy, naturally they were ecstatic, but to get to that point, they had to endure the typical stomach-churning that comes with every game Andy plays at Lynah. It's hard enough being a hockey parent, but being the parent of the goaltender, particularly a goaltender who was born and raised in town, adds an extra level of angst.

"It's nerve-wracking," Dave admitted. "Your stomach starts turning cartwheels at about noon on a game day, and then it takes about an hour after the game to come down from that adrenalin rush. It's either an extreme high or an extreme low. When things are going great you're on top of the world, but when things aren't going well for the team or Andy's not performing as good as he'd like to, it's tough. The community is great, they're very supportive, but it's also a very demanding hockey town."

When Cornell's assistant director of athletic communications, Brandon Thomas, went into the Big Red locker room to inform sophomore forward Rodger Craig that members of the media wanted to talk to him, Andy hatched a plan.

"That was his first interview since he's been here at Cornell, so we wanted to give him a little something to chuckle about," Andy said of Craig, one of three teammates that he shared an off-campus apartment with over on Cook Street, just off the main drag through campus, College Avenue. "I said to the guys it would be funny if we all piled out there (into the interview room) while he was doing it, and the captain (Keir Ross) said, 'OK boys, you want to do it?' and the team was in on it."

As Craig finished explaining how his first goal of the season, midway through the third period, capped a rally from a 2–1 deficit and lifted the Big Red to a thrilling 3–2 victory over Union that enabled Cornell to tie the Dutchmen for first place in the ECAC standings with one game left, the team cheered for Craig, who smiled sheepishly at his goofball teammates.

"That's something special because he's one of my best friends on the team," Andy said of Craig, who had struggled most of the year and had been a healthy scratch for all but thirteen games. "Unfortunately he's been out of the lineup the majority of the season, but he never gave up, and he made the most of his opportunity tonight and hopefully he can keep it going."

With a tie at Clarkson and a win at St. Lawrence the previous weekend, the Big Red set up this showdown for first place with Union, and Andy was up to the task against Dutchmen goalie Troy Grosenick. Grosenick was the only goalie in the ECAC who ranked above Andy in the three main statistical categories—wins, goals-against average and save percentage. But Andy stopped twenty-eight of thirty shots, while John McCarron, Greg Miller, and Craig all found a way to beat Grosenick. And the fact that his buddy, Craig, was the one who finally broke the Dutchmen was a bonus.

Unfortunately, this big victory became meaningless twenty-four hours later when the Big Red lost to tenth-place RPI, 2–1, in overtime. Coupled with Union's 5–3 victory over Colgate, Cornell ended up where it began the weekend, two points behind the Dutchmen in the final standings. John McCarron's goal 8:18 into the third period gave Cornell a 1–0 lead, but Andy was beaten for the tying goal with just 2:20 left in regulation, and then gave up the winner with only nineteen seconds to go in the extra period.

"As a coach, you're like, 'How could you not be ready to win a league championship on your home ice, in front of your home fans, on Senior Night?'" coach Mike Schafer said. "After that big win Friday night, to come out and follow it up with the way we played tonight, it was like two different teams."

The Big Red still secured a first-round bye for the ECAC tournament, but while Andy said that was the primary goal, he added, "It would have been nice to have the regular-season title along with it."

LONG WEEKEND

For some strange reason, as the second overtime period was coming to a close, Andy was feeling as strong as he had all night. "I was back there in the crease and I felt like my game was getting better as the game went on," he said. "I felt my sharpest in the second overtime and I don't know how that happened because everyone else was really tired."

The clock was ticking inside two minutes to go in the fifth period, and Andy was already mentally preparing himself for a third overtime in Game One of the Big Red's best-of-three ECAC quarterfinal series against Dartmouth at Lynah Rink. After all, more than sixty minutes—the length of a regulation game—had elapsed since the last goal had been scored, by Dartmouth's Kyle Schussler midway through the second period, which forged the 3–3 tie the teams were still entangled in, and it didn't look like anything was changing.

But then it happened, seemingly out of nowhere. Cornell senior defenseman Sean Whitney, who hadn't scored a goal all season, worked himself free for a shot from the right faceoff circle and rifled a wrister that rang off the crossbar and went into the net behind Big Green goalie Joey O'Neill. Game over. Big Red, 4–3 winners in the longest game ever played in the fifty-four-year history of Lynah, a mark that would last less than a day.

"Thank God it was over because we were two minutes away from having to play a third overtime," Andy said. "It didn't look like either team was going to score because guys were getting tired. It's hard to create offense when you're fatigued like that, but luckily he got it over with."

Game Two was delayed forty-five minutes because earlier in the afternoon the Big Red women played nearly two full games—119 minutes and 50 seconds to set a new Lynah length record—before it defeated Boston University, 8–7, in a wild NCAA quarterfinal game that advanced Cornell to the women's Frozen Four.

Mercifully for the folks who work at the rink, the Big Red men needed only the three regulation periods to dispatch Dartmouth, 3–1, and move on to the ECAC semifinals in Atlantic City. Dustin Mowrey, Locke Jillson, and Whitney all scored in the first 8:21 and Andy, coming off a forty-six-save performance, stopped twenty-seven of the twenty-eight shots he faced in the clincher.

"The mood walking into the locker room was pretty upbeat," Andy said of the second game. "We were a shot away from being on the other side and being down one game and having to play for our season, so just to be able to go into a game not having to worry that this might be our last game was huge."

Of the upcoming semifinal game at Boardwalk Hall against red-hot Ivy rival Harvard, Andy said, "We're excited. We prepare all year to be in a situation like this and one of our goals was to get there because once you get to Atlantic City it's anyone's tournament and you have a chance to win a championship."

NICE CONSOLATION

Even though the bus pulled up in front of Lynah Rink at around five o'clock Sunday morning following the trip home from Atlantic City, and Andy wouldn't get into bed for at least another forty-five minutes, he knew he'd be up in time to watch the NCAA tournament selection show that would be airing at noon on ESPNU.

And he was. "I'm a big fan of college hockey," he said, "so I enjoyed watching the show and hearing about the other teams."

Of course the team he was most interested in was the Big Red and, as expected, Cornell was selected for the sixteen-team field that would be participating in college hockey's showcase event despite the fact that it did not win the ECAC tournament.

The Big Red were smoked 6–1 Friday in the semifinals by Harvard, killing their hopes of winning a thirteenth ECAC title. But rebounding from one of his, and the team's, worst games of the year, Andy recorded his sixth shutout of the season less than twenty-four hours later, a twenty-five-save masterpiece in the pressure-packed consolation game, and the Big Red defeated Colgate, 3–0.

"We pretty much knew if we won that game we'd probably get in," Andy said. "We weren't really crunching the numbers too much, but we felt based on what we had done during the regular season that if we got one win down there we'd get into the NCAA tournament. We didn't want to have to rely on that as much as we ended up having to, but it worked out."

Cornell had beaten Harvard at Cambridge, 4–2, and tied the Crimson, 2–2, at Lynah in a pair of hard-fought regular-season games. But with Harvard's only chance for an NCAA bid dependent on winning the ECAC crown, the Crimson played a spectacular game. They scored two goals in each period and Andy's six-goal yield was a career-worst.

"It was one of those games where as a team we didn't play very well, Harvard played a great game, and I didn't play as well as I would have liked to, so the combination of those things didn't get the job done for us," Andy said.

The loss meant that Cornell was playing for its season against Colgate, a team it had lost to on back-to-back nights a little less than two months earlier. And for Andy, he had some additional baggage on his shoulders. Last year at this venue, he'd been torched for five goals in less than half of the ECAC championship game against Yale. Now with another clunker on his plate, he had to play the biggest game of the year having allowed eleven goals in his last four and a half periods in Atlantic City.

"One of the things I've always prided myself on is that it's always about the future," he said. "You can't dwell on the past or look in the past whether it's a positive or a negative. For me it's not about the last save I make, but the next shot I face, so it was turning the page after a disappointing performance and realizing what was most important wasn't how poorly I played on Friday night, but the performance I had to give on Saturday."

It was a beauty, and with Sean Collins, Dustin Mowrey, and John McCarron scoring, the Big Red improved to 18–8–7, a record for which they were rewarded with a spot in the NCAA Midwest Regional as the fourth seed.

"It's going to be fun," said Andy of what would be his first NCAA tournament experience, a game against top-seeded Michigan in Green Bay, Wisconsin. "Obviously Michigan is a great team, with a great history in that program, but the history of our program speaks for itself as well, and throughout this year we've played some other high-profile programs with some big names and we've had success. We have to focus on ourselves and prepare ourselves to perform to the best of our ability."

FALLING SHORT

As a collective group, hockey players are among the toughest athletes you'll find anywhere, and they have the stitches and the scars and the false teeth to prove it. But for all their grit and their rough-and-tumble nastiness on the ice, their tears are as wet and salty and come as easily after a heartbreaking, season-ending loss as anyone else's.

And so, in their locker room at the Resch Center in this small city where NFL football is king, tears were flowing freely from the ducts of the Big Red players following a 2–1 loss to Ferris State in the regional championship game.

"That's one of the toughest experiences you have as an athlete," Andy said. "Those guys are your brothers and we're a big family and it's tough to lose because we're all such competitors. At that moment you realize your season is over and you know you're never going to be with this same group of guys again, it's tough, and it's sad. And it's hard for the seniors because we feel like we let them down."

Moments after the final horn sounded, and the traditional handshakes had been exchanged, the Big Red gathered in their room and coach Mike Schafer called the four departing seniors—Sean Whitney, Locke Jillson, Sean Collins, and captain Keir Ross—to the middle and the rest of the players encircled them and Schafer, arms and shoulders locked.

"Coach addressed the team and then everyone pretty much took their turn giving the seniors a hug and letting them know how much we appreciate them," Andy said. "It was a really emotional scene, a lot of shedding of tears."

The fourth-seeded Big Red advanced to the title game by taking out the region's number one seed, Michigan, 3–2, on another huge goal by Andy's roommate, Rodger Davis, 3:35 into overtime. "Rodger is one of my best friends so that was great to see," Andy said. "He only had two goals, but the other one, if he didn't get it against Union, we probably wouldn't have been in this position, and then he extended our season again with the goal against Michigan."

That game started terribly for the Big Red as Michigan scored 1:11 into the first period when Andy allowed back-to-back rebounds in one flurry and

Luke Glendening banged the second one into the net. And it appeared to get worse twenty-two seconds later when Kevin Lynch scored on another rebound. However, after Schafer called a timeout to calm his team down, the officials reviewed the play and determined it was no goal because Andy had been interfered with on the play.

Now settled down and feeling fortunate, the Big Red got back into the game when John McCarron rifled a slap shot from the right circle that beat Michigan goalie Shawn Hunwick just inside the far post during a power play midway through the first period. Cornell took a 2–1 lead forty seconds into the second when Ryan scored from the slot off a nice setup from Collins on a two-on-one rush.

Andy was terrific the rest of the period as the penalty-happy Big Red had to kill off nearly ten minutes of shorthanded time with Andy stopping all thirteen shots he faced in that wild stretch. Deep into the third period it was still 2–1, but Michigan finally got the equalizer with 4:01 left as Lynch scored on a rebound.

The overtime didn't last long as Ryan scooped up a loose puck in the Cornell zone and sent away Dustin Mowrey on the left wing. Mowrey carried into the Michigan zone where he fed Greg Miller for a shot that Hunwick made a nice save on. However, he kicked the rebound right back into the slot where Davis was crashing through and he had a virtual layup on his backhand into an open net, touching off a wild celebration.

During the break before overtime, Andy wasn't nervous at all, even though if he allowed the next goal, the season was over. "A lot of times people think going into overtime that it gets more stressful, but it just got more and more fun as the game went on," he said. "If you know in the back of your mind that you've put in all the work and all the preparation, then your play should take care of itself. You work all year to be in situations like that, and when you start to have an impact on the game and you're in the middle of it, things start to get easier and you realize it's just another hockey game and you're prepared for it."

Cornell and Ferris State played it close to the vest throughout a tedious first two periods before things opened up in the third. "It was one of those games that was kind of a stalemate; two teams playing great defense and limiting the chances," said Andy. "You could hear guys on the ice wondering if anyone was going to score."

Well, Ferris State did eleven seconds into the period. Cornell's Eric Axell snapped his stick on the opening faceoff and with the Bulldogs already on a power play, this was a big problem. "Eric had to skate to the bench to get a new stick and it basically gave them a five-on-three zone entry and they took advantage of it," said Andy. Ultimately, Andy made two saves, but lost control of the second shot and Garrett Thompson swept it into the net. "That was kind of unfortunate, a broken stick, a couple bounces, and it was 1–0," said Andy.

Cornell answered just 1:21 later when Mowrey broke in on right wing and whistled one through the legs of Ferris State goalie Taylor Nelson, and then the Big Red spent almost seven consecutive minutes on the power play, fruitlessly trying to produce the go-ahead goal. Finally, just as the man-advantage time was expiring, Ferris State was able to break out two-on-one and Andy Huff neatly set up Jordie Johnson who beat Andy over his glove with a slap shot from the left circle for what proved to be the winning goal.

The Big Red pushed for the equalizer, and Nelson made a superb glove save on John Esposito with a minute left while Andy was pulled for an extra attacker, and that was the last good chance Cornell had.

"It's disappointing that we didn't go as far as we wanted to and we left some unfinished goals on the table," Andy said. "But in a situation like that, how much can you dwell on the past? It's only going to hurt even more, so we tried to take some positives out of it. There were so many great things we did this year, and we left our hearts on the ice and we had to realize that."

MELTDOWN

Andy didn't need a reminder that the Big Red hockey season was over, but he got one a few days after the return from Green Bay when the maintenance crew at Lynah Rink melted the ice. "Yeah, I guess that's it," Andy said. "It's weird looking down and seeing the concrete."

In a couple weeks the Cornell players returning for the 2012–13 season would begin their off-season workout regimen, but there would be nowhere to skate, not for several months, and that was OK with Andy. He'd had enough, at least for a little while.

"They'll bring the ice back in July because that's when the Cornell youth hockey camps start, so the only hockey stuff we'll do is we'll get together as a group and go out on the concrete with a tennis ball and play ball hockey, have a little fun," he said. "It reminds you of the days when you were young and playing street hockey. And I won't be putting any goalie equipment on. I'll have a little fun stick-handling and shooting and just being with the guys."

With the ice gone, the pads put away, and no more practices or games, Andy suddenly had time on his hands, and just like his freshman year when the season ended, he wasn't quite sure what to do with it.

"That's the weirdest part when the season is over; I'm back to being a regular student and I feel like I have so much time, but for some weird reason it feels like work builds up even more," he said. "During the season you're stressed out and feeling like you can't accomplish what you want to accomplish from an academic standpoint, but once you're done with the season, you have so much more time, yet I almost feel unproductive."

But he's not going to feel too guilty because it would be a well-deserved respite for Andy after such an impressive year for the Big Red. He was one of only two goalies in the country who played every minute of every game for his team (Kent Patterson of Minnesota was the other). He was the first Cornell goalie to do so since Darren Eliot in 1982–83, and the first Big Red sophomore to do it since Laing Kennedy in 1960–61. Because of that, his won-lost record of 19–9–7 mirrored the team's final mark and he finished with a 2.12 goals-against average, a .919 save percentage, and six shutouts. He put together the second-longest scoreless streak in school history, and then had another shutout run that was the ninth-best in school history. He established a new individual best with forty-six saves in the ECAC quarterfinal opener against Dartmouth, and he earned first-team All-Ivy honors, second-team ECAC All-League.

Looking back, his was one of the finest season-long performances a goalie at Cornell had ever had, and that's saying something considering this is a school that has produced netminders such as Eliot, Ken Dryden, Brian Hayward, David LeNeveau, and Ben Scrivens, all of whom went on to the NHL, most notably the iconic Hockey Hall of Famer, Dryden. "That's one of the reasons I came to the school, because of the goaltending tradition," Andy said. "It's something special. It's something I use to motivate myself. I'm trying to follow in their footsteps."

If he continued on this track, by the time he was done playing on the East Hill Andy would be creating new footsteps for others to follow in. And as an Ithaca native who chose to attend Cornell and play hockey for the Big Red for so many reasons, but one definitely being the opportunity to perform in front of family and friends, that's something he was striving to do.

"Being a local guy I want to prove myself that much more every time I step on the ice, not only because I want the team to win and represent Cornell University, but just because I want to be one of the best to ever play here," he said. "I may be here in Ithaca for the rest of my life, I don't know, so I want to leave a mark."

SPRING

GREG ZEBRACK

PENN BASEBALL

It wasn't his native Southern California, but it sure felt like it could be. Who said global warming was a bad thing? Certainly no one who lived in the Northeast in the non-winter of 2011–12. It was sixty degrees on this mid-January day in the City of Brotherly Love, and if Greg and a few of his Penn teammates were so inclined, they could probably have gone over to Meiklejohn Stadium and taken some infield or shagged some flies.

Two weeks from now, when Ivy League teams could officially begin spring season practice, there was no doubt that Quakers coach John Cole would have the team over there on a day like this, taking advantage of a rare chance to be outdoors in the baseball preseason. But because the Quakers were only permitted per NCAA regulations to do individual workouts right now—six-on-ones, they're called, where one coach works with six or fewer players on various fielding and hitting drills—they were inside the newly-constructed bubble-covered practice facility named Penn Park.

"It's pretty nice," Greg said. "We can have full team scrimmages in there. Last year we were in an old, crappy armory that had a rubber track surface, and we were in there most of the time because we only got outside maybe twice (before the annual season-opening trip down South). We went out one day after it had snowed and we were on Franklin Field and we tried to be out there and it was like thirty degrees, and the other day we went out it was about twenty-three degrees. This is much better."

There were definitely some days last year when Greg was inside that old, crappy armory wondering what the hell he was doing on the other side of the country, trying to get ready for baseball season in conditions that were better-suited to alpine skiing. But after a stellar first year playing for the Quakers when he earned first-team All–Ivy League honors batting .336 and leading the team in slugging percentage (.596), on-base percentage (.449), runs (thirty-five), home runs (seven) and total bases (eighty-seven), Greg could look back and say his eyebrow-raising move from SoCal to the Ivy League of all places was the decision that reinvigorated what had become his stalled quest to become a professional baseball player.

A quick scan of the 2012 Ivy League baseball rosters revealed that all eight Ancients had at least a couple Californians. But no one else had a kid like Greg, who was drafted by the Los Angeles Dodgers out of high school but who declined to sign so he could accept a scholarship to play at the University of Southern California, once one of the iconic programs in college baseball and college sports.

"Yeah, you don't see that too often." Cole said of the unique dynamic of a talented, already-drafted West Coast kid coming East to play baseball when usually, overwhelmingly, it's the other way around. "It's tough to keep the best kids in the East here because they want to go where they can play."

But that was the problem for Greg. In order to play, he had to do it the opposite way. His year-and-a-half at USC was grossly disappointing, the future didn't look much better, and if he harbored any hope of making baseball his career, he knew he had to make a change. He just never could have envisioned it would be as drastic a change as transferring into the Ivy League.

"Baseball's not like football," Greg said, citing the example of former USC quarterback Mark Sanchez. "He sat for a few years and then started one year and he was a first-round draft choice. In baseball you can't do that because it's a developmental sport. You have to play. My goal is to play pro ball and I needed to develop. You need to get at-bats. When coach Cole called me, he was like, 'Why do you want to come to Penn?' and I just said, 'I want to play baseball.' Plus it's a great school, so why not? It wasn't a bad choice."

GAME OF HIS LIFE

Born in Los Angeles, raised and schooled in the San Fernando Valley, in attendance for Dodgers games at Chavez Ravine from the time he was a baby, and a year-round participant in baseball whether he was playing for youth, school, or upper-level amateur teams, Greg had never really wanted to do anything else but play baseball.

His mother, Ivy (how's that for a forewarning of what was to come in

Greg's life?), was born in Germany but grew up in New York; his father, Jeff, was born and raised in Southern California, and that's where he and Ivy settled to raise Greg and his older sister, Sara. Jeff had always been a baseball fan, but he wasn't much of a player, as tennis was his sport, and still is. He started taking Greg to Dodger games in a stroller, and before Greg was in kindergarten he was throwing a ball around and watching games on television whenever he could.

"I've always been big into baseball," Greg said. "It's funny, I have a little cousin, Gabe, and he's just like I was. He's obsessed with baseball, been going to Dodger games since he was a baby like I did."

Greg didn't play Little League, he played Pony League, and there's a difference, and not just because it's two separate organizations. "We have a big thing; Pony Leaguers think Little League is kind of crap," he said with a smile. "We were stealing bases at seven years old; in Little League you can't steal bases until you're about twelve. I wish we could have played in the Little League World Series. I'm convinced our twelve-year-old team would have won that tournament. We'd play teams from Northridge Little League and we killed them, it was a joke."

It's not hard to understand why. The 2011 American League MVP, Ryan Braun of the Milwaukee Brewers, is just one of dozens of former North Valley Youth Baseball Pony Leaguers playing pro ball. This was the baseball environment Greg grew up in, with top-notch competition and games and tournaments that were played year-round because, well, it's California.

Greg enjoyed success at every youth level, and that continued in high school. He attended a small private school, Campbell Hall in North Hollywood, and was a four-year varsity letter-winner in baseball (he also played football). During his time the Vikings won two California Interscholastic Federation (CIF) regional championships. He was the CIF player of the year as a sophomore and an all-state selection as a senior.

When he wasn't playing for Campbell Hall, he was augmenting his resume on the highly competitive Southern California amateur circuit, including scout ball in the fall which is a key component for players looking to get recruited by college programs or drafted by professional organizations, or both. Basically, major league clubs organize teams of promising players with their own scouts coaching and managing, and the weekend games are contested in front of other scouts and coaches.

"It's just a way for the scouts to see the players, and it's really good competition," said Greg, who played whenever he didn't have a conflicting football game. "Especially for me, coming from a small school like Campbell Hall where most of the games were against lesser competition, going there you're playing with the top players. Pretty much every big-time guy in Southern California who gets drafted played scout ball."

During the fall of his sophomore year he played for the New York Yankees scout team and its home field was the University of Southern California's Dedeaux Field, named for the legendary former Trojan coach, Rod Dedeaux, who built USC's baseball dynasty beginning in the early 1940s, maintained it for forty-five years, won eleven College World Series titles, and sent dozens of players to the major leagues including Ron Fairly, Don Buford, Tom Seaver, Dave Kingman, Roy Smalley, Fred Lynn, Mark McGwire, and Randy Johnson.

Greg's parents raised him as a UCLA fan, but the Bruins were a non-factor in baseball. With its historic pedigree, USC is where Greg longed to play, and that feeling only intensified that fall when he was practicing and playing there. "It was a dream to play there, absolutely," he said. "When I was growing up it was Mark Prior and Geoff Jenkins and all these guys who went to the big leagues. They were going to the College World Series and when you talked about college baseball it was USC. If they wanted me to play there I was going in a heartbeat."

A little more than a year later, that dream began to take shape.

NEW YORK STATE OF MIND

Baseball is the ultimate game of nuance, and all of its perfect imperfections are what attract us to the sport, the same as they did our parents, and their parents, and their parents.

The soft breeze that blows through the stadium on a summer night, the wafting aroma of hot dogs and roasted peanuts, the sheen of freshly cut grass, the roar of the crowd when the home team scores a run or prevents one. It's a game that tantalizes the senses, but it is the nuances of the game that set it apart from the other sports. Albert Pujols can turn on a fastball and drive it over the fence for a four-hundred-fifty-foot home run. But Ichiro Suzuki can leave the bat on his shoulder and draw a walk, steal second base, take third on a grounder to the right side, and score on a wild pitch, a run that counts the same as the Pujols long ball. Ball or strike? Fair or foul? Hit or error? Safe or out? Take a pitch or swing away? Fastball or curveball? Bunt or steal? Tag up or hold?

Greg knows all about the whimsicality of baseball. In the summer of 2007 before his senior year of high school, he was given the opportunity to play in the prestigious Area Code tournament, a week-long series of games held at Long Beach State University, where some of the best high school players in the country compete against each other in front of hundreds of scouts representing Major League Baseball as well as countless colleges.

The Northeast team run by the New York Yankees needed a few players, and Stewart Smothers—who at that time was the Yankees' Los Angeles–area scout—knew Greg and recommended him as well as three other California kids including Cade Kreuter, the son of then-USC coach Chad Kreuter. An amazing perk for this team was that it was invited to go to New York and have a practice and scrimmage at Yankee Stadium the week before the tournament started, and the kids from California, as well as their families, were flown in for the event and put up at a Marriott in midtown Manhattan.

"Pretty cool," Greg said.

Not to mention pretty fortuitous for Greg because nuance came calling that afternoon when he stepped into the batters' box at the most famous of baseball cathedrals, the same box where Derek Jeter and Mickey Mantle and Joe DiMaggio and Babe Ruth have stood. With his adrenaline pumping in his first at-bat, Greg tried to rip the cover off the ball, but instead wound up fisting a sickly blooper that barely made it out of the infield. Rather than lope to first, he exploded out of the box and didn't stop running until he'd slid safely into second, his sheer hustle turning that seemingly harmless single into a double.

"I really didn't have a good scrimmage, but on this one play I hit something off the nob over the first baseman's head and it had a weird spin and went into foul territory and I just kept going," Greg recalled. "A scout or a coach can watch you play one game and you might have a bad game, or you might walk twice and not have a play in the field so they can't see anything. You have to try to do something to grab their attention, whether it's your attitude, or how you run out a ground ball. You never know when it's the last time they're going to see you play."

Chad Kreuter was watching intently from the stands, primarily because his son was playing, but also to see if there were any potential recruits in his midst. When he saw Greg make that play, Kreuter, who cobbled together a seventeen-year major-league career with seven different teams, knew there was.

"I caught coach Kreuter's eye because it was a very aggressive play off a terrible swing and that stood out for him," said Greg. "After the game we're on the subway going back to the hotel and I was sitting with him and he kept talking about that play. He told me I'd get a call from his assistant, coach Burton, and then a couple days later I committed."

TROJAN TRANSFER

If all had gone according to plan on this mid-February night, Greg would have been starting his senior season at USC and patrolling center field at Dedeaux Field in Los Angeles for the Trojans' season-opening game against Jacksonville University. Instead, he was in Philadelphia taking batting practice at Penn's Meiklejohn Stadium on yet another unusually balmy day in a winter that had been remarkably cooperative from a baseball perspective.

"This winter has been great, we've actually been outside a lot, probably 50 percent of the time," said Greg of the Quakers, who had been practicing for two weeks, and were still two weeks away from opening their season down in Florida. "Last year it was hard going down to Florida because we were hardly ever outside. For me coming from Southern California, I had never done that before where you haven't caught a fly ball outside for months. Everything's different outside, the ball bounces differently, it's a whole different game, even running when it's windy. I think we'll be better prepared for the start this year."

And once they got to Florida, coach John Cole knew he'd be penciling in Greg's name every day on the lineup card, center field, batting second, or third, maybe even fourth.

"He's an aggressive player, and he really enjoys the game and works his trade," Cole said. "He's got some tools you need. He's an above-average runner, he'll go get the ball in the outfield, and he's got power in his hands. He's not a massive person, probably five-eleven, but he has thunder in his hands, which you can't teach, so he has real good power for his size and that surprises people. He handles things during a game really well, and he's a guy I have a lot of confidence in."

It seemed as if then-USC coach Chad Kreuter had plenty of confidence in Greg, too, when he welcomed him to the Trojans back in the fall of 2008. But after procuring a scholarship from the only school he really wanted to play for, Greg's dream of helping the once-mighty Trojans return to their former glory as the preeminent college program in the country turned into a veritable nightmare.

During the noncompetitive fall season when the team plays mainly exhibitions and intra-squad scrimmages, he seemed to be right on track for a starting spot in the Trojan outfield. Sure enough, come February 2009, there he was out in right field on opening day against Long Beach State.

"Freshman year fall I played really well," he said. "The only person I hit behind was Grant Green, who was a first-round pick (thirteenth overall by the Oakland A's), and I think I surprised the coaches coming from a small school. And then in the spring I was playing OK in practice and I ended up starting as a freshman, but I struggled in the first few games and didn't hit well, and I was out of the lineup and never got back into it."

He started five of the first seven games, managed just one hit in fourteen at-bats, and spent the rest of a disappointing year pinch-hitting, pinch-running, or playing late-inning defense. "I had never not started a game my entire life, so when I came in there, I kind of expected that I was going to work hard and I was going to start, and I did that. So it was disappointing when I didn't play well and didn't start again."

Greg hoped to turn things around as a sophomore, but by the end of fall ball he was told by Kreuter that nothing was going to change in the spring. That's when Greg decided he needed to move on, Kreuter agreed, and to his credit he helped Greg—with an assist from famed sports agent Scott Boras, whose son, Shane, was a Trojan teammate and friend of Greg's—land at Penn.

"Chad called and said, 'Listen, this kid is stuck behind a couple players, he's a good kid and he has some ability, but we don't see him playing for us right now,'" Cole said, recounting the conversation he had with Kreuter. "After he was here, Greg told me Scott Boras helped steer him here. Whatever the reason, thank you Mr. Boras. That was good for us."

Boras had no connection with Penn, but Greg said, "He's a huge fan of education and when I mentioned that I was thinking about the Ivy League, he thought it was a great idea. He said Penn was a great school, I'd play every day, and he said big leaguers have been drafted out of there like Doug Glanville and Mark DeRosa."

Greg recalled being in New York's Madison Square Garden one night watching a Rangers hockey game during a visit with his sister who was in school in New York, and his phone rang and it was Boras. "I went out into the concession area to talk because he was helping me with the whole transferring process and he really thought Penn was a place I'd want to be. He's one of those people who, if he tells you to do something, you probably should do it. He's very convincing with what he says, and I'm sure a lot of MLB general managers have gotten that feel with him, too. He's probably the smartest guy I've ever met, and he helped me a lot."

What Boras could not help Greg with, though, was the laborious negotiation of Penn's transfer rules. First, Penn did not accept mid-year transfers, so that meant Greg needed to spend the spring of 2010 at Santa Monica Junior College. Second, once Greg was accepted for enrollment at Penn, he had to undertake the tedious process of figuring out what classes would allow him to be eligible to play baseball in the spring of 2011 once his NCAA-mandated one-year transfer probation period was up.

"The rules are crazy," Greg explained in an exasperated tone. "At Penn, before your junior year you have to have 40 percent of your major done in order to be eligible, and before senior year it's 60 percent. I was a business major at USC, but I couldn't get into Wharton here, even though I wanted to, because I didn't have enough credits. So what was tough was to figure out what major I could do where 40 percent of my classes would go toward that major. That was a pain in the butt, but I ended up going with communications. I had to go in person to different counselors and advisors and tell them I needed this class to transfer, or I can't play. But they don't care about that. It's not like USC where the teachers are introducing their kids to football players. Here they don't care if you're an athlete, so it was really hard. I wasn't totally cleared until the end of 2010 fall. There was something new every day and there were times when I was thinking I'm going to be here and not be able to play, so that was hard. Once I figured it out, it was a big relief."

WHIRLWIND TRIP

Greg knew the day was coming because his Grandma Zebrack had been ill for quite some time, so when she passed away this week at the age of seventy-six due to complications from Alzheimer's, he was mentally prepared. What he wasn't ready for was the whirlwind adventure he was about to embark on—a circuitous journey from Philadelphia to Los Angeles to Orlando—so that he could attend the wake and funeral, and then join his teammates for the start of the season.

"It's been pretty hectic, a tough week, but I'm getting through it," Greg said as he enjoyed a much-needed day of rest at the condominium complex where the Quakers were staying before they would begin the second segment of their ten-day visit to Florida with five games in the next six days. "It was a crazy start with a lot going on."

Last Wednesday Greg was staring at three midterm exams, and knowing this, his parents decided not to tell him that early that morning his grandmother had died. "They just wanted me to focus on my exams and not worry about logistics, but they called the coaches and told them what was going on, and then I found out later in the day."

The team was scheduled to fly to Orlando the next morning, and then meet nineteenth-ranked Stetson University Friday night in the first game of the Bright House Invitational. Greg made different arrangements. He hopped on a flight to Los Angeles at five-thirty in the morning Philly time Thursday, spent the next thirty-six hours with his family, then took a red-eye to Florida and made it in time to suit up for the Quakers' second game Saturday morning.

"I got in around six-thirty in the morning, went to the hotel, had breakfast, got on the bike for a little workout because I was so out of it—I hadn't really slept in a couple days because it was so busy—and I just went to the field and played the game," he said. "After that we came back to the hotel and had some dinner and then I just knocked out for the night. Got up again and played Sunday. Yeah, pretty hectic."

Not to mention emotionally draining because he was very close to his grandmother, and disappointing from a baseball standpoint because the Quakers lost all three games.

Without Greg on opening night Penn took a 14–1 beating at the hands of a very good Stetson squad that didn't need any help but got some in the form of three Penn errors, which opened the door for six unearned runs, and nine walks by the pitching staff.

The next day was much better, though it still ended in a 4–3 extra-innings loss to Georgia State. Working on no sleep, Greg made his debut and in five plate appearances he had a single, a double, was hit by a pitch and scored a run. With Penn trailing 3–1 in the sixth, Greg singled and scored on a Spencer Branigan double to right-center, and Austin Bossart's RBI double in the seventh tied the score. Georgia State won in the eleventh thanks to a walk, a botched pickoff attempt, and a wild pitch that plated the final run.

Sunday was another disaster as Southern Illinois got to Penn starter Matt Gotschall for seven earned runs in four-plus innings and the Quakers didn't have enough offense to overcome that in an 11–4 loss. Greg had a single, scored a run, and drove in one.

"Saturday was rough," Greg said. "That was a game we should have won, but we couldn't get a clutch hit. And Southern Illinois we didn't think was going to be that good, but they were big and physical and we were tied through four, but walks killed us and we made a couple errors and that'll always kill you. We just have to tighten it up a little bit, play better defense and get the bats to come alive and we'll be all right."

TEMPLE OF DOOM

All the reasons why the Quakers had stumbled out of the box this season were on display during the home opener at Meiklejohn Stadium on a remarkably perfect and unexpected seventy-five-degree mid-March afternoon.

"That was tough," Greg said after Penn blew an early 5–0 lead thanks to a combination of poor relief pitching and a lack of clutch hitting and lost to crosstown rival Temple in eleven innings, 11–9. "We came out ready to go, which was good because that was our problem in Florida, we were taking the punches early instead of delivering them."

The season-opening Florida trip had resulted in a 3–5 record as the Quakers, after losing all three in the Bright House Invitational, took three of five games in the Russ Matt Tournament. There was a 13–2 blowout of Bowling Green, a 3–2 nipping of Northeastern, and a 7–3 victory over Fairfield along with an 11–4 loss to Western Michigan and a 15–3 pasting at the hands of North Dakota State.

"We're disappointed with the start," said Greg, who batted nine for twenty-six (a .346 average) in the seven games he played down South. "We've had chances and the other teams aren't really beating us, we're beating ourselves. If we play our best game and they play their best game and they win, you tip your hat. The games we've been losing we've been beating ourselves, we haven't really played a complete game, which is the unfortunate part. Some of these teams aren't really earning their win, we're helping them."

Such as Temple.

The afternoon started so well for the Quakers. Greg drew a first-inning walk and scored when Ryan Deitrich cranked a three-run homer to left to highlight a four-run opening salvo. And then Greg's sacrifice fly in the second plated Penn's fifth run.

Temple scored a pair in the third, then freshman starting pitcher Connor Cuff worked his way out of trouble in the fourth and fifth and departed having allowed only those two runs on four hits and two walks. However, the Quakers had to rely on a bullpen that had been pyrotechnic early in the year, and sure enough, the Owls began pecking away and finally caught up when Steve Nikorak touched Cody Thomson for a no-doubt-about-it three-run homer to left-center in the eighth.

The Quakers spent the next three innings threatening to win the game, as they had runners in scoring position throughout, while Vince Voiro—their best starting pitcher—was shutting Temple down in a rare relief performance. No one could come through with the clutch hit, though, and when freshman Sam Horn took over for Voiro in the eleventh, Temple erupted for four runs, two more than Penn managed during a spirited bottom-of-the-inning rally.

"We couldn't put together any more rallies," said Greg, who finished one-for-three with a walk. "We'd have a good at-bat, then a bad at-bat, and we couldn't get anything going. A team like Temple who's struggling, they lost yesterday, you have to keep punching them and knock them out. We started walking guys and we let them back in the game. We had some chances and we couldn't pull through, so it was a tough one."

HITTING STRIDE

It's not too often that a batter misses hitting for the cycle because he lacked a measly single, but that's what happened to Greg at Meiklejohn Stadium during Penn's 11–4 thumping of Villanova.

"In a selfish way my last time up I wanted to bunt for the single, but you can't bunt when you're up seven runs," Greg said with a laugh, reciting time-honored baseball etiquette. Instead, he drew a walk in the seventh inning to finish off a glorious day that also included a three-run home run in the first, a two-run triple in the second, an intentional walk in the fourth, and a two-run double in the fifth. It was a hell of a line in the box score, three-for-three with seven runs batted in.

"I had some good times to hit with a bunch of runners on base every time I came up, it seemed like," said Greg, who in the past three games had gone six-for-seven with four runs scored, eight RBIs, and six walks. "I'm starting to swing it pretty good, finding my rhythm."

The lack of a single wasn't anything new for Greg lately. When the Quakers went down to Charleston, South Carolina, to play Charleston Southern a couple weekends earlier, Greg had three hits in twelve at bats—two doubles and a home run—as Penn lost two of three. Last week in a 6–3 victory at Villanova his lone hit was a triple. And in three games against Lafayette and this one against Villanova, Greg had only one single among his six hits, and his three extra-base hits enabled him to establish a new single-game career-best for RBIs.

"It was a pretty fun day," said Greg. And if it couldn't happen in an Ivy League game, he was thrilled that it happened against a Villanova team he considered to be pretty cocky, and in a game that doubled as a first-round matchup in the annual Liberty Bell Classic, which pits the Philadelphia-area teams against one another with the championship game held at Citizens Bank Park, home of the Phillies, a few weeks hence.

"The year before I got here they killed us (17–5 in 2010) and I heard they kind of snapped off that we were a joke," said Greg, who didn't get a look at the Wildcats until last week because Penn did not play Villanova in 2011. "Even when we played them last week at their place, they kind of arrived nonchalantly, took batting practice, and you could just tell they weren't giving us too much respect. Our assistant coach (John Yurkow) said they were thinking they were going to roll over us and that gives you some extra motivation, so it was nice to beat them last week. And we kind of knew they were pissed about it; when we shook their hands you could see it in their faces and they knew their coach was going to be ripping them new ones. Today we thought they'd come out aggressive, but we got on them in the first couple innings and it was almost like they gave up after that. That was awesome."

After a rough start, the Quakers had started to play better and this was their fifth win in their last eight games, raising their record to 8–9 as they headed into the start of the Ivy League schedule this weekend with two games against Yale and two more against Brown, all at home.

"This was a big game from a pitching standpoint for us," said Greg. "Hitting-wise we knew we'd start coming around. The hitting will always come around with repetition and more at bats, but the pitching is the big question. We have two bona fide aces (Vince Voiro and Connor Cuff), but the other two spots and the bullpen are a big question. The freshmen have to step up, and they have. Now the concern is we haven't played any back-to-back doubleheaders yet like we do in the Ivy League. It will be interesting to see how we respond in those back-to-backs because it's always a grind those fourth games of the weekend, but we're starting to play defense and we're starting to pitch, so we're clicking at the right time."

NUMBERS DON'T LIE

One of the simple joys for a baseball fan, one that has been passed down from generation to generation, is opening the sports section of the morning newspaper and poring over the previous days' major-league box scores. And even though more and more fans in the technology age go to the Internet for their information, the concept remains the same.

Baseball is a game that thrives on numbers. Its averages and percentages are an integral part of the fabric of fandom, more so than any other sport, because those neatly tabbed box scores tell the story of every game, day after day after day. Greg spent countless hours in his youth reading the box scores in the *Los Angeles Times*, and one thing he came to learn is that box scores are not biased. The box score doesn't differentiate between a solidly struck line-drive single and a blooper off the end of the bat; a hit is a hit. Nor does the box score care if a fly ball was caught by an outfielder standing still, or by one making a highlight-reel headlong dive; an out is an out. It doesn't matter how a player produces the numbers, just that he produces them.

When the Quakers opened their Ivy League schedule the first weekend of April with a doubleheader sweep of Yale and a doubleheader split with Brown at Meiklejohn Stadium, Greg went a combined seven-for-fourteen at the plate. It was a four-game body of work that certainly did wonders for his batting average and, in the end, it's the numbers that count, not how they were achieved. Still, in breaking down his at-bats, Greg was left to rail against the box score evidence that indicated he had a great weekend.

"What's funny is that even though I had a good weekend, I didn't really square anything up, and I wasn't happy with it," Greg said. "The results were good, but I didn't think the process was that great. I was getting hits, but I wasn't hitting the ball hard. When I'm hitting doubles, you can tell I'm driving the ball."

For instance, the semifinal game of the Liberty Bell Classic when Greg went three for four with two ringing doubles and scored twice as Penn knocked off LaSalle, 9–4, to earn a trip to Citizens Bank Park for the championship game in two weeks against St. Joseph's.

"Yeah, today I was driving it," Greg said. "I was hitting the ball hard and, not just getting hits, I was squaring balls up and they were traveling."

This victory was Penn's eighth in its last ten games, and Greg thought the recent resurgence boiled down to elevated confidence. "Coaches always talk about it, teams start believing in themselves, teams start coming together, everyone gets on the same page, all those clichés, but when it happens it's amazing what a team can do. This past week we beat Villanova twice, got off to a good start in the Ivy, and now we beat LaSalle. Something has clicked, we're buying into the team goal, and we know we can be a good team and win games."

For Greg, he knew why he had found his stroke at the plate: Games, games, games.

"It was our fifth game in three days, but I like that, I like playing every day. That's why I've always played well in summer ball because you're playing every day and you get in a groove. You don't have two games and then have three days off, you're getting consistent at-bats. Whenever I play a lot, that's when I hit better."

Greg was hit by a pitch in his first at-bat and struck out looking his next time up. In between, Penn scored four runs in the second inning to take a lead it never relinquished. Greg laced a double down the left-field line in the fifth, but was stranded, and after LaSalle made it 4–2 in the bottom of the fifth, Rick Brebner homered for the Quakers in the sixth. Greg then doubled to left again and trotted home on Ryan Deitrich's home run to left-center that put the game out of reach at 7–2. Greg capped his three-hit day with a single to right in the ninth, and after he stole second, he scored his second run on Deitrich's double.

There was much work to be done in the interim—eight Ivy League games and a rematch with LaSalle—but the Quakers couldn't help but already be excited for their game at Citizens Bank Park, when they would seek their first Liberty Classic championship in the twenty-one-year history of the event.

"I've never played in a game in a big-league park, just played at Dodger Stadium for a couple workouts," said Greg. "I'm really excited; it should be fun, but winning the game is the main goal."

THE MISSING STRIKE ZONE

The most difficult aspect of managing in the Ivy League is figuring out a way to get the most out of your pitching staff without blowing it out once the grueling back-to-back weekend doubleheaders kick in.

"There's a lot to think about, and it's really tough because you only have so many arms," said Penn coach John Cole.

Because the League prefers that its student-athletes concentrate on classes during the week, it schedules most of its athletic contests in all sports on weekends. In baseball it does them two at a time because there are only so many weekends available during the spring season, so you can imagine the strain four games in two days can produce for a pitching staff.

Obviously not every game can be played on a weekend, so Ivy teams are allowed to sprinkle in a limited number of non-League games during the week, though it prefers that whenever possible those are against nearby schools to minimize travel. For instance, outside of its season-opening sojourn to Florida, and its trip to Charleston Southern, the rest of Penn's non-League baseball schedule was against teams from the Philadelphia area such as Villanova, LaSalle, Lafayette, Temple, and in the coming week against St. Joseph's in the Liberty Bell Classic championship game.

Juggling his staff on the weekend is daunting enough for Cole, but mixing in a Tuesday or Wednesday game can really be a nightmare, especially if the Quakers had a particularly tough weekend where the bullpen had to be utilized more than he hoped. "In the mid-week games we have to be flexible and move guys around," said Cole.

So when the Quakers hosted LaSalle on Wednesday, April 11, Cole's plan was to pitch by committee, meaning he would use a bunch of pitchers for no more than an inning each, two at the max. Unfortunately, the committee apparently hadn't recovered from the previous weekend's road trip, during which Penn dropped a pair at Dartmouth before sweeping Harvard in Cambridge.

"We pitched terrible," Cole said after an 11–4 loss to LaSalle. A total of ten Penn pitchers had combined to walk ten batters, hit four others with pitches, and allow eleven earned runs on nine hits. "That's why the score was what it was."

Penn had blown the first game at Dartmouth a few days earlier as ace Vince Voiro, thanks to a couple errors and a wild-pitch third strike, gave up three runs in the bottom of the sixth of a seven-inning affair to lose, 6–3. The Quakers lost the nightcap, 11–2, as Greg's two-run homer in the eighth was the lone highlight. With two games at struggling Harvard the next day, Penn knew it had to sweep to stay within shouting distance of first-place Cornell in the Lou Gehrig Division, and it did, 7–0 and 8–5, with Greg homering in the second game.

But then came the dud against LaSalle, a game in which the Quakers were hoping to continue building momentum off their sweep of Harvard as they headed into a critical four-game series at Princeton that very likely could determine the fate of their season. "Yeah, that was the idea," Greg said. "They did not deserve to beat us today; we gave it away and that's frustrating."

The good news was the loss to LaSalle didn't matter in the Ivy standings, but if the Quakers hoped to win their division and get into the Ivy championship series, they needed to get past it, go down to Princeton and win at least two of the games, preferably three or, ideally, all four.

"This is the biggest weekend of the year coming up against Princeton because if we get swept we're out of it, and if we lose three out of four we're pretty much out of it," Greg said.

BIG-LEAGUE DREAMS

For those three hours on the evening of April 17 when the Quakers were playing in spectacular Citizens Bank Park, just the mere fact that they were competing on that beautifully-manicured major-league diamond would, years from now, override the disappointment of the final result, a 6–3 loss to St. Joseph's in the championship game of the Liberty Bell Classic.

They would probably forget the score. They might even forget who they played against. But they wouldn't forget every at bat they had, every pitch they threw, every chance they fielded, every time their name appeared on the giant JumboTron scoreboard—or all the noise one crazy fan was making in the disappointingly tiny crowd of 302 that was nestled into the forty-five-thousand-seat home of the Philadelphia Phillies. "One fan was pretty rowdy, so that's always nice to see," said Penn designated hitter and Philly native James Mraz. "I wish we could get more of those guys at the Meik."

"It was pretty awesome, to be honest," Greg said. "Playing at a big-league park is a once-in-a-lifetime experience for a college player. Now, hopefully, it's not the last time I play in a big-league park because that's my goal, to do that for a living, but it was really cool to be there."

Playing at the Bank was by far the highlight of Penn's season, and thanks to what happened the previous weekend, it likely won't be surpassed. The Quakers' hopes of winning the Ivy League's Lou Gehrig Division took a major hit as they lost three of four games at Princeton to fall to 6–6 in the League, four games behind first-place Cornell and three in arrears of Princeton.

"Pretty disappointing, because now we're in trouble," Greg said, referring to Penn's slimming chances of getting into the League championship series, the winner of which gets a berth in the NCAA tournament.

In the seven-inning opener of the first doubleheader, Mike Ford of the Tigers had a no-hitter through six before Greg broke it up with a solo homer leading off the seventh. Penn went on to score three runs, but that wasn't enough in a 7–3 loss. In the nine-inning nightcap, Greg hit another solo homer in the eighth to give Penn a 2–1 lead, Ryan Deitrich homered in the ninth to make it 3–1, and then the Quakers watched in horror as Princeton scored three runs with two outs to pull out a 4–3 victory.

"The walk-off game really sucked," said Greg. "Getting walked off on is one of the worst feelings in baseball. Especially when we were actually up two runs and they came back to win. That was brutal."

The next day, Greg found a way to feel even worse in the seven-inning opener. Austin Bossart's two-run triple capped a four-run Penn uprising in the sixth that broke open a scoreless battle and gave Penn a 4–0 lead. But in the bottom of the inning, Greg made a costly error that helped lead to five Tigers runs.

Thankfully, Greg had an opportunity to make amends in the top of the seventh. "I've gotten better in recent years at realizing, 'OK, I screwed up, get over it, be mentally tough, get to the next play and figure out what to do.' Kyle Toomey led off with a triple and I came up with one out and I'm thinking, 'There's no way you're getting me on this at bat after I had that misplay.' I thought they were going to pitch around me, but the guy threw a slider in the zone and I fouled it off and I was kind of shocked it was in the zone. So I'm thinking, 'If you throw another one in the zone I'm gonna crush it,' and he threw a hanging slider and I got a double. That was a good feeling, knowing that I could come back and get that hit after making that mistake."

Penn went on to win, 7–5, with two runs in the ninth, but the euphoria was short-lived when Princeton won the finale of the four-game set, 13–7, despite Greg's four-for-five performance.

The Classic championship game was an opportunity to take some of the sting out of the Princeton losses, but the Quakers' offense was silenced by five St. Joe's pitchers, and nine Penn hurlers combined to walk nine Hawks. Still, while the result was unsatisfactory, Greg really enjoyed the evening.

"The surface was unbelievable. The grass at our place sucks, but the grass here is ridiculously nice. Visually it took a couple innings to get used to playing there. Usually from the outfield you're looking up and you see nothing, and here you're looking up and you see three layers of stands, even though they were empty, so it was a little surreal. But then we settled in and you realize the pitchers' mound is sixty feet away, the bases are ninety feet apart; it's the same game, just a different place."

Greg finished one for four at the Bank, a double to left in the fifth. Not a great line for the Quakers' leading hitter, but he said he was proud of how he reacted to playing on that stage. "I was pretty calm; my heart wasn't beating crazy fast when I had my first at bat and I remember talking to Vince Voiro, our top pitcher, who was drafted last year, and we were both saying this isn't the last time that we're going to be playing here. When I was playing catch in the outfield I was thinking that I can see myself doing this every day, that this could never get old. It was such a motivation; that's what it really was. I was out there thinking this is what I want to do every single day. That's how I thought about the night."

WHAT A RELIEF

When Greg stood up in room twenty-eight of Williams Hall, handed in his Spanish test, and walked out the door, just like that, it was over. That was his last class, and all he had left to do was finish one paper, and take one more final exam, and his undergraduate days would be complete.

"That felt pretty good," he said. "It's kind of weird knowing that I'll never have to go to class again."

Unlike many Penn students who would go on to law school, or med school, or graduate school, Greg was moving on, hopefully to a career in the big leagues. But while baseball was his passion, school had always been important to Greg, and as his two-year stint at Penn was coming to a close and he was only a few weeks away from earning his degree in communications, it had been hitting him just how special it was to attend an Ivy League institution.

"I don't like to say that everything happens for a reason, but I really think it was the right decision to come here," he said. "I've been happy with how things have played out; happy about baseball, but also academically and socially; absolutely it was the right decision. This has made me a better person and a smarter person and has helped me transition into becoming an adult."

Which was just a little different than the one year that Greg played for USC in the winter and spring of 2009. "It was a great bunch of guys, great chemistry and we loved each other," he said. "We lived in a suite, eight of us, four rooms, and the discussions were about baseball and girls."

Laughing at the thought, Greg then added, "We'd go out to eat and you try to split the bill and nobody could figure it out. Here, that's pretty easy. And here they're talking about fixed income divisions, economics, derivatives, and all this cool and interesting stuff. It's just a different place. I got eighteen-ninety combined on my SAT, which was the second-highest on the team at USC, but here it's like the second-lowest on the team. I'm not saying USC didn't have smart people, but my girlfriend here is a biological basis and behavior major, she's premed, applying to her MD PhD program in neuroscience; she's basically a genius. Here, you can have full conversations with really smart people."

Greg's old Trojan teammates wouldn't have much trouble figuring out what went wrong with Penn's 2012 season. The Quakers had been beset with pitching injuries the past few weeks, the guys who weren't hurt hadn't pitched well, the offense had been failing in too many clutch situations, and the result was a sabotaging stretch where they had lost eight of ten games. And with three losses in four home games against first-place Cornell last weekend, the Quakers' fate was sealed: Cornell was 13–3, Penn was 7–9 (16–20 overall), and with only four games left, that meant the Quakers were officially eliminated from contention in the Lou Gehrig Division.

"We just couldn't hit all weekend," Greg said. "We might have hit two balls hard all weekend. It was unbelievable. It wasn't that their pitching was overpowering, they just pounded the zone and we didn't hit them."

In the first and third games the Quakers suffered identical 3–0 shutout losses, managing just eight hits combined, only one by Greg. In the second game Cornell scored five runs in the second inning and cruised to a 9–5 victory. Finally, Penn broke through in the last game as Ryan Deitrich tripled and scored the winning run on a Cornell error in the seventh inning for a 4–3 victory.

"Our offense this weekend was nonexistent," coach John Cole said of his team, which batted .233 in the four games. "We pitched pretty well, so if we had swung the bat I think we would have been all right. But Cornell's a good club. That's why they're in first place, because they pitch and play defense."

HOLE IN THE SWING

After the rough four-game series against Cornell, which came on the heels of an equally disappointing four-game series against Princeton, Greg placed a call to Encino, California, to his hitting coach, Reggie Smith Jr.

If the name sounds familiar, it should. He's the son of Reggie Smith, one of the best switch hitters in baseball history, who spent the bulk of his seventeen-year major-league career with the Red Sox, Cardinals, and Dodgers, compiling a .287 average with 314 home runs and 1,092 RBIs.

"He's a pretty big influence on me," Greg said.

When Greg was enduring his struggles at USC in the fall of his sophomore year, one day he went back to his high school to take some extra batting practice and talk to Rob Glushon, a family friend who was also the assistant baseball coach at Campbell Hall. "I was swinging at bad pitches in the dirt, just not hitting anything," Greg recalled. "Rob is really good friends with Reggie and he said, 'I'm setting you up with Reggie and he'll change your career.' You're going to him, I'm making you do it.' He called Reggie and I went there the next week and I've been hitting with them ever since."

Reggie Jr.—RJ, as Greg calls him—had actually done the bulk of the work with Greg, so when Greg called the other night to lament his recent slump, the two hashed it out.

"I talk to RJ often when I'm hitting poorly," said Greg. "A few weeks ago at Lafayette I went oh for four, and the way I felt then was the way I felt last weekend. I wasn't hitting, I was missing pitches right down the middle, so I texted RJ and he called me. Sometimes you need a different voice. I'll text him or call him and say this is what I'm doing. He knows my swing so well so the other night he told me one thing, use your legs and keep turning. In practice today I was hitting much better."

Unfortunately, those good strokes didn't carry to the weekend, and Greg closed his Penn career on a real downer, going three for sixteen in four games against Columbia, three of which were embarrassing ten-run losses.

"Yeah, it was a disaster for the team and a disaster for me," Greg said.

The four-game series was a home and home, the first two at Meiklejohn Stadium where the Quakers lost in nightmarish fashion, 12–2 and 13–3. The teams traveled to New York to finish off their respective seasons at Columbia's Robertson Field at Satow Stadium and Penn managed an 8–5 victory before losing an 11–1 laugher.

"We couldn't pitch, we couldn't throw strikes—the only guy who threw strikes was Vince—and you're not going to win many games when we do that," Greg said. "It was the same story: walked guys, hit guys. They capitalized, and we couldn't get any rhythm going on offense. It couldn't really get much worse."

UNCERTAIN FUTURE

Three days had passed since Greg swung and missed at a high fastball for the final out of a terribly disappointing season for the Quakers. That 11–1 loss to Columbia left Penn with a 17–23 overall record, 8–12 in the Ivy League which was last in the Lou Gehrig Division, six games behind first-place Cornell.

Greg led the club in home runs (seven), RBIs (twenty-eight), runs (thirty-four), doubles (eighteen), walks (seventeen), sacrifice flies (five), stolen bases (ten), total bases (ninety), and slugging percentage (.697), and his .343 batting average was second only to Spencer Branigan's mark of .350.

He left Penn ranked second in career slugging percentage (.625), third in on-base percentage (.448), seventh in batting average (.339), tied for eighth in home runs (fourteen), and tenth in doubles (twenty-nine). His time wearing the red and blue was short, but he left an indelible mark on the program, even though his batting prowess did not translate into team success, as the Quakers finished below .500 both years he was there.

Coach John Cole only wished Greg was coming back for the final year of eligibility that he was still allowed by the NCAA, and he let Greg know that, more than a couple times, during his exit meeting with his departing center fielder.

"He seemed pretty pissed off that I wasn't coming back next year," Greg said. "I think he expected me to come back for a fifth year; there was a little lack of communication, and it was my fault. He found out about a month into the season that I was graduating and not coming back, and I guess I hadn't communicated that to him properly, but my plan all along was to get drafted and go. He said a few times, 'I wish you were coming back,' and I was like, 'OK, I get it, but I'm not.'"

Greg's hope was that he would be picked in the Major League Baseball First-Year Draft in June, and if he was, he'd pack his bags and head wherever the organization that chose him told him to go. If he got passed over, he would use his last year of NCAA eligibility to play college baseball, but it wouldn't be at Penn because the school does not allow graduate students to play sports.

Greg's father had been in touch with USC coach Frank Cruz, who was an assistant coach when Greg was there a few years back, and Cruz was confident that a roster spot would be available for Greg in the fall if need be.

"Coach Cruz thinks I'm going to get drafted, but he said he got some guys into grad school last year, and he could most likely get me in," Greg said. "It's the only place I'd want to go. I really don't want to move to a different part of the country again just to play for one year, I'd rather stay home in L.A. and play there in the warm weather. Plus, it makes a difference for scouting. There are scouts that come to our (Penn) games, but in the Ivy League you're at such a disadvantage as a position player. If you hit .400 the scouts just think it's because you're playing lesser competition, and if you hit .300 or below, they're going to say this guy can't hit. The scouts don't always stay for the entire game to see all your at bats. At USC, every scout is there watching the nine-hole hitter through the ninth inning. I know I'd have a chance to get drafted out of there next year if it doesn't work out next month."

And he was growing concerned that things might not work out. He did not finish with a flourish, as he went thirteen for forty-four in the final twelve Ivy games, nine of which were Penn losses. His two-year body of work was solid, but in a what-have-you-done-for-me-lately world, his ill-timed slump was the last impression scouts had of him right now.

"I definitely think it's a concern," he said. "Obviously you hope that one bad game or series doesn't paint the whole picture for a scout. Albert Pujols hasn't hit a home run in a month, so you know the good players don't always play well every day. But I'm worried that a scout might say, 'I saw him play this game and he didn't play well,' so I've been a little stressed out about it."

The hardest part of this was that with the season over, and the draft still a month away, Greg couldn't do anything but sit and wait.

"I have a lot of pride, and I always want to prove myself, but there's nothing I can prove right now, I can't change how I played at the end because there's no more games," he said.

That's the reality that about 99 percent of Ivy League senior athletes must face: Once they've played their last game in the Ancient Eight, they've probably played their last game, period. Greg believed he'd be part of that 1 percent that played beyond the Ivy because if he didn't get drafted this year, he could look to 2013. He had always wanted baseball to be his career, and he was prepared to chase the dream until the dream could no longer be chased. And then, if and when that happened, he'd have that Ivy League degree in communications to fall back on.

"To be able to have a chance to go play pro ball with an Ivy League degree in my pocket, it doesn't get much better than that."

KYRA CALDWELL

COLUMBIA TRACK

When she looked up at the clock and saw her times, Kyra didn't have much of a reaction, and her indifference had nothing to do with the typically stoic demeanor she displays on meet days. Quite simply, neither race—the 400-meter dash nor the 4 × 400-meter relay—had measured up to the lofty standards of the multiple-record-holding Columbia senior. Sure, for mid-January, in the first meet of the indoor track and field season, it was good to win twice, but the results didn't exactly stir Kyra's soul.

"It wasn't the best; it was OK," Kyra said. "I was able to win the 400 and we won the relay so that was good, but there's a lot to improve on."

When the day was complete, the Columbia women placed fourth in the six-team West Point Invitational at Gillis Field House with seventy-seven points, and Kyra had been fully responsible for ten points, and partially responsible for ten more points. Kyra crossed the finish line in 58.49 seconds in the 400-meter dash, half a second in front of her closest pursuer from Monmouth College, but nearly two seconds slower than her personal best time of 56.67 set a year earlier during a tri-meet at the Armory Track and Field Center in New York, which serves as Columbia's home track. In the relay, Kyra and teammates Yamira Bell, Miata Morlu, and Uju Ofoche combined to run 3:57.98, which was downright glacial compared to some of the times the Lions have compiled since Kyra joined the team in 2009.

Like she said, lots of room for improvement, but that's what Kyra had been seeking in all aspects of her life since she was a little girl. From the time she was in elementary school, at an age when she really shouldn't have had a care in the world, Kyra knew there was a better life out there somewhere, and if she worked hard and paid attention to the things that were important, she would have a better chance to experience it.

As a young African American girl growing up in predominantly black

Ypsilanti, Michigan, in a home with a father who was a drug abuser and a mother who wouldn't stand for it so she threw him out and ultimately divorced him, Kyra knew she had obstacles in front of her. But she also came to understand that many children in the community where she lived had fractured home lives, and it came down to this: She could let her situation hold her back the way it was so many of those other kids, or she could find a way out. She chose the latter, her path lighted by learning, and that light continued to shine brightly as she closed in on the end of her undergraduate days at Columbia.

"There's a history of drug abusers in my family," she said. "I was pretty much aware of it the whole time; it wasn't hidden. That helped to fuel me to want to do well in school. I've always wanted to be the best, get straight A's, and I was very interested in learning. I loved going to school and reading, and that definitely had a big influence on me wanting to do well in school."

Her father, Willie Caldwell, grew up in South Carolina and later New York City before settling in Ypsilanti, where he was a high school basketball star, though not the top gun on the team. That was Fred Cofield, who went on to play college ball at Oregon and Eastern Michigan before being selected in the fourth round of the 1985 NBA Draft by the New York Knicks.

After his playing days ended, Willie just couldn't find his way, and he fell into the street life. He had fathered a child out of wedlock—Kyra's half sister, Kagyn—while he was still in high school, and being a teenage father, coupled with the pressures of being the oldest of six siblings growing up without a father and with a mother who was a drug abuser, proved too much, and he, too, turned to drugs.

Willie did not go to college. He had trouble keeping jobs, and even after he seemed to be getting on track when he married Kyra's mother, Kerri, he couldn't kick his drug habit. The Caldwells had another daughter together, Kendra, and in those early days as a couple they both held jobs at the University of Michigan in neighboring Ann Arbor, Willie as a janitor, Kerri in patient transport for the university hospital. But by the time Kyra was nine years old, Kerri could no longer deal with Willie and they separated and later divorced.

"In the area I'm from, certain parts of the city are drug infested, and my father was a substance abuser and it was a lot for my mother to go through," Kyra explained. "For a while my mom didn't work, so we didn't have a lot of money. We were on the low spectrum of poor. But them splitting up was a good thing for me and my sister because then we didn't have to experience some of the things that come with drug abuse. For me it was good, I was happy they split up, and I just thought we could move and be happy, but life was still a struggle."

Church often provided refuge and solace for Kyra. "Growing up we stayed close to the church community," Kyra said. "We went three times a week, and that was our family. We had lots of friendship and fellowship and it was a place where there were no drugs." But in her alone time, when she just needed to get away from everything, Kyra read. Voraciously.

Kyra was the star of the accelerated reader program at her school. "In fourth grade I was reading books that were tenth-grade level," she said. "You would read books and get a certain number of points for each book, and I was like the top reader in the whole school. I would read the chapter books because they had the most points. I would come home every day and read. I played sometimes, but there was a certain period where I just wanted to read, and that carried through middle school and high school."

Her favorite books when she was younger were the Cat Who mystery novels written by Lilian Jackson Braun, and those memorable characters— reporter James Qwilleran and his Siamese cats, Koko and Yum-Yum—were basically her best friends.

"I loved reading those," she said with a knowing smile, adding that Harry Potter books were forbidden by her church-going mother because they involved witchcraft. "Reading helped me go into a different world."

SHUTTING DOWN

One of the hallmarks of Kyra's track career at Columbia had been her consistency, so the fact that she had been consistently inconsistent in the first month of the indoor season was starting to grind at her psyche.

"I feel like I'm having a pretty bad season," she said a day after she was a nonparticipant in the Millrose Collegiate Invitational at the Armory Track and Field Center. "This season has been so up and down, dealing with injuries and trying to get my body healthy. I've won some races, lost some races, but the most important thing to me is improving my times every year and defending my titles, and I haven't been doing that."

The problems began all the way back at the indoor opener at West Point when she felt some pain in her hip and hamstrings, ailments that had plagued her clear back to her high school days. "We had our blue and white intra-squad meet before Christmas break and I felt really good there, no pain in my legs," she said. "I was happy that I ran well and I felt no pain. But then when I got back to school I started hurdling and then I started feeling pain."

If there was one thing Kyra had learned during her first three years of college competition, it was that the bodies of track athletes are like finely tuned machines. Every part has to be firing precisely in order to succeed because in this sport, hundredths of seconds can be the difference between winning a race or finishing out of a point-scoring position.

"You can run through it to a certain extent, like when I got injured back in high school, I was still running through it, but you can only do that for so long," she said. "In college, your body has to be really into it. I'm not sure right now where I am."

Since West Point, Kyra had endured a string of disappointing results. At the annual Ivy League tri-meet with Dartmouth and Yale, she ran the 60-meter hurdles in 9.08 seconds after winning that race last year in that meet in 8.74. In the 400-meter dash she ran 1:01.34 to finish fifth, well off the 56.67 she ran to place third a year ago. And while she and her three teammates did win the 4 × 400 relay again, they did so in a time that was nearly seven seconds off the 2011 pace, and about eighteen seconds slower than the Ivy League record time the Lions posted in the 2010 outdoor championships.

At the Metropolitan Indoor Track and Field Championships, things went a little better as Kyra won the 60-meter hurdles in 8.64 seconds, then took second in the 200-meter dash in 24.79 as Columbia finished first as a team, ahead of the thirteen other New York–area schools.

But the two most recent meets had been a nightmare. In the New Balance Collegiate Invitational at the Armory, Kyra ran only one race—the sixty-meter hurdles—and she didn't even qualify for the finals. Running in the eighth preliminary heat she clocked 8.91, fourth in her five-woman group, a time that was nearly a second slower than what the eventual winner ran in the finals.

And then in the Millrose, Kyra didn't run anything, her hip flexor and her hamstring too sore to allow her to compete. "It's just been a really disappointing season so far," she said.

Compounding matters for Kyra was the fact that she wasn't exactly coasting home academically in the final semester of her undergrad days. "I'm taking a pretty heavy load for a senior," she said.

She had a concentration in religion, so she was taking two classes to fulfill her requirements—African American Prophetic Tradition, and Defining Marriage. She was also taking classes in biology and statistics, both of which she needed for medical school, and she had a weekly three-hour physics lab. Add to the class work her track practice schedule, which included more than ten hours of running, stretching, lifting, and commuting back and forth from campus down to the Armory, and you wonder—as you do with all of these Ivy League athletes—how they fit everything in.

Then, there's also the babysitting gig for a couple hours every Tuesday, watching the two children of one of the doctors at Columbia Medical Center.

"I met them through a friend who was babysitting," Kyra explained. "There's a lot of people in the neighborhood around Columbia who are faculty, and my friend who worked for them was moving away and she referred me. I have a lot of siblings, so I'm always taking care of people, so it kind of reminds me of being back home a little bit. Maybe I do like kids; maybe it's just something I don't want to admit. It's good money, the hours are very flexible, and it's a good networking thing because I was able to work in the doctor's lab last summer. At first I thought it was going to be kind of overwhelming, but I'm working through it."

FINDING HER OWN WAY

When Kyra was in fifth grade, she was tethered to the Willow Run school district because it was within those troubled borders that her mother had taken up residence. Of the three districts in the area—Ypsilanti and Lincoln being the others—Willow Run was the worst, and Kyra knew that if she stayed there, her dream of going to college would be more difficult to achieve.

"I wanted to be in the Ypsilanti district because I thought it would be better for me in high school and would put me in a better position to get into a better college," she said. "I knew Willow Run was pretty bad. There was a lot of violence around it, there were fights in school, drugs, just a lot of bad influences, and I didn't want to be in a situation like that."

So, as a fifth grader, Kyra took it upon herself to see if she could transfer.

"I actually called around, got the information, and went to the schools and got the paperwork that I needed to transfer to the other school," she explained. "I started school in Ypsilanti and then we moved to Willow Run when I was in first grade so I kind of knew the difference. Ypsilanti had more diversity, and there were more resources at the school. I presented it to my mom and she allowed me to do it, but I had to persuade her because she worked and she didn't want to have to drive me everywhere."

And so Kyra started down the road that led to the Ivy League. The first step on the journey was school, which she always enjoyed. "I remember being in middle school, I really wanted to be a doctor, and for a while I was getting these anatomy and biology books and just trying to memorize them because I thought when I get to college I'll be ready because I'll have memorized all this stuff. That phase ended up dying off because I just focused on what I had to do for school. School was never really hard for me, and I've always tried to go above and beyond. I would study on my own and read on my own. When teachers told me to do things, they would say, 'Do well here and you can go on to college' and I would listen to that. But not a lot of people in my community did. They weren't as focused as me, I guess. For me, I just thought listen to the people around you and use the resources around you to get where you want to go."

Her grades alone were going to give her an opportunity to pick and choose where she'd like go to college, especially knowing that she'd be eligible for the maximum amount of financial aid, given her parents' divorce and combined income level. But when she added the athletic component to her resume, the doors opened even wider for Kyra.

For much of her time in middle school Kyra was prohibited from playing sports because her mother could not get her back and forth to practices and games, plus, she needed Kyra to help out around the house. "But I begged her to let me do basketball in eighth grade and she allowed me to do it," Kyra said. "Most times I had to get my own ride because she couldn't do it, or I just walked from the school to my cousins' house and I would try to get a ride home. And by this time my father was getting his life straightened out and he would help me. He was very supportive and he started becoming more involved with the family again."

Kyra can admit it now, but she didn't want to back then: She was merely an average basketball player, and she was never going to be able to play at the college level. "I worked hard, but it wasn't the best experience because I felt like the girls who didn't work hard got more playing time, but they were just better, so that's how it was."

However, playing basketball ultimately led Kyra to the sport that became her passion, the sport that helped lead her to Columbia, where she became one of the most decorated track athletes the school has produced.

"In my freshman year, the track coach came to the games because he was really into the community and very supportive, and he said I should run track," Kyra said. "I always had to worry about getting rides, so I didn't know if I could do it, but I tried it, and I really liked it."

Which shouldn't have come as a surprise. When she was younger, she was a member of the mileage club at Willow Run. During recess the kids would run around the bases at the baseball field and they would earn one token for every trip. Kyra was the fastest runner, and also the most prolific, and she earned a trophy for her efforts.

"I was always fast," she said. "I wasn't making the shots in basketball, but whenever we would do sprints I was always in the lead in those. So I knew I could do it. The track coach, Tom Micallef, was also a biology teacher, and on his wall in his classroom he had all these newspaper clippings of girls he coached, all-Americans, state champions, all-state. Every day I would look at that wall and think to myself, 'This is what I want to do. I want to be all-conference, then all-state, and then all-American.' Those were my goals."

OUT WITH THE INDOOR, IN WITH THE OUTDOOR

The indoor track season officially came to a close in early March in Nampa, Idaho, and the lone Columbia athlete at the NCAA Division I Indoor Track and Field Championships was long-distance runner Waverly Neer, a freshman from Russiaville, Indiana, who capped a sensational individual season with a fifteenth-place finish in the 3,000-meter run. And it would have been even better if she hadn't tripped about 600 meters from the finish, causing her to break her stride and fall further back in the pack.

"It was very exciting, and I'm really happy for her," Kyra said. "She's a very talented athlete. She ended up having an incident in the race and she fell, and if that hadn't happened she would have been in position to be All-American."

Kyra wished she had been there, too, but her indoor season ended after Columbia won the biggest Ivy League indoor meet, the Heptagonal Championships at Cornell's Barton Hall the final weekend in February. It was a historic day for the Lion women, as this was the first time they'd ever captured the team title, scoring 124 points to easily out-pace runner-up Cornell. But for Kyra, it was an exercise in frustration.

"I was really happy about the Heps, but individually it didn't go well," Kyra said. "I was really happy for the team, but I definitely had bittersweet emotions about not performing my best."

Kyra's physical problems—the persistent pain in her hamstring and hip flexor—simply would not allow her to compete at the level she was accustomed to, and she was far from her peak at the meet. She participated in her two best events, the 60-meter hurdles and the 4 × 400-hundred relay, and while she was able to contribute points to the cause, it wasn't what she was hoping for.

She qualified third in the 60-meter with a time of 8.68 seconds, but in the finals she ran fourth in 8.79, which gave the team four points, not the first-place ten she had produced in both 2010 and 2011 when she won the race in times of 8.69 and 8.52, respectively. In the relay, she and her teammates Yamira Bell, Uju Ofoche, and Miata Morlu, placed second in 3:46.88, well off the 3:39.46 that Kyra, Ofoche, Morlu, and Sharay Hale had run to win in 2011.

"It was disappointing because I had never gotten anything but first in the hurdles since freshman year," Kyra said. "Last year we won the relay and the year before we set the Ivy League record outdoors in the relay in 3:35. What we ran this time wasn't close to that."

Kyra also tried to give the team a chance to accrue points in the 200-meter dash, but after running 24.7 earlier in the season at the Metropolitan Indoor, her 25.5 prelim didn't qualify her for the final. So upon returning to New York, Kyra and coach Willy Wood decided it was best that she take some time off to get ready for the start of the outdoor season.

"We shut it down after the Heps just so I could give my body some rest and build it back up," she said. "I'm feeling a lot better, not having the pain in my hip flexor. I was feeling pain everywhere, but right now I'm not having those issues anymore. I went to a kinesiologist, and he told me I needed to get more flexible in my hip flexor. He said it was really tight and touching some nerves that were causing pain. He gave me a series of exercises and stretches, and I took a week off before I started training again, and I'm feeling pretty good. It's good that I'm getting better, but it has been pretty hard to get injured early on in my career in high school, then get better and run well, and then get hurt again and not be able to make progress."

In two weeks, the final segment of her college athletic career would begin with the opening outdoor meet at historic Franklin Field in Philadelphia. "I hope I'm ready and can run the way I want to run," she said, only a hint of pessimism detectable in her voice.

FRESH START IN THE FRESH AIR

Kyra is a devout Christian and trusts the Lord will take care of her, and as the outdoor season got underway Saturday at the University of Pennsylvania's Franklin Field, she felt that was what He did.

"I felt good, and I just have faith that God will continue to bless me and allow me to bring my times down," Kyra said. "I know it's in me, I know I can run it again."

The Big Five and Friends meet included Philadelphia-area schools such as Penn, Temple, Villanova, Lehigh, and LaSalle, with the Lions the lone out-of-Pennsylvania invitee. Kyra's specialties in the outdoor season were the 100-meter hurdles, the 400-meter hurdles, and the 4 × 400 relay. There was no relay on the schedule, and for Kyra there was no 100-meter because she false-started in her prelim and was disqualified.

"I was like 'oh man,' but it didn't tear me apart," she said. "I hadn't really practiced with hurdles in a while because I was just trying to get my body back into the rhythm of running and running without pain. I warmed up really well and I was trying to get familiar with the hurdles and I was just a little too excited at the start. It's not even like a crazy competitive meet, so I don't know why I did that."

The results were quite a bit better in the 400, as she ran a 1:01.36, the second-fastest time by an Ivy League runner this year, and just .04 off the pace of winner Jade Wilson of Temple. Her time was right around where she usually was at this point in the outdoor season, but normally she would have had a better indoor season to prepare and that wasn't the case this year because of her injuries, so to rip that one out of the blocks this early was encouraging. "I usually drop more and more each week, so for this early, I felt pretty comfortable and it was good to get used to getting over those hurdles again. I definitely think I can run faster."

Her personal best time in the 400 is 57.98 at the 2010 ECAC Outdoor Championships at one of her favorite tracks, the oval at Princeton, and she really thought she could get there by the end of the season. "This is the earliest I've run the 400 meters in a season. I ran that [57.98] in late May that year. Because the season is so long, I think I'm on the right track. For me right now it's just about repetition."

And in class, it's all about closing strong, and that's what Kyra was trying to do. "This is the homestretch of college, I'm going to graduate in a month and a half and I've got two fifteen-page research papers to write and three exams in the next month," she said. "The first paper is for my Defining Marriage class, and I'm going to do something on African American gender roles. The other one is for my African American Prophetic Tradition class, and I'm doing it on Fred Shuttlesworth, who was a civil rights activist in the 1960s who was part of the big three with Martin Luther King and Ralph Abernathy. They were all big players in Project C, which was the campaign to desegregate Birmingham in 1963."

While there was still much work to be done this semester, she was also peeking into the future, which was bearing down on her. "I'm starting to think about what I'm doing next year. I'm applying for research programs, and I'm excited about the next stage of my life, but I don't know where I'm going to be, I haven't outlined it. I know I'm taking a year and then applying to med school, and in that year I want to do research, so hopefully I get into one of these research programs."

CLEARING HURDLES

Kyra will never forget the first time she ran the hurdles in a high school race, a 100-meter distance her freshman year.

"I had been doing well, I was able to do the three-step pretty naturally, which is good for the 100 hurdles, and then the first meet I hit one of the hurdles and it slowed me down and I lost and I was really upset because I had practiced and knew that I could do better," Kyra recalled.

One of her teammates was senior Tiffany Ofili, among the best high school runners in the state of Michigan and probably the country, who, during her time at Ypsilanti won state titles in the 100 and 300 hurdles, the long jump, and as a member of the 4 × 100 relay team while graduating as class Salutatorian.

"Tiffany talked to me about it, and it was nice because obviously she was someone that I really looked up to," Kyra said of Ofili, originally from Nigeria who came to America on a British passport, then went on to star at the University of Michigan where she won three NCAA championships in the 100 hurdles and two in the 60 hurdles before signing an endorsement deal with Adidas and becoming a top-flight performer on the professional circuit.

Ofili's advice that day to Kyra was to forget that race and move on, and after shedding some tears, that's what Kyra did, and her high school career flourished thereafter.

"I wasn't fast at all when I started, I ran the 400 in like 1:13 the first time I did it indoors, but the coach was very encouraging. He'd say, 'Good job; this is where you are. Do this, that, and you can get to here.'"

And like Ofili, the coach knew what he was talking about, too. Tom Micallef led the Ypsilanti girls' track team for twenty-seven years, and during his tenure the Phoenix enjoyed several perfect conference seasons and won numerous Michigan state championships including back-to-back titles in 2004 and 2005 just before Kyra joined the program. Dozens of his athletes went on to stellar collegiate careers. Some, like Ofili, went pro, and it was his keen eye that saw greatness in Kyra as she was running sprints during basketball practice.

"He was a huge influence on me," Kyra said of Micallef, who also had coached her father, Willie, in middle school basketball back in the day, and in 2007 was inducted into the Michigan Interscholastic Track Coaches Association Hall of Fame. "I knew I wanted to keep going with track and he kept encouraging me and he was a really nice person. He really cared about everyone on the team and he was a big part of the community in many sports. In our area, our state, we had a really good track team. It was a really good program; there was a lot of pride in the program, and it helped me and pushed me because I wanted to be a part of that legacy."

As a freshman Kyra made it to the regionals in the 300-meter hurdles, and beginning with her sophomore year she began to add to her repertoire, as she ran the 100 hurdles and was on both the 4 × 100 and 4 × 400 relay teams. And then, in the summer before her junior year, she was recruited to run AAU track for a team that was based in Romulus, Michigan, and that experience was pivotal because it proved to her that she had upper-tier talent and could compete against the best runners in the state.

It was at that point when she knew track was the sport that was going to help write her ticket to college, and she needed to focus solely on that. Playing basketball and being a cheerleader, which she had picked up when she entered high school, had been fun activities, but they no longer fit in her schedule. Unfortunately, that realization occurred too late for her to avoid suffering her original hamstring injury. One night, while performing a round-off during a routine at a boys' basketball game, Kyra landed awkwardly and tore a tendon in the area of her hamstring near her butt.

Although she was able to compete for Ypsilanti that spring, and for the AAU team that summer, the injury bothered her throughout that period, and after a relatively pain-free junior year, it gave her more trouble as a senior, and it was still the root of her physical problems all these years later as she struggled to get through her final season at Columbia.

Fortunately, her talent and her desire enabled her to keep improving her technique and her times, and as she blazed around area tracks winning more races than you can count, the mail started coming in from dozens of colleges asking her if she'd be interested in spending four years running for their program. As early as fifth grade Kyra had made the decision that she was going to college and she began taking steps to assure that it would happen, and the track component wound up playing a key role.

FAMILIAR SURROUNDINGS

Kyra couldn't really explain it, but Weaver Track and Field Stadium on the campus of Princeton University had always been one her favorite places to compete. "Yeah, that track is always pretty good to me," Kyra said. "I really like that track."

It was good to her again during the annual Sam Howell Invitational in early April, as she ran the 400-meter hurdles in 59.64 seconds, a time that beat the other six collegians in the field, and was just four-tenths of a second off the pace set by winner Wendy Fawn-Dorr, one of several professional runners who were competing.

Princeton was home to a few competitions each year, and that had always been fine with Kyra because she had broken sixty seconds in the 400 hurdles in six finals there through the years, most notably her personal record of 57.98 in the 2010 ECAC Outdoor Championship. And this latest trip around Weaver qualified her for the NCAA East Regionals in Jacksonville, Florida, in late May, meaning she would have a chance to earn a berth in the NCAA National Championships at Drake Stadium in Des Moines, Iowa, in early June.

As if that wasn't exciting enough, the opportunity to test her skills against Fawn-Dorr was an added bonus as well as a personal thrill.

"I was nervous for a split second when I saw her," Kyra said, referring to the presence of Fawn-Dorr in the lane next to her, "but then I was like, 'I'm just going to get as close to her as I can.' She was the only one seeded above me and she's one of my role models, someone I really look up to. I was happy to be able to run against her and I ran really well, the best I've run all year. She transferred to Penn State and was a distance runner originally, but she got into an accident and couldn't run long distances anymore because of health issues, so she trained to be a sprinter, a 400 runner. She worked really hard, and her last two years of college she wasn't on the radar, but she got faster and got a contract."

Kyra loved the open meets because she still wanted to pursue running as a pro while she attended medical school, and running against the likes of Fawn-Dorr and others gave her an indication of where she stood.

"This is an Olympic year, and pro runners train all around the country and they only have a few track meets where it's strictly pros, so in these open meets you have a lot of runners coming together," Kyra explained. "The pros can get a good workout, and they'll get some good competition because they have to get times to compete and get better and they use these meets as sort of a marker to see where they're at. And it also gives collegiate runners a chance to step up and run with the pros."

The rest of the day wasn't so good as Kyra ran what she called "a terrible" 100 hurdles, placing fifth in 14.95, while the 4 × 400 relay team took fourth in 3:54.45. "I had some technical problems with my start, and it was the slowest I've ever run in college," she said of the 100. "I shook it off in the 400 and ran great, and then the relay did not go well. One of the girls had a bad ankle, and another girl just really isn't in shape, and I didn't run my best."

In one month Kyra would be sitting with thousands of other seniors, a sea of Columbia blue on the Morningside Campus, and there was no doubt that as she daydreamed during President Lee C. Bollinger's commencement address, she would hearken back to the time, not so long ago, when she was initially deciding where she was going to pursue her athletic and academic dreams.

The initial batch of inquiries from schools interested in her as a track athlete included some of the true Division I powerhouse athletic institutions. From the familiar Big Ten there was Ohio State, Michigan State, and hometown Michigan, next door to Ypsilanti in Ann Arbor where her friend and mentor, Tiffany Ofili, was furthering her greatness by winning conference and NCAA championships. There were some Big East schools, including Syracuse and South Florida, there were Mid-American schools like Miami of Ohio, and among the Ivies, there was Princeton (oh, if she'd only known then how much she was going to like that track) and Columbia.

"Colleges started being interested in me junior year when I won states, went to nationals and was fifth, which made me all-American," she said. "I was getting letters from everywhere, but in the end it was Michigan and Columbia. At Michigan, Tiffany was there and I could have followed her, had her as a role model, but also it would have been like, 'Kyra Caldwell is going to be the next Tiffany Ofili,' and I'd always be that. I wanted to be Kyra, so that was part of why I didn't go to Michigan. The other Ivies were on the same level, but it came down to where I could make my own path. And location was important. Columbia was Ivy League, and it was in New York."

Kyra had changed her mind a couple times regarding her field of study, and when she chose Columbia she was favoring business. "Two years into high school I was taking accounting and business classes and I was thinking I could be a consultant and make a lot of money, and New York was a good place for that. I also thought it was a place where there wasn't a big star runner, a place where I could start my own legacy. And another big factor was to get away, get into a new environment, meet different people. It wasn't that I needed to go to an Ivy League school, I just wanted to go to a good school, and I knew I could do it. I had worked so hard for so long and I was near the top of my class. I just felt like I could apply anywhere and pray and have faith that I would get in anywhere."

When the acceptance letter came, naturally, Kyra's mother was worried that her daughter was going so far away, and she was going to miss all the help Kyra provided taking care of her sisters. "But," Kyra said, "I felt this is the way I could help my family, coming here and doing well."

She got off the business consulting track pretty quickly, thought about economics and realized that wasn't for her, and finally in sophomore year, medicine was back on her radar just as it had been in grammar school when she tried memorizing anatomy and biology books. "I saw my roommate was doing medicine, and I was so interested in it, the biology labs, it made me excited, and I knew I had to pray about it and it was something that I was supposed to do and wanted to do. I was a little indecisive, but deep down in my heart I knew I should be doing medicine, so I switched over."

In the next month, Kyra and her teammates would be on a whirlwind schedule. First there was the George Mason Invitational in Fairfax, Virginia, followed by another big trip as the Lions would be heading to Auburn, Alabama, for the War Eagle Invitational. And then would come the big finale to her career, starting with the historic Penn Relays at Philadelphia's Franklin Field, the Ivy League Heptagonal Championships, also at Franklin Field, the IC4A/ECAC Championships at Princeton, and the NCAA East Regional, for which she had already qualified, in Jacksonville, Florida.

And with papers needing to be researched and written, exams to be studied for, and practice and training and rehabbing at their collective peak, Kyra was as busy as she had ever been. Then again, she knew it was going to be this way when she chose to come to Columbia.

"It was hard at first because I was always used to being at the top of the list in high school, but at a certain point here you have to realize you're not like all the other students, because you have athletics," she said. "In high school, it was a matter of just doing the homework. If you did it, you got credit. Of course you had to perform on tests, but here, it's not just about finishing the work. You can do the work and spend ten hours on it, but if you don't do it right, you're not going to get a good grade. And if you get a C here, it's like an F. People don't get F's here.

"So if you want to do well in both, you have to have balance. You can't stay up all night and study if you have a meet or practice. Either you have to manage your time wisely, or something has to give a little bit. Some people can be all-American and national champion, and be all straight A's, but it's pretty tough at Columbia. Here, everybody is in the same situation. You can go to the library at four in the morning and someone is there already. That's what I learned right away here. Everybody wants to change the world, so everyone is the same in that aspect, but as athletes, we have to find the right balance between practice, meets, and studying, and it's tough."

ANOTHER INJURY SETBACK

One of the things Kyra loved about running track when she was first discovering the sport was the feeling of bliss that came over her as she pumped her arms and legs and felt the breeze she was creating blow through her hair as she ran past her opponents on the way to the finish line.

"I would run and forget everything, and it's like you're just floating," she said. "You don't remember much during a race; you're not in a trance, but it's just this feeling of free floating. That's how I feel when I run and I'm at my best, not hurting, not distracted by anything else."

Kyra missed that feeling because for much of her time at Columbia, that bliss had been absent. She had been hurt, obviously she had been distracted by the challenging demands of Ivy League academia, and she hadn't been able to make the strides she thought she was capable of when she first began wearing Columbia blue.

And then, just when it seemed like this final season was taking a turn for the better with her strong effort in the 400 hurdles at Princeton, there was another setback at the George Mason Invitational. During her preliminary heat in the 100 hurdles, Kyra struck one of the hurdles on her approach and in trying to prevent herself from falling to the track, she overstretched her trail leg—the one with the bad hamstring—and tweaked the injury again.

"Every time these things happen it's worse than it feels," she said. "I walked off the track and fell to the ground and I was like, 'Oh man, what if I can't run the 400 hurdles' because the 400 is really my main event; it's the one that I love doing, and here I could barely walk. I went to the trainer (Andrea Ditrani) and I was like, 'OK, it's not that bad, I can run through it' but then she said, 'No, you're not going to run' and I just started bawling. I've been having some troubles with the short hurdles all year so I was frustrated with that."

Kyra spent the next week getting treatment in the hope that she could participate Saturday at Auburn, a big meet that brought together schools from all over the country as well as several professional competitors. When it was time to board the plane for the trip South, coach Willy Wood figured Kyra wouldn't be able to run, but he wanted her to come along in the hope that she could, and because she deserved to be there with her team.

"I trained and went down, and my coach said maybe if I felt better I could run, but I decided not to run," she said. "I warmed up and I didn't feel better, so he said, 'Maybe you'll feel better tomorrow' but I didn't. It's just hard, I feel like I've dealt with pain a lot and it's hard for me to draw the line between pushing through this or maybe needing to let my body heal."

The problem was that time was running out for healing. Now it was the week of the prestigious Penn Relays, one of the sport's great events, and beyond that there was Ivy Heps and the NCAA Regional. Kyra needed to be healed because she was literally limping to the end of her collegiate career and it saddened her that she hadn't had the chance to compete at her optimum level for pretty much the entire indoor and outdoor seasons.

"A meet like Auburn, we're not trying to win it as a team, so for me, it would be to just try to run a (personal record) which would be great," she said. "There were three professional runners in the heat I would have been in and no one ran faster than my PR. Just to see them running and knowing I could have been in the mix and potentially could have won, it was painful. I saw a girl I had beaten the year I was at my best; she wasn't even near me then, but now she's running after college. So I saw that and I was like, 'Wow, I want to be out there competing and doing what I love doing.'"

She had hope for the Penn Relays, because she always has hope, that's just her personality. By not running at Auburn, she would have gone nearly two weeks since reinjuring herself at George Mason, so with a little luck, and some blessings from God, perhaps she'd be able to get into the blocks at Franklin Field unencumbered by pain. At this point, that's all there was left to hope for; not to win, or better her personal record, but to just have a chance to run, which used to be such a joy.

SLOW MOTION

Kyra knew it wasn't going to go well, and for an athlete, there isn't a worse feeling than knowing you are going to fail at something you should never fail at given your skill and training. Her leg did not respond as favorably to the nonstop treatment she had been receiving, and on the first day of the Penn Relays, Kyra ran a 400 hurdles race unlike any other in her college career.

"I felt all right, I was on anti-inflammatory, so the pain wasn't bad, but the strength just isn't there," Kyra said after crossing the finish line seventh in her eight-woman preliminary in 1:04.73, a time she hadn't seen on the clock since her high school days. Including all eight of the heats, Kyra's time was fifty-second-best, and nearly seven seconds slower than the winner of her particular race, Latoya Griffith of Illinois, who ran 57.88.

"I thought I was ready and I wanted to test it, to see if it was just mental. I was in the second heat, and it was a pretty fast heat. It was good to be in a fast heat like that, and once again my PR is 57, so to be there, but not be there was very frustrating. Even though I had the injury, my mind-set was to go out and do my best. It's the last Penn Relays, and I thought I could win it if I ran my best time, but I did not do that."

Kyra returned to the track with her 4 × 400 teammates Uju Ofoche, Miata Morlu, and Yamira Bell, to run in the only other event she was entered, but the results were just as disappointing. All seven teams in the race were from the Ivy League, and the Lions finished sixth in 3:51.98, more than ten seconds behind winning Princeton, with Kyra's 1:00.6 opening leg the slowest of the four Lions.

"My team was counting on me, so I wanted to run, but then it came around and I ran bad," said Kyra, whose career best leg in the relay was a 54.0. "I know who these girls are and usually by the first curve I'm breaking the stagger, and the last 150 it's just me. And this time I couldn't do it and everyone just passed me."

The Ivy League Heps at Princeton, the last conference meet for Columbia, were up next, but after this, Kyra was already facing the possibility that she might not be available. "I know I need to take time off and that's where I'm at right now," she said. "I'm just going to take it day by day and if I feel like I'm up to it and I feel like I can contribute then I'll run, and if not I'll hold off until regionals because I've already qualified. I have faith in my teammates that they will do a good job (in the races she would run), but we want to make sure no one else wins them because we'll need the points. So I have to make that decision."

There was very little for Kyra to smile about this season, and that trend continued at the Heps. Entered only in the 400 hurdles, she ran a mediocre 1:01.36 prelim, which qualified her for the championship race, but in the eight-woman final she had nothing left and ran 1:03.79 to finish last, more than four seconds behind winner, Molly Glantz of Cornell.

However, a ray of sunshine shone down on Kyra a few days before the team left for Philadelphia when she and fellow track athlete Kyle Merber were each presented the Connie S. Maniatty Outstanding Senior Student-Athlete awards, the highlight of the ninety-first annual athletic awards banquet, the Varsity C Celebration.

"It was kind of crazy because I've been going through so much the last year and a half with the injuries, so it was amazing to see my hard work and my accomplishments that I had my first two years be acknowledged," Kyra said. "I was a little discouraged at first because when I got nominated I didn't really think I had a chance because this past year has been rough, but they look at the whole four years of your career. So when I won that award that made me pretty happy to see that the things I've done didn't go unnoticed and my school had my back. They remembered the good times."

The ceremony was held inside Levien Gymnasium, and almost all of the varsity athletes were in attendance as each Columbia team was recognized, and individual awards were announced. So to watch two of his finest win the prestigious his and hers Maniatty was quite a thrill for track coach Willy Wood.

"I know the levels of work and commitment they put in over the last four years, so to see it manifest itself in such a way was very cool," said Wood. "Both of them are so dedicated to what we were doing and they are two people who performed at a high level; they bought into the program, and they were phenomenal athletes who were really driven."

Among the list of Kyra's achievements that were presented to the audience were her six Ivy League championships—two each in the outdoor 100-meter hurdles, indoor 60-meter hurdles, and outdoor 400-meter hurdles—and her four relay championships, two each indoor and outdoor at the 4 × 400-meter distance. Also, it was noted that she was the Most Outstanding Competitor of the 2010 Ivy League Outdoor Heptagonals, that she was the first Columbia athlete to ever win the title in the 100 hurdles as a freshman, and that she helped the Lion women win the indoor Heps for the first time in school history a few months earlier.

"I think the thing I learned the most is that life isn't perfect, sometimes you get hurt and things don't work out, but you have to keep getting back up, and I think I did that," Kyra said.

Such as she did at the Heps. Her prelim time wasn't close to her best, and she knew that if she hoped to just score some points for the team (the top six finishers count), let alone win, she was going to need to be much better. But she couldn't do it.

"It was an improvement from the week before, but it wasn't where I wanted to be," she said. "I went into the final race with faith that I would be able to pull it out, but it didn't work out. My first half was good, but when I really have to pull from my strength base in the second part of the race, which is instrumental for me, that was hard to do."

With that in mind, she skipped the IC4A/ECAC Championships at Princeton, because the only chance she would have to run close to her potential at the NCAA Regional was to get some rest, keep taking treatment, and hope that her leg would allow her to take one more shot at collegiate glory. But in keeping with this season of discontent, Kyra had nothing in Florida. A week after graduation, she ran her preliminary heat in the 400 hurdles in 1:00.99, last in her eight-woman group, and that wasn't nearly good enough to make it into the semifinals, let alone the finals.

"It was better than Heps, but it still wasn't good," she said. "The first half of the race was great, but I couldn't maintain it. It was a terrible year, not what I expected, especially after running fifty-seven (in the 400 hurdles) my sophomore season and ending my collegiate career in the sixties, that's not exactly ideal."

Her immediate future was uncertain regarding both the next step toward medical school and her possible pursuit of running on the professional circuit, assuming she could get her body to cooperate.

"Obviously I'm keeping my options open," she said. "My sophomore year when I ran that fifty-seven I was thinking in two years I'll be running fifty-five no problem and that's professional and I can get a contract, then still pursue medical school. I've been running track for eight years, so what do I do now? I feel like I have some more years, though, so I'm going to rest it up and try it again in a few months. Anything is possible."

Coming from where she came, raised in a single-parent home in Ypsilanti, Michigan, to where she was today, a graduate of Columbia University, she was living proof of that.

MELANIE BASKIND

HARVARD WOMEN'S LACROSSE

The first day of February meant it was back to work for Melanie. Not that she ever really took any time off.

"It's been pretty hectic with school and everything," she said, referring to the epoch between the end of soccer season and the beginning of lacrosse season as the Crimson held their first official practice.

Catching up with Melanie was laborious because the energetic senior never actually slowed down. Barely a week after the 3–0 NCAA soccer tournament loss to Boston University last November she had her lacrosse stick in her hands and was participating in the minimal informal team workouts that are allowed by the Ivy League, "Just to get the feel of it back." She closed out the first semester in high style academically, which is nothing new, of course. And she also flew out to San Francisco right after exams for the job interview with Acumen, which proved to be an eye-opening experience.

"I didn't get the job, which was good," she said. "I kind of got freaked out by the office scene and I didn't think it was a good fit for me. I kind of decided that even if I had gotten the job, I wouldn't have taken it. So now I'm thinking that I want to spend a year abroad. I applied to a bunch of travel and public service scholarships the school offers, and I had to put together proposals on why you want to go, and what you would do with the funding."

After spending time with her family over the holidays, she was back on campus weeks before she was required to return, working in the library, crafting those proposals, and spending countless hours in the gym pounding a treadmill to get in shape for lacrosse.

There is an unmistakable vibe around the team, and it was clearly evident as coach Lisa Miller put the players through drills under the bubble that was erected inside Harvard Stadium during the winter months, allowing the historic venue to be functional for spring sport practices. "There's a lot of excitement going into the season, a lot of hype and expectation that came with the success we had last year and knowing we only graduated one senior and brought in a big freshman class," Melanie said.

Harvard closed 2011 ranked twentieth in the Intercollegiate Women's Lacrosse Coaches Association poll thanks to a 10–6 record, 5–2 in the Ivy League. That victory total was the Crimson's best since 1994, and it was the first time since 1997 that they had appeared in the IWLCA poll. However, there was disappointment at the end of the year when they lost a heartbreaker in the Ivy League championship game, 12–10, to Princeton, denying them an automatic invitation to the NCAA tournament. And what was frustrating about that is the other two teams who participated in the Ivy tournament, Penn and Dartmouth, both received at-large bids to the NCAA despite their first-round Ivy losses.

The hope for 2012 was that the Crimson would take that next step and win their first Ivy title since 1993 and earn their first NCAA bid since 1994.

"In sport you live for today," Miller said. "So you can't really look at last year's success and say we're just going to have it this year. We're looking forward to it. We have a tough schedule, but the kids are really excited about it."

GIRL FOR ALL SEASONS

Melanie grew up in Massachusetts, Lucky Mkosana was born and raised half a world away in Zimbabwe; she is white, he is black; she went to Harvard, he attended Dartmouth; her goal was to become a doctor, his was to play professional soccer. They were different in so many ways, but they had one thing very much in common with soccer players of any age, on any continent: A passion for what the legendary Pelé refers to as "the beautiful game" that was as clear as the top row on the eye chart.

This was evident for Melanie even when she was five years old and her little T-shirt came down past her knees when she was playing in the youth leagues around her suburban hometown. She was always one of the smallest kids on the pitch—come to think of it, she still is—but she was a little tornado of energy, running and dribbling and scoring.

She was about to turn ten years old in the summer of 1999 when Brandi Chastain ripped off her uniform top after scoring that instantly famous penalty-kick goal to clinch the World Cup for the United States. As one of the millions who watched on television that day, Melanie remembered being perplexed by the fact that people were saying women's soccer was irrelevant before that seminal moment because to her, soccer was the most important thing in her life.

"I was already so into soccer at that point, and to hear people saying soccer was dead before that, I just thought maybe it is to some people, but not to me."

Melanie dabbled in Little League baseball with the boys, and she played ice hockey, but the bulk of her time was spent on soccer, as she played on school teams, youth league teams, advanced summer club teams, and winter indoor teams. And the more she played, the better she got. Chastain? Mia Hamm? Abby Wambach? Watch out, here comes Melanie Baskind to a World Cup near you.

But then in her freshman year at Framingham High, a woman named Stacy Freda, the girls' lacrosse coach at the school, opened her eyes to another game. Melanie's older sister, Julie, had been playing lacrosse for several years, but Melanie's only exposure to the sport was to occasionally pick up one of Julie's spare sticks and try to play catch with her. Freda knew Melanie was an outstanding athlete, and she knew she could teach her the requisite skills to turn her into a standout laxer. The trick was to convince her to try out for the team. With Julie chiming in, Melanie's ultra-competitive nature got the best of her, she agreed to play, and soon a new passion was percolating.

Soccer always came naturally to Melanie because she began playing as a little kid and grew up with the game, improving by leaps and bounds at every interval. Lacrosse was different. Before she went out for the high school team as a freshman, she'd never done anything more than play catch with Julie, so to start learning the game at her age when she'd already enjoyed so much athletic success took some patience. All of a sudden she wasn't going to be one of the best players, she was going to be one of the worst, at least for a little while. A very little while.

Working in her favor was the fact that girls' lacrosse was still establishing a niche in the New England region. Because there weren't many youth programs at the time, Melanie's learning curve wasn't as steep because she wasn't all that far behind the other girls who were playing. That and because she's a natural at pretty much everything she does.

"Soccer is so much more developed; everyone plays growing up, so it's really hard to put together a great high school team," she said, meaning the talent was so widely dispersed that many other schools had just as competitive a roster as your own. "Lacrosse was such a new sport, with no feeder programs, so it was possible for one coach to train athletes and get one team really good. And that's what coach Freda was able to do. I wouldn't be playing lacrosse if it wasn't for her. Our team wouldn't have been good if it wasn't for her. She picked all these athletic kids from the high school, threw them all together, taught us to play lacrosse, and a couple years later we were winning state championships."

From the moment she stepped onto the field, Melanie was one of the best pure athletes; she just needed some work on the finer points of lacrosse. "I could always catch and throw and I was always really fast, but for some reason I really had trouble with cradling," she said with a smile. Once she mastered that, she became one of the best players on one of the best teams in Massachusetts. By the time her days at Framingham were done, Melanie was one of the most decorated athletes the school had ever produced. She played a starring role in the Flyers' back-to-back state lacrosse championships in 2006 and 2007 which included a fifty-game winning streak; she was an all-State and all-American selection in both soccer and lacrosse; and in her senior year of 2007–08, the *Boston Globe* selected her in the fall as its Division 1 Girls' Soccer Player of the Year, and later in the following spring as its overall Female Athlete of the Year.

So what's a two-sport high school star supposed to do with a resume like that? It seemed clear at first for Melanie: Soccer would be the sport she played in college. Going back to her sophomore year she had been sending communiqués to schools gauging their interest in her as a soccer player, and many responded with recruiting letters and brochures that must have driven her local mailman to a chiropractor. Then the lacrosse letters began arriving without prompting from her, because with Framingham doing so well, recruiters were seeing her play and she didn't need to drum up interest. Yet even though she had immediate and noteworthy success in lacrosse, she hardly paid attention to the lacrosse inquiries she received. In her heart, soccer was still number one, and that—and only that—was what she was going to play at the next level.

"I'd been playing soccer competitively my whole life and I always knew that I wanted to, if given the opportunity, play soccer in college," she said. "You invest a lot of time and money playing in those showcase tournaments and all that, training and putting time and energy into it. I was set on playing college soccer. Lacrosse kind of came out of nowhere, but I never wanted to play lacrosse when I was going through the recruiting process."

In fact, while she wouldn't change a thing from her high school days, for a while she was worried that her newfound love of lacrosse was going to derail her pursuit of the soccer and academic mix she was seeking in her college search. That was because as much as she loved playing lacrosse, her involvement prevented her from competing in the Massachusetts Youth Soccer Olympic Development Program with the other top-level, soccer-specific athletes, many of whom she'd grown up playing with and against, but now was lagging behind in the recruiting process.

"Playing ODP, that's how you get onto regional and national teams where a lot of the big scouting and recruiting comes into play," Melanie explained. "My club team wasn't well known, and, for example, I sent letters to Princeton and Yale and didn't even hear back from them. I had plenty of smaller schools looking at me, but I wasn't getting much attention from most of the big schools. I wasn't a top-one-hundred recruit or a player that people were talking about because I wasn't playing ODP. So Harvard was a big surprise."

So, feeling quite fortunate that she landed in Cambridge and would have an opportunity to play soccer, she was convinced that her multiple-sport days were over. "Absolutely I wasn't going to play lacrosse," she said.

But when that lacrosse itch surfaced after her first soccer season, she had to scratch it, and once she negotiated the drama of recognizing that she wanted to play lacrosse, and it was OK with Harvard soccer coach Ray Leone and her soccer teammates, she got to work. "If I'm going to do anything, I'm going to do it all in," she said. "That's how I am with school, studying, with my friends, my family. I'm just a very intense person, so I knew I wasn't going to half-ass it."

During Christmas break in the middle of her sophomore year, Melanie hooked up with several players she once played lacrosse with at Framingham including her best friend, Kristin Igoe, who went on to play for Boston College and earned a place on the United States national team; Shauna Kaplan, who was also a dual-sporter in lacrosse and soccer at the University of New Hampshire; and Devin O'Leary, who played lacrosse at Stonehill. They whipped her back into shape, and when spring rolled around, Melanie was as ready as she was ever going to be after a two-year layoff.

"It was very interesting; I knew every single player on the lacrosse team, at least knew their name or from waving to them on the street. But I didn't know the freshmen, and they were like, 'Who is this girl who came out of nowhere?' I had been listed on a lacrosse recruiting website in high school, so some of the older girls knew I had played, and the coach had been saying since I came to Harvard, 'Do you know Melanie Baskind? You have to get her to play lacrosse.' So I had been talking to them, and they knew it was a possibility and they knew I might try it. I was nervous, but it went smoother than I thought."

That's because her natural athleticism offset the technical aspects of stick work that she needed to get reacquainted with. In her first season, Melanie led the team in ground ball recoveries with forty-one, was second in goals with thirty-two, and she helped the Crimson achieve just their second winning record (8–7) in eight years. After another fine soccer season in the fall of 2010, she was at the center of a lacrosse program revival in the spring of 2011. Named a captain after having played just one season, Melanie was fourth in goals with twenty-eight, and once again topped everyone with thirty-three ground balls.

She was a captain again this year, too, and soon, the final segment of her magnificent athletic career at Harvard would begin with a lacrosse game against cross-town rival Boston University.

UNDERDOGS NO MORE

Unfortunately, things did not get off to a very good start. It was way too early in the season to panic, and Melanie wasn't the type who ever would, but following a rather sloppy opening 11–9 victory over BU where Melanie scored goals on all three of the shots she attempted, the Crimson were waxed 12–6 by Cornell in the League opener.

"I wouldn't go so far as to say it's a disturbing trend, but everyone is taking a step back," Melanie said following the loss to the Big Red. "There's lots of conversations about what our problems are, how do we go about fixing them, and how can we learn from this and turn it around pretty quickly because if we keep playing the way we're playing, given the schedule we're playing, it's going to be a really long season."

Against BU, Melanie said, "We were happy with the win, but BU came out firing and we didn't necessarily play our best game. It was encouraging that you could have a bad day and find a way to get it done and grind out a win." But there was no overcoming their bad day against Cornell, as the Big Red took control with a four-goal run in the first half and never relinquished the lead. "It was a big loss," Melanie said. "All the Ivy games are huge; you only get one shot at them and we just dropped one."

Melanie had an unusually quiet day statistically against Cornell as she did not score a goal or record an assist, but she wasn't too concerned about that. "As a midfielder I'm not a goal scorer in the same way that I am in soccer as a forward," she said. "I play defense in lacrosse as much as I play attack. I would have liked to be the person to get things turned around when things weren't going well, so I was disappointed in my performance from that perspective, but it's not something that I will harp on or think about. I don't play for the stats."

Melanie surmised that one of the issues the Crimson was facing was the lofty expectations that had been placed on them. "We're not an underdog anymore, and I think people are a little bit nervous and are playing not to lose rather than playing to win. There's that feeling of, 'What if we lose, what if we don't meet people's expectations,' and that hasn't been there in the past. These are all things that I'm confident we can get over, but it's tough right now, it's not a good feeling."

And in order to accomplish that feat, Harvard was going to have to do it against a grueling schedule, as the next two games were against ranked teams—James Madison and Penn. "It'll be interesting to see what happens this next week," Melanie said. "It's a tough schedule, which makes it fun."

ROCK BOTTOM

What happened was the Crimson pulled out a thrilling 9–8 victory over thirteenth-ranked James Madison when Danielle Tetreault scored 1:39 into the second overtime, which Melanie thought would set the Crimson straight. "It was a great win," Melanie said. "We were feeling pretty good after that, but honestly, it's hard at this point to think back to how good that felt because we're in such a slump right now."

That's because since that day at Soldiers Field when Melanie had two goals and an assist and Jess Halpern had three goals to key the takedown of James

Madison, the ceiling had collapsed on the Crimson. There was an absolutely horrific meltdown against ninth-ranked Penn that saw Harvard blow a 10–5 lead with 16:23 left to play on the way to a 14–13 overtime loss in Philadelphia, their twelfth straight loss to the Quakers, a streak that extended back to 2000. Then came another gut-wrencher at Johns Hopkins when the Crimson put on a three-goal rally in the final six minutes to tie the score, only to lose 8–7 on a Blue Jays goal with nineteen seconds remaining in regulation. And then at Harvard Stadium, playing against cross-town rival Boston College and her best friend, Kristin Igoe, Melanie and the Crimson dropped a 7–5 decision in a game that really wasn't as close as the score indicated. Incredibly, in a season where the Crimson were thinking they would be in the hunt for the Ivy League title, they were 2–4 overall, 0–2 in League games, and it was going to take a Herculean effort to even qualify for the four-team Ivy League tournament.

"This is really taking a toll on my mental state for sure," Melanie said, her chuckle offering evidence that she was only half-serious. "It's been driving me nuts. You feel a lot of pressure to pinpoint a problem and then fix it, but it's not that easy; if it was easy it would have been taken care of. But we seem to fix one problem and then we have another one."

After the surprising and lopsided loss to Cornell in the second game of the year, the Crimson worked hard on cleaning up the sloppy play that killed them that day. It worked in the victory over James Madison, and it sure seemed to be working at Penn. "We played a fantastic forty-five minutes against Penn, and then I think we got a little bit tired, a little complacent, and we panicked a little, and a good team will take advantage of that," said Melanie. "It was a big slap in the face losing that game; that one really hurt. That's the one team I've never beaten in the two sports; Penn lacrosse. I'm 0–4. Not meaning to sound dramatic, but that was probably one of the most disappointing results I can remember."

Against nineteenth-ranked Boston College, Harvard fell behind 5–1 in the first fifteen minutes, was down 7–2 with just eleven minutes remaining, and then made the final look respectable when it scored the last three goals, one of them by Melanie. Melanie's former teammate at Framingham, Igoe, matched her output with a goal, but the national team member also scooped five loose balls and caused two turnovers, one of her typical stat-line-filling performances that made her one of the best players in the country.

"She's my best friend, so there's always a big rivalry in there," Melanie said.

"She's a fantastic player, but it sucks to lose two years in a row to her. It's a big in-region game; it was our first under the lights at our stadium since the bubble has come down, and we just didn't perform."

THE BIG STAGE

Her career in athletics had given Melanie a deep reservoir of memories that would last a lifetime, and on a sunny Saturday afternoon on the last day of March 2012, she added another to the pool when the Crimson participated in a doubleheader at Gillette Stadium in Foxboro, Massachusetts, home of the NFL's New England Patriots since it opened in 2002.

"Playing at Gillette was unbelievable," she said. "It's something that we knew we were doing, but it didn't really hit me until we pulled up and saw the stadium and you're like, 'Wow.' To think what that really meant, playing at Gillette, the first women's collegiate sporting event to take place there, it was really cool to be a part of. Walking on the field, going in the locker room before the game, taking pictures; it was really cool. We were excited about the opportunity."

Unfortunately the Crimson were given an extremely difficult task in this momentous event, having to play the second-ranked team in the nation, Syracuse University. And despite a gallant effort, Harvard just couldn't stay with the talented Orange and lost, 10–6.

"We played pretty well, but turnovers continue to plague us," said Melanie, who had her best game of the season with three goals and two assists. "They were a great team; they really push the ball in transition, which is something we haven't really seen from many teams, and we tried to slow them down the best we could, but in the end they nipped us probably three or four times with that."

Syracuse, which was playing without one of its best players, Michelle Tumolo, who was sitting out because of a red card she'd received in the previous game against UConn, raced out to a 6–2 halftime lead. Melanie took the game over for a five-minute stretch early in the second half as she scored three straight for Harvard to cut the deficit to 7–5, but her eleventh career hat trick wasn't enough. Syracuse scored three of the game's final four goals including a pair by its leading scorer, Alyssa Murray, to pull out the victory and send the Crimson careening to 4–5.

"The environment was great; there were a lot of young girls there. We had an autograph session afterward, so you could see all the hype around the day," Melanie said. "It was a great day for women's lacrosse, with some of the best teams in the country (top-ranked Northwestern, the national champion six of the past seven years, survived a scare in the second game before defeating fourteenth-ranked Ohio State, 13–12, in overtime)."

The Crimson had undertaken one of the most challenging schedules in the country, but Syracuse—coached by Syracuse grad and men's lacrosse legend Gary Gait—was clearly a notch above anyone else they had seen. "The biggest difference wasn't skill-related," Melanie explained. "I mean they weren't scoring behind-the-back goals, they're not doing things that we aren't capable of doing, it's just another level of discipline and better decision making. It's a smarter game; they don't make mistakes and they capitalize on our errors. They have very few unforced turnovers, they just make the right plays at critical moments, and they have a swagger about them that they feel like they should win and are going to win and we're still trying to figure that out."

It looked like the Crimson were making progress in that endeavor leading into the showdown with Syracuse. They snapped their three-game losing streak with a 7–5 victory over Yale for their first Ivy League win, and then took down Stanford, 10–4. The victory over Yale was certainly a strange game, as Harvard jumped out to a 7–0 halftime lead with Melanie scoring twice, and then held on as Yale scored the only five goals of the second half. There wasn't as much angst against Stanford, as Harvard opened a 5–0 lead by the break, then kept piling on in the second half in taking a 10–1 lead.

Next up, the Crimson would fly to Virginia to take on the ninth-ranked Cavaliers, but at this point the nonconference games were an afterthought. The only chance Harvard had to make the NCAA tournament was to win the Ivy League tournament, and there was still a lot of work to be done to even qualify for that four-team event. That's why Melanie called the victory over Yale, "Massively important. Every Ivy League game is a must-win now."

PLANNING FOR THE FUTURE

What little free time Melanie had outside of lacrosse practice and games and her class work had been devoted to preparing for a pretty important interview. She would speak before a committee in the Fellowships Office that would decide which graduate students were getting school funding for a wide variety of activities.

"I'm anxious, I just want to get it over with," Melanie said. "It was a crazy process putting the proposal together with the essay, transcripts, letters of recommendation, a budget proposal, all this stuff."

Melanie's senior year had been a roller coaster ride both on and off her two fields of play, the latest valley being a 12–6 loss at Virginia. In looking ahead to graduation, her original plan was to work for a year before starting medical school. She spent time in the fall researching companies and opportunities, and she went on a couple of interviews. Neither worked out, and that was a good thing because now she had completely altered her game plan.

"I just decided it's something that I need to do," she said of her decision to—drumroll please—go to Africa.

During the soccer season Melanie concluded that she wanted to participate in the Coaches Across Continents initiative that was founded by 1991 Harvard graduate Nick Gates, a former Crimson soccer player. Similar to the Grassroot Soccer program that was founded by Dartmouth grad Tommy Clark, which helped enable Lucky Mkosana to come to Dartmouth to study and play soccer, Coaches Across Continents had made a huge impact on the youth of Africa, and now India. It was designed to have experienced soccer coaches assist developing communities using a specially designed soccer education curriculum with the ultimate goal of helping young people to become modern leaders in their communities.

"It's doing unbelievable things abroad, using soccer to teach things like female empowerment, HIV awareness, health and wellness, conflict resolution," Melanie explained. "It was started by a Harvard soccer player, and these are the people that make Harvard amazing. A lot of times we get caught up in sports, but there's so many other things that people do on campus that they're passionate about; it's very inspiring."

Melanie originally was hoping to go to Africa and lend a hand for a couple months and then return to America to work and prepare for med school. Now she wanted to spend the year in Africa, and her proposal included working for Coaches Across Continents as well as an orphanage in Kenya.

"One fellowship is for the full year and one is for six months, so I really hope I can get one of them," she said. "But if I don't get anything, I'm still going to go and fund-raise as much as I can. I'm definitely doing Coaches Across Continents, and I'd like to stay over there as long as possible. I've always worked, and I don't spend too much here [at Harvard], so I've got some money saved up that I can use. Ideally I'd like to use that on other things and have a buffer between this and med school, so I'm keeping my fingers crossed for funding."

Of course if she didn't get it, she'd be immune to the disappointment given the way lacrosse season had gone. Against a very good Virginia squad, the Crimson got off to a horrible start and were down 6–1 by halftime, and all they could do was trade goals for the final thirty minutes.

"The consistency is where we're hurting ourselves," said Melanie. "We feel like we haven't played anywhere close to where we should be, and yet we're still staying in these games. We were down two goals to Syracuse, and there were opportunities that we had in the Virginia game where we could have closed the gap. So the fact that we're not playing well and hanging with these top-ten teams is motivation in itself, but it gets more and more frustrating trying to figure out why we aren't putting things together. We're at a point in our program where we're nationally competitive. Trying is good enough at a certain point, but we need to start executing things now. We're not happy just staying with these teams, we want to win."

GETTING OFF THE MAT

When Harvard lacrosse coach Lisa Miller put together the 2012 schedule, she knew with absolute certainty that it was going to test the Crimson the way no schedule had ever tested them. But there was a method to her madness.

"For Harvard to be able to compete within the Ivy League, we have to step outside and play top nonconference competition," Miller explained before the season began. "The schedule is built to prepare us to play Princeton, and to play Dartmouth, to play Penn. If we can run with Stanford, Virginia, and some of the other nonconference teams on the schedule, we'll be able to compete in the Ivy League. It's a tough schedule, but if you like to compete, it's a lot of fun."

The meat-grinder slate of games was also supposed to give Harvard a leg up in the battle for at-large bids to the NCAA tournament if, by chance, it failed to win the automatic bid that was awarded to the Ivy League tournament champion. However, to that end, it only helped if you won some of those games. "Yeah, the idea is to do well out of league to put yourself in position where you get enough big wins that it doesn't matter what happens in the Ivy tournament, and we're not really in that position," Melanie said with a laugh.

That's because in the four games the Crimson played against nonconference teams ranked in the top twenty, they lost three of them to Syracuse, Virginia, and Boston College. And with six losses in their first ten games overall, including a tepid 1–2 start in Ivy play, the Crimson were in danger of not even qualifying for the Ivy tournament, let alone the NCAA tournament.

"This is definitely the toughest schedule I've ever played, lacrosse or soccer," Melanie said. "I think if [Miller] had the option to play this schedule every year, or harder, she would, the idea being you prepare for the best, and you get better every game."

It took a while, but that finally began happening for Harvard in mid-April. Because only four of the eight teams qualify for the Ivy tournament, the Crimson were operating with no room for error and they put together three stellar efforts in wiping out Brown, 16–8; defeating Holy Cross, 10–4; in the last non-League game; and then a pulling 10–7 upset of eighteenth-ranked Princeton, which vaulted Harvard into a third-place tie with the Tigers and Cornell, drafting just behind Penn and Dartmouth.

"I don't think it was about confidence, it was a feeling of if we stuck to the game plan and put everything together we could beat anybody out there, and it was just a question of doing that," Melanie reasoned. "We've struggled to play sixty minutes and struggled to stay in structure and play within ourselves. It was more our ability to execute, so doing that in the Princeton game made it that much better to come out on top."

The teams split twelve goals in a wild first half of action, and Melanie had the sense the Crimson couldn't continue to run and gun with the Tigers. So the Crimson defense stepped up and held the Tigers to one goal in the final thirty minutes, and after Melanie scored the go-ahead goal that made it 8–7 with just over twenty minutes left to play, leading goal-scorer Danielle Tetreault pumped in a pair of unassisted markers in the final sixteen minutes. After that, Harvard goalie Kelly Weis had very little to do with protecting that margin because the Crimson had possession of the ball most of the rest of the way.

"We've had our backs against the wall, and we've responded pretty well to it," Melanie said.

TRIP OF A LIFETIME

The glow of the Princeton victory was wonderful, but it wasn't like Melanie had an opportunity to revel in the renewed hope Harvard now had of qualifying for the Ivy tournament. There were what she termed the seven "end-of-the-year things" she needed to complete before she walked through Old Yard in less than a month to receive her diploma, meaning she was fine-tuning papers and projects and preparing for final exams. There was another game, a 10–3 walk-over at Columbia during which she had a goal and controlled four draws as the Crimson continued their impressive turnaround with their fourth victory in a row. Oh, one other thing: "I got the fellowship; I'm going to Africa," she said with glee regarding the news that Harvard was going to pay for her to spend a year in Africa as she tried to do her part to help change the world.

When she walked out of the Office of Career Services and strolled down Dunster Street the day she presented her proposal, she had a pretty good feeling about what had transpired in front of the four committee members she met with. "I got the impression that it went really well," she said. "It was much less about my project proposal than I thought it would be; it was much more about them getting to know me as a person."

When she found out via e-mail that she'd been awarded the full-year fellowship, "I was in my room and I was running around seeing if anyone was home and nobody was, so I was just kind of smiling by myself, and then I called my parents."

It was way too early in the process to define exactly what she'd be doing, but once she arrived in early July she would go right to work in the Coaches Across Continents program for a couple months, then move on to an orphanage in Kenya where she would help establish an after-school soccer program, and teach English and science classes. She also hoped to find time to travel the continent, and one item on her bucket list was to visit the Gombe Stream National Park in Tanzania where Jane Goodall—the British primatologist, ethologist, anthropologist, United Nations Messenger of Peace, and founder of the Jane Goodall Institute—had spent nearly five decades studying the social and family interactions of wild chimpanzees. And, if possible, while she was in Tanzania she wanted to climb Mount Kilimanjaro, the highest mountain in Africa.

"I'm just winging it right now, it's kind of open-ended, so I'm interested to see what I end up doing," she said. "It feels awesome, though. I'm really excited. But there's a lot to do before then."

For instance, finishing off her athletic career on a high note, something that had become a tangible possibility thanks to the sudden late-season lacrosse resurgence. After a slow first-half start, the Crimson ran away from Columbia as the defense held the Lions to a mere three goals, a season-low. Danielle Tetreault led the offense with her second straight four-goal game, and Harvard remained tied for third place in the Ivy League with Cornell and Princeton heading into the final weekend of play as it vied to secure one of the four tournament spots.

"There are a ridiculous number of situations that can take place, and there could actually be a five-way tie for first and that would mean a team could win the League and not make it to the tournament," Melanie said. "We could be the one seed or not even get in at all. All I know is if we beat Dartmouth, we'll at least be in the tournament."

A LITTLE HELP NEVER HURTS

Melanie was sitting in her room thinking about what a crazy lacrosse season this had been, and she smiled and shook her head in wonderment when it took another interesting turn. Despite all their troubles, which extended past the halfway mark on the schedule, Harvard officially clinched one of the four available berths in the Ivy League tournament when Penn defeated Princeton on the final Friday of the regular season, eliminating the Tigers from contention.

"This has been the most extreme in terms of the ups and downs," Melanie said of a season that began with two early Ivy losses, but now had the Crimson heading to Philadelphia next weekend to join Cornell, Dartmouth, and host Penn in the tournament where the winner would earn an automatic bid to the NCAA tournament. "It's pretty unbelievable to think of where we were a month ago. It wasn't pretty."

The Crimson were 4–6 after their loss at Virginia, and Melanie recalled the gloom that pervaded their plane ride home. "We've been laughing about that when we're talking about the low points, and we've been saying, 'Do you remember that flight home from Virginia?' It was a lot of the same at that point, it was so frustrating because we'd already had the same conversation over and over about what is going on, what can we fix, how can we spark change here? The first time you have that conversation you feel pretty good that you've identified the problems, let's fix it. But the third, fourth, fifth time you're having that conversation, self-doubt creeps in and you think maybe we can't change this, maybe this is how our season is going to go and we don't have the tools. I would never say that out loud to the team, but that's how I was feeling on that ride home."

Free of the burden of having to win, the Crimson put together a solid effort and knocked off the tenth-ranked Big Green, 7–5, at Harvard Stadium. "It was a really exciting win," she said. "I think we are peaking at the right time. Obviously we were thrilled to clinch a spot in the tournament, but we wanted to win the game and continue to feel good about our chances in the tournament."

Dartmouth led 2–1 at the half and extended the lead to 3–1 soon after the break, but then the captain did what she had been doing—be it lacrosse or soccer—for four years at Harvard. Melanie came up big in the clutch as she scored back-to-back goals 1:13 apart to tie the score. The Big Green scored next, but the Crimson tallied four of the game's final five goals as Jenn VanderMeulen set up Mikayla Cyr twice for the tying and go-ahead goals, then scored the clincher with eight seconds left after Dartmouth had closed to within one.

"This was a game between two very good lacrosse teams," said Melanie. And one of them would be going to Philadelphia riding a five-game winning streak. "It's huge going into the tournament. We had some low points in the season and fighting through those made us more competitive and smarter. Now that we know we're playing on a level we have been trying to reach all year, we're a lot more confident going into this weekend."

NO MORE SPORTS

When Melanie and her Crimson teammates entered the expansive and breathtaking lobby of the Ritz Carlton Philadelphia on the evening of May

3, their eyes widened, their jaws dropped open, and it was immediately apparent this wasn't a Microtel or a Hampton Inn.

"We walked in and we were kind of blown away," Melanie said, laughing at the thought of seeing the stately Roman columns that greet visitors as they enter this world-class hotel in the heart of downtown Philadelphia. "I don't know how we ended up there, I guess they had a hard time getting reservations anywhere else and they didn't have a choice. We were all walking around in our Ritz robes in our rooms. We went out with a bang on this trip."

Sadly, there was that whole "out with a bang" aspect of the journey down to Philadelphia. The Crimson got off to a terrible start the next night in their tournament semifinal game against top-seeded host Penn and ultimately lost, 9–5, bringing an end to their season, and to Melanie's magnificent athletic career.

"It didn't have as big of an effect on me as I would have thought," she said, referring to the realization that as soon as that final horn sounded, it was over for her, and she'd never wear a Harvard uniform again. "A couple of the seniors said there were particular moments where they got emotional knowing we were going to lose and this was going to be our last game, but it didn't really hit me like that. I just wanted to win the game because I'm competitive and we hadn't beaten Penn lacrosse and I wanted to make it to the championship game. It was much more about being in the moment and wanting to win that game than it was being the end of playing sports here."

The team had bused down from Cambridge, tooled around the Ritz for a while, then retired to their rooms because fourteen players, including Melanie, had to take various final exams the morning of the game in a meeting room that had been reserved at the hotel. Melanie's was in her elective class that examines Africa and the making of a modern continent, and she expected it to be a breeze, and it was. "I wasn't too nervous because it's a pass-fail class and I really liked it so I had paid very close attention to the lectures all year. I knew I'd be fine, but some of the other girls were taking their exam in Science of the Physical Universe and they were a lot more nervous than me."

It was just another day in the life of Ivy League student-athletes. Even though they were playing the most important game of the season later in the evening, there is no preferential treatment regarding school work. The rest of the students were taking these same exams back in Harvard classrooms, so the only concession the lacrosse players received was the opportunity to take their tests while they were on the road.

"This is what we do, and we're all pretty good at it at this point," Melanie said of the ability to juggle athletics with unyielding academics. "This was magnified a little bit because we're at a tournament, but we kind of do this every day. You're a student at Harvard and then you have to step away from that before you go across the river to the athletic side, whether it's for practice or a mid-week game or you're traveling somewhere on the bus. You learn to switch on and off to the different modes."

By noon the exams were done, and following a shoot-around at the Dunning-Cohen complex—where the tournament was being held because the Ivy League track and field championship meet, the Heptagonals, was being contested at Franklin Field—the Crimson returned to the Ritz to do a little more studying and resting before they went back to Dunning-Cohen for the game.

The Quakers scored three times in the first five minutes before Jess Halpern broke through for Harvard, but then Penn's Meredith Cain scored three in a row over the last ten minutes of the first half for a 6–1 lead.

Down 7–1 early in the second half, Melanie responded with two goals in a row, giving her twenty-seven for the season and at least one goal in the final eleven games of her career. Harvard would eventually get within 8–5 with four minutes remaining, but it never scored again.

"I really never felt we were out of it just because of the way the possessions were going," Melanie said. "We had the ball so much in the second half. I hit a post, someone else hit one, we missed two open nets when the goalie was out and we shot wide, so it just felt like it wasn't our night."

A month ago, Melanie would have been thrilled to have this opportunity to play in the Ivy tournament because at that point, it seemed like a remote possibility. However, the Crimson closed with a rush, and they made it, so as she walked through the high-five line at the end, she couldn't feel bad about what had happened.

"The easy answer would be to say it was disappointing, and it is," she said of a 9–8 record that fell well below what she and the Crimson were anticipating this season. "But in the end I'm so proud of the way we turned it around. It's so hard to make a change like that midseason, and we ended up beating Princeton and Dartmouth and put together a five-game winning streak, so we were in position where we could have won the bid. So yes it was disappointing because the expectations were high, but it was a good season, and I'm extremely grateful for the games we did win and for the girls I got to play with. I'll look back on it positively."

There was one more term paper to turn in, and when that happened, Melanie's undergraduate days at Harvard would be complete. She would leave Cambridge with a bachelor of arts in neurobiology, a secondary degree in global health and health policy, and a citation in Spanish, putting her right on track to enter medical school next year after her sojourn to Africa. She would put away her cleats having scored twenty-seven goals in four soccer seasons, seventh-most in Harvard history, and eighty-eight goals in three lacrosse seasons. She pulled on a Harvard uniform 115 times, captained three of her teams, won three Ivy League soccer championships, was named to seven all-Ivy teams, and as a senior she earned Ivy women's soccer player of the year and Harvard's distinction as its female athlete of the year, and she was a first-team Academic All-American in both sports.

With no more games or practices, she didn't quite know what to do with herself. For someone who was used to being on the go twenty-five hours of the day, all of a sudden there was down time, and with it would likely come reflection on a four-year epoch of her life that she will never forget.

"What I'm feeling now, it's a really big sense of accomplishment knowing that I'm going to get a degree from Harvard, a school that I never thought I would have the opportunity to go to, a school that, even if I did have the opportunity to go to, that I wouldn't be sure I'd be successful at," she said. "There's a sense of pride looking back on the last four years and realizing what I've accomplished and being able to walk out of here feeling good about what I've done, the grades that I've gotten, and the success I enjoyed in athletics. It's weird because it hasn't hit me that I'm finished. I guess it will eventually. I'm a little scared for when it does."

EPILOGUE

When Tommy Amaker stepped onto the Harvard campus to interview for the vacant men's basketball job in the spring of 2007, he could feel history and tradition and achievement oozing from every building at America's most prestigious university.

"You are exposed to greatness from every direction here," said Amaker, who at that time was referring not to the downtrodden basketball program he was inheriting, but to the institution and all that it stood for.

Amaker knows of what he speaks. He played college basketball in the mid-1980s under the now legendary Mike Krzyzewski at Duke University, often referred to as the Ivy League of the South. Duke is a place where academics are every bit as important as athletics, and just like the eight schools that comprise the Ivy League, there are no concessions. If you can't make the grades, you can't wear the uniform.

"That's my background; it's the way I'm wired," said Amaker. "It was the same at Duke when I played there; I was a product of that at Duke. These kids at Harvard, and in the Ivy League, they are students and they are athletes, and we understand that and they understand that. The main thing coach Krzyzewski said was that the institution is the pillar; it's the attraction. And it's the same at Harvard."

It was that very premise that linked these nine student-athletes. All were tremendously talented athletes in high school, and they could have gone to any number of Division I universities to play their respective sport. But it wasn't all about sports for Ona McConnell and Alex Thomas of Yale, Melanie Baskind and Keith Wright of Harvard, Lucky Mkosana of Dartmouth, Andy Iles of Cornell, Sheila Dixon of Brown, Greg Zebrack of Penn, and Kyra Caldwell of Columbia.

They were looking for more. They were looking for the ultimate challenge of both body and mind, and they wanted to be measured against the very best in environments that demand the very best.

"These kids are tremendous," Amaker said. "It's very challenging, without a doubt, to have the kind of expectations and standards we have in terms of academics, and to also participate for your university on an intercollegiate athletic team and give the kind of time you have to give to succeed. But these kids coming to Harvard and the other schools, this isn't the first time they've been exposed to high rigors academically and athletically. And like I tell the kids being admitted to Harvard, if they didn't think you were able to handle this, they wouldn't have admitted you to come here."

For Kyra, Melanie, Keith, Alex, Lucky, and Greg, the Ivy League experience was complete. All six graduated having distinguished themselves in the classroom and in their respective athletic arenas, because that's what the vast majority of the more than eight thousand Ivy League student-athletes do.

"It's definitely a feeling of accomplishment; a lot of hard work went into these four years," Keith said, a statement that every one of the six graduates would echo.

Sheila, Ona, and Andy were not done with their undergrad days. Sheila had one more year to go at Brown, Ona had one more year left at Yale, and the baby of the group, Andy, still had two years remaining at Cornell. In some ways, they envied the graduates, but they also knew that college was a wondrous time in a young person's life, and they were happy knowing that they still had some time left to experience whatever might come their way.

Here's what the nine men and women were up to as the curtain came down on the 2011–12 school year:

MELANIE BASKIND

Johnny Cash once sang that he'd been everywhere, and so, it seemed, had Melanie in the weeks immediately following Harvard's May 24 commencement. She and two of her best friends and fellow Crimson graduates, field hockey player Georgia McGillivray and track athlete Christine Reed, left Cambridge in the minivan of Reed's parents, and embarked on a celebratory cross-country journey.

"It's been a blast," Melanie said one night while relaxing in Las Vegas near the end of the trip. "It was in the works since about December. We took off the day after graduation, and it's been awesome." The girls hit New York City, Washington, D.C.; Atlanta; Montgomery, Alabama; New Orleans; Austin, Texas; Carlsbad, New Mexico; the Grand Canyon; Vegas; Los Angeles; and San Francisco. As graduation presents go, this was a pretty good one, but let's face it, the two-sport captain and owner of a bachelor of arts degree in neurobiology deserved it.

On the day of graduation she reflected on her arrival at Harvard four years earlier, and how to this day she still finds it amazing that she was able to attend America's most prestigious university, let alone excel the way she had both in the classroom and on her two fields of play. "Graduation definitely made me appreciate being at Harvard," said Melanie, who found out while she was still on the road trip that she had earned one of the highest honors in women's lacrosse as she was named the Intercollegiate Women's Lacrosse Coaches Association's Division I Scholar-Athlete of the Year. "Like I've said, I feel very fortunate to have had the chance to go there. It really hits you strongly at the end, it's just a place with so much tradition, and you realize how lucky you are to be able to walk away with a diploma."

Melanie estimated there were about thirty thousand people crammed into Harvard Yard for the morning and afternoon ceremonies, and that included her parents and sister, and her grandmother on her mom's side who made the trip over from Syracuse, New York. Harvard's undergrads receive their diplomas at their residences between the morning and afternoon sessions, so that meant Quincy House for Melanie, and then after lunch she settled in to listen to Indian-born journalist Fareed Zakaria, an editor-at-large for *Time* magazine and host of his own show on CNN, speak eloquently on the hope and promise of a world that, in his view, has been in much worse shape than it was in 2012.

A few weeks after returning from her dash across the United States, Melanie boarded a plane at Logan International bound for Africa, a part of the world she never dreamed she would have a chance to see, at least not until she went to Harvard. She will spend a year on the African continent, visiting places such as Zimbabwe, Zambia, Namibia, Kenya, and Tanzania, teaching soccer to the children as part of the Coaches Across Continents initiative, but also participating in numerous public health endeavors including conducting tests for the AIDS virus at an orphanage in Kenya.

Only then will she get on with the rest of her life, as she will apply to, and ultimately attend, medical school.

"It will just be a really neat experience being in a developing country and doing something completely different that I've never done before," she said before leaving. "The soccer piece is really cool. It's a world sport, and I feel like it's something you always read about, but I've never seen it with my own eyes, the power of soccer and the impact it can have around the world. I'm pretty excited to use my soccer skills to do some positive things, especially as a female. That's one of the things that excites me most about the program is the role that females in particular can play in serving as role models for young girls."

KYRA CALDWELL

There wasn't an overwhelming feeling of excitement for Kyra as her May 16 graduation ceremony approached. It was raining in New York, so that put a bit of a damper on the festivities in the middle of the Morningside Campus, and her mother, Kerri, was staying with her, and that had Kyra "a little stressed out."

"At first it just felt like any other day," she said. "I'll walk across the stage and listen to this person (President Lee C. Bollinger) talk about something boring. But then when I actually put on my cap and gown, and I met up with some of my classmates and took pictures, it was like, 'Wow, this is really it.' I'm about to graduate from Columbia, I'm done with that phase of my life.'"

It was a momentous day for Kyra's family because she became its first member to graduate from college. And she had her own rooting section on hand to pay tribute to her. Both of her parents and their new spouses were there, two of her sisters, one of her best friends, members of her dad's family who live in Brooklyn, even an uncle from Cleveland. "I felt a lot of love and support," she said. "To see all my family there, that was amazing because everybody was so proud. I knew I was the first to graduate, but it didn't really seem like it was a big, big deal to me because I know I have a lot more school left with medical school. But it did feel good to be done with all my Columbia classes, and it was like one thing off the list. And I know being an Ivy League graduate will open a lot of doors for me."

Kyra was going to spend the summer in New York doing research for an orthopedic surgeon at Columbia Medical Center while simultaneously beginning the process of getting ready to apply to medical school, though she wasn't quite sure where. And, after resting her injuries, she was going to get back into training because she wasn't quite ready to give up hope of running professionally.

SHEILA DIXON

At the end of the spring semester Sheila found herself in a bit of quandary. Brown students need to be on track with their credit hour totals at various checkpoints throughout their undergraduate stay, and because Sheila had to drop her Symbols in American Politics class very late when she realized she was probably not going to pass, she was one class short for someone finishing her junior year, so she had to go back to Providence in late June to take a summer school class in financial accounting.

"I dropped the class because the grade was weighted on only two assignments, a midterm and a paper," Sheila explained. "I did poorly on the midterm, and then the paper, it was my last one and I thought I could do it, but it became too much and I decided I couldn't do it. So in order for me to be where I'm supposed to be, and so I don't have to take five classes next semester, I'm taking the summer class."

This, however, was a good thing on a number of fronts. First, she wasn't sure what she was going to do with her political science major, and she had given some thought to perhaps turning to accounting. "When I was in high school I loved math and numbers and I wanted to pursue accounting, but Brown didn't have an accounting program," she said. "Depending on how this class goes, I might come back to Albany (after graduating from Brown in 2013) and do accounting."

Second, being back at Brown gave her an opportunity to continue getting her new apartment situated for the fall. She and teammate Carly Wellington said goodbye to dorm life and decided to become roommates in an apartment building that is literally on the campus grounds, just down the street from the campus bookstore.

Third, she was able to work out at the Brown facilities, and she sought help from Bears men's assistant basketball coach T. J. Sorrentine, hoping he could fine-tune her game to the point where she might be able to consider playing professionally in Europe after graduation. "Because of NCAA rules, I can't work with our coaches, but I can with the men's coaches, so T. J. Sorrentine has been helping me with some guard stuff," Sheila said. "I'd really like to see what my chances are of playing overseas. My coach thinks I have the potential to do it, so I have to continue to improve and be better than I was last year."

The fact that she was about to start her senior year excited her because she was anxious to see what the next phase of her life was going to include.

"I wish I was graduating this year, but other than the academic stresses, it's been such a great and fun journey," she said. "In some ways I don't want it to end, but I'm also excited about closing this chapter and moving on to the next one and see where I'm going to go after Brown."

ANDY ILES

Andy finished off his second year at Cornell with a 3.58 grade point average and that earned him a spot on the College Sports Information Directors Association's Academic All-District At-Large Team. And at the hockey team banquet Andy—who was a first-team All-Ivy selection and a second-team all-ECAC choice—was given the Nicky Bawlf Award as the MVP, and the Joe DeLibero-Stan Tsapis Award for skilled efficiency, unselfish dedication, and hard-nosed competitive desire.

"Once hockey ends, school really becomes a grind," Andy said. "Those last few weeks when papers and projects are due and then we have two weeks of exams, but I made it through."

After having entered Cornell thinking he would be studying biological sciences, he officially changed his major after the semester was over when he was accepted into the Dyson School of Applied Economics and Management. Though he has hopes of playing professional hockey after he graduates in 2014, he knows he needs a reliable backup plan, and the academic goal was to earn a business degree with a double major in marketing and accounting.

A few days after his final test in mid-May, Andy boarded a flight bound for the Dominican Republic to lend his support to the El Portal De Belen Foundation, which was incorporated by Father Ronald Gaesser, a former pastor of Ithaca's St. Catherine of Siena Parish, who also did ministry work at Cornell before retiring and moving to one of the poorest sections of the Caribbean island.

"It was an amazing experience," Andy said of the ten-day trip, on which he was accompanied by Big Red teammates Greg Miller, Cole Bardreau, Kevin Cole, Nick D'Agostino, and Dustin Mowrey; coach Mike Schafer and his two sons John and Luke; and a few others.

The foundation was formed for the purpose of raising funds and providing contributions and grants to support the care, well-being and Catholic development of needy children in the Dominican Republic. Andy's group was tasked with starting construction on a building in the community of Bosque Arriba that would serve as a chapel for Mass and parish events as well as a classroom/meeting room, and it would also be used as a future hurricane shelter. In seven days, they erected four cinder-block walls, getting the project off to a rousing start.

"Father Ron brings groups down there to start projects and help further the mission and give opportunities to kids and families in the Dominican Republic," Andy said. "We were about an hour and a half from Santa Domingo, so it's in the countryside and it's really poor. I've done stuff locally, and it's something I'm pretty big on and want to get more involved in, but this was the first time I'd gone out of the country."

As for his summer, he went to Boston and stayed with his older brother, David, while working at a couple hockey camps. He helped mentor youth hockey goalies, and also did some learning of his own in sessions with several goalie coaches he had wanted to meet. He wasn't back home in Ithaca for too long before he hit the road again, up to Toronto, to do more teaching and learning at hockey camps because he always feels like there's something new he can incorporate into his game.

Heading into his junior season, Andy would be looked upon as one of the team leaders and a major cog for the Big Red as they looked to defend their Ivy League championship, perhaps add an ECAC championship, and hopefully make a deeper run in the NCAA Tournament.

ONA McCONNELL

Myotonic dystrophy may win out in the end because, as of now, there is no cure for the neuromuscular disease that afflicts Ona. But while it may continue to weaken her body and make the most simple of life's tasks ever challenging, and it may eventually relegate her to a wheelchair, at the end of her junior year at Yale, she was kicking its ass.

In fact, she referred to herself as an official "bad ass" after she and field hockey teammates Maddy Sharp and Jessie Accurso traveled to Pocono Manor, Pennsylvania, to compete in the Tough Mudder challenge.

"It was the coolest thing ever," Ona said of the twelve-mile course where competitors had to negotiate through twenty-six obstacles including mud, fire, ice water, ten-thousand volts of electricity, twelve-foot walls, and underground tunnels to get from start to finish and earn the right to call themselves a "bad ass." "My major worry was that I wouldn't finish, but I did."

The three girls went to the Mudder to raise money for the Myotonic Dystrophy Foundation, of which Ona was the youngest board member. "It was an amazing day," Ona said of the event, and the fact that the three Bulldogs received more than $1,300 in donations.

After finishing out the school year strongly, Ona was presented with two awards at Yale's year-end banquet. The F. Wilder Bellamy Jr. Award is given to a junior who best exemplifies the qualities for which the alumnus is remembered, including personal integrity, loyalty to friends, and high spiritedness in athletics, academics, and social life. She also received, for the second year in a row, the Amanda Walton Award, for being someone who demonstrates the ability to confront challenges and displays the courage to overcome them, while inspiring teammates with her work ethic and unselfish attitude.

A few days after the Mudder, Ona flew to California, where she spent a month at Stanford Hospital working as a clinical researcher in the neuromuscular department under Dr. John Day, one of the leading researchers in myotonic dystrophy. She saw several patients whose symptoms were further along than hers, and her mother, Karen, could not comprehend how she was able to keep such an optimistic view. "I don't know how she did it; I'm not sure I would in her place," Karen said.

But Ona refuses to feel sorry for herself, and she said the reality of what she will likely be confronting did not resonate. "When I went to the conference in Florida (in December, where she delivered one of the keynote speeches) I saw a huge amount of people with my disease," she said. "I don't really have trouble seeing other people with it because every situation is so different.

You just hope that they are dealing with the complications they have. I'm able to separate my life from their life. When I was in California, I spoke to the head of the lab who does research, and working there made me more positive about the future because he was saying he really thinks five to ten years down the road there may be a treatment."

When her stint at Stanford was complete, she flew home to London to begin a busy summer during which she was taking two classes offered by Yale so that she could get her credit hours total in line. And, with coach Pam Stuper leaving instructions for her team to make sure they watch field hockey games and start getting mentally prepared for the 2012 season, Ona figured she might as well do it right. The Summer Olympics were held in London, and Ona procured tickets for one day at the field hockey venue. "Very excited about that," she said.

Amid all the fun and interesting things she did in the spring and summer, Ona had to deal with her condition, which was worsening. She had begun to notice it was getting tougher for her to negotiate flights of stairs, and her cramping had become more acute, which had her worried about the start of field hockey practice.

"I need to figure out how to deal with that because I think it will affect my running," she said. "I'm going to have to push through it and do my best."

In other words, do what she had been doing ever since her diagnosis.

LUCKY MKOSANA

When Lucky was picked in the second-round of the Major League Soccer draft in January 2012 by the Chicago Fire, just the third Dartmouth player ever selected, he was confident that his transcendent skills would enable him to earn a roster spot and begin his career as a professional soccer player, the only job he has ever wanted.

However, because Lucky was not a United States citizen and did not have a green card, only a P1 visa, he was classified as an international player. And per the roster rules of the top professional soccer league in the United States, only 152 international spots are available and must be split equitably between the nineteen MLS clubs. Thus, with their allotment filled, the Fire could not retain Lucky and had to release him.

"I was training in Chicago for two months and they tried signing me, but they couldn't because they didn't have foreign spots left, so that was a tough situation for me," said the only Ivy League player drafted in 2012. "I knew it was possible, but I thought Chicago was going to sign me. I went early in the second round, so it was one of those unfortunate things."

So Lucky spent a few more weeks training with the Fire while his agent tried to find a team for him to sign with, and that ended up being the Harrisburg (Pa.) City Islanders of the United Soccer League Pro, soccer's version of triple-A baseball.

Lucky had to miss Harrisburg's home game against Wilmington on June 9 because he returned to Hanover to participate in Dartmouth's graduation ceremony. With the school on a trimester schedule, its students report later to school, but also are taking exams into late May, so graduation is traditionally held in early June, last of the Ivies. Lucky did not want to miss it, and neither did his mother, Ayda, who flew from Zimbabwe to listen to the Baker Library Bells chime as her son joined the procession through Dartmouth Green to conclude his wondrous journey from the dusty roads of his homeland to becoming an Ivy League graduate with a bachelor of arts degree in geography.

"This is her first trip to the U.S. and she's really excited," Lucky said. "She's staying with my American family, the Kahans, so it's a great time. And I'm excited to go back because I miss being at Dartmouth. I'm still on the e-mail list, and with trying to find a team and figuring things out, I miss everyone. But I think I made the right decision graduating early (after the second trimester in March). It was nice to not have to worry about school, no more papers or projects or studying, so I felt really free when I was training with Chicago."

Lucky—who was awarded in absentia at Dartmouth's annual athletic awards ceremony the Alfred E. Watson Trophy as the Big Green male athlete of the year—finished the 2012 season as Harrisburg's leader in goals (six) and points (sixteen) despite playing in only sixteen matches. That performance led to the MLS's Philadelphia Union signing him to a contract for the 2013 season.

His coach at Dartmouth, Jeff Cook, was thrilled by the news, but as wonderful a soccer player as Lucky is, that's not what Cook will remember most. "Despite all of his on-field accomplishments, this person is one of the most humble and respectful young men that I have ever worked with," Cook said. "His personality and kind nature have endeared him to our community, and he means the world to myself and my family. As his coach, he is without question one of the most talented individuals I've ever coached, but he's a great person, and we're all going to miss him."

ALEX THOMAS

When last we left Alex, he and his Yale football teammates were licking their wounds following a 45–7 thrashing at the hands of archrival Harvard in The Game. It was a terrible ending to what had been a disappointing 5–5 season, and things didn't get any better for the program a few weeks later when Bulldogs coach Tom Williams resigned amid controversy. While his 0–3 record against Harvard was part of Williams's downfall, his demise was cemented when it came to light that he may have lied on his résumé about being a candidate for a Rhodes scholarship while a student at Stanford in the early 1990s. Williams said in a statement that he was encouraged to apply for the scholarship by Stanford's fellowship office, but acknowledged he never did. However, it was clearly an embarrassment for Yale, and the school was more than happy to close the Williams era.

As for Alex, he spent a couple weeks trying to cope with the fact that his football career was over, and then a light bulb went off in his head, because the reality was it didn't have to end. "I thought I came to terms with football being over after the Harvard game, and then once the realization set in that football was over, I couldn't deal with it," he said.

So, Alex joined several of his teammates who were training for Yale's pro day in March 2012, a workout day that most Division I schools host to give their athletes who are eligible for the NFL Draft a chance to strut their stuff in front of pro scouts. But neither Alex nor any of his teammates, nor for that matter any players from the Ivy League, were drafted, so Alex made the decision to pursue playing professionally overseas.

"I think I did well, but nothing ever came of it," he said of the pro day. "I did it as a last-ditch effort because you never know, but my numbers weren't outstanding, my season stats weren't outstanding, so there wasn't anything to grab the attention that I would have needed. So I looked into playing abroad. A few of my former teammates have done it in the past and said it was an amazing experience. It's more just a way to continue playing for another year and give yourself more time to figure out what to do in addition to having an absolutely incredible experience for a year getting paid to play a sport you love."

Alex was exploring leagues in Italy and Spain, and he was hoping Italy panned out. "I was in Rome studying abroad last summer and I've fallen in love with Italian culture, so I definitely want to go back," he said. "I've been contacting teams in Italy, so hopefully I'll start getting some feedback pretty soon."

In the meantime, Alex reveled in being a Yale graduate, a feat that seemed so remote way back in that first semester of freshman year when he thought they'd be throwing him out of school because he wasn't succeeding in class. "I'm officially a Yale graduate, and it's kind of hard to believe," he said. "Very cool."

Alex had three spring classes, plus he had to write his senior thesis, a twelve-thousand-word essay on the disproportion of population between slaves and white men in Jamaica and the problems that were associated with the disparity. "It was a year-long activity, but in football season I was much more busy and couldn't put the effort in that most people can in the first semester, so the bulk of my research was done in second semester and all of the writing," he said. "I passed, so that was good news."

After listening to legendary television journalist Barbara Walters deliver a speech on Yale's Class Day, the ceremony prior to graduation day, Alex received his bachelor of arts diploma in history on May 21, and by the time it was in his hands, he said he was pretty much "all ceremonied out."

The gist of Walters's speech was that the graduates should look long and hard for their bliss, and once they found that, that's what would make them happiest. Football has been in Alex's blood since his days playing Pop Warner in Ansonia, and since he wasn't quite sure yet what he wanted to do with his Yale degree, football was still his bliss.

"I know guys that are working now who kind of wish they had done it postgraduation," Alex said of playing overseas. "I figure this is the only time in my life where I can continue playing, so I'm hoping it works out."

KEITH WRIGHT

Harvard graduate. "Nice ring to that," Keith said.

But as happy and proud as he was to get his bachelor of arts degree in psychology, and "end this part of my journey and get ready to start the next part" Keith knew graduation day wasn't so much for him as it was for his mother, Sabrena.

"It meant a lot to her to have her first child graduate from college and not just any college, but Harvard," he said. "It's ours as a family, it took a lot of work from everybody in this family to accomplish a goal that not many people accomplish. She was happy, extremely proud. She wasn't all that emotional, no crying or anything, just happy for me, and I was happy for her. The graduation, walking across the stage and them calling your name, that's for the parent and I was glad to give that to her."

Since Harvard's exit from the NCAA Tournament in March, Keith had been busy finishing off his classes and preparing for what he hoped would be the next phase of his basketball career, playing professionally somewhere. He attended the prestigious Portsmouth Invitational Tournament where every year, sixty-four seniors are invited for a four-day, twelve-game showcase in front of scouts from all across the NBA and several from European teams. In his three games, Keith averaged eight points and seven rebounds, and came away from the experience feeling like he'd done his best.

"It went well," he said. "Those things are really guard dominated so for a big man to showcase what they can do, you have to run the court as hard as you can, rebound, block shots, and play defense and make open shots when you can and I think I did all that."

After Portsmouth, Keith chose Derrick Powell of Excel Sports Management, who happens to be a step cousin from his father's wife's side of the family and has known Keith for many years, as his agent. "At the end of the day I have to be with someone I know and trust," Keith explained. "He never pitched to me that he wanted to represent me until after my senior year. He said, 'Please don't think our relationship has been based on me becoming your agent.' He has connections and I trust him, and I know he'll do right by with me or he'll have to suffer the consequences of my step sisters."

Powell got Keith a workout with the Boston Celtics in May, and Keith thought he performed to his capability. "There were six of us and I was in there with some really good guys and showcased what I can do, and I think I surprised those guys," he said. "I couldn't really sleep the night before; I was nervous, and then the next day I went to the practice facility and I just remembered thinking that I had nothing to lose. Thinking of where I came from, it was a great honor and a privilege to practice in front of any NBA team, let alone the Celtics."

Keith continued to work out at Harvard throughout June, often with his ex-Crimson teammate and roommate Andrew Van Nest, and also with Harvard assistant coach Brian Adams. But when the NBA Draft rolled around in late June, Keith was not selected, and so Powell went to work exploring overseas possibilities in one of several European leagues.

Always someone who exudes positivity, Keith was confident that something was going to work out, but if it didn't, he was ready to move on with the rest of his life and put that hard-earned Harvard degree to work. "When I went to Harvard I wasn't thinking about playing ball after college," he said. "Anything I do in basketball right now is just icing on the cake."

GREG ZEBRACK

By the time the exhaustive three-day, forty-round Major League Baseball First-Year Draft was complete in early June 2012, and more than twelve hundred players including his Penn teammate Vince Voiro and twelve other Ivy Leaguers had been selected, Greg was left staring into space wondering why his name was nowhere to be found on the board.

"I was pretty devastated and depressed when I found out I wasn't going to be drafted," said Greg, who really felt it was a foregone conclusion after a final season with the Quakers in which he'd finished tenth in the League in batting (.343), first in slugging percentage (.657) and doubles (18), fourth in on-base percentage (.448), and third in total bases (90), played a reliable center field, and was an Academic All-Ivy and All-Big 5 choice. "You ask the question what more do you have to do? I had a good summer in a really good league, I didn't have a great last two weeks of the Ivy season, but I hit with a high average, stole some bases, and played good defense, so I thought I'd be OK."

He wasn't. So after sulking for a day or two, he jumped into action and began the process of enrolling in the business school at USC to begin work on his MBA and utilize the final year of his college eligibility playing for the same Trojan team he had begun his college career with back in 2009.

"I met with coach (Frank) Cruz before the draft, and then after the draft when I wasn't picked he talked about getting me into school and getting things going," Greg said. "USC had already called the compliance office at Penn and gotten the release, so it moved pretty quickly. It's a lot easier to get into a big-time athletic school than it is an Ivy League school."

Despite the obvious disappointment, Greg's attitude remained upbeat, because he truly believed things would work out and he would get his chance to play professionally. "Baseball has never come easy for me," he said. "I went to a small high school, so I had to fight to get noticed by big-time D-I programs, and then when I found out I wouldn't be playing much at USC, I had to transfer and move to the East Coast and prove myself again. You have to look at the bright side of things. Luckily I still have another year to play. All these challenges make you stronger, make you more powerful, because if you can overcome these things it makes you a better person. People turn out to be successful when they have some setbacks."

And if by chance nothing changes and he doesn't get drafted in 2013, then by the age of 23, he'll have a bachelor of arts degree in communications from the Ivy League, and he'll be on his way to earning his MBA. "I want to play baseball, and hopefully the draft works out next year, but if it doesn't, I have some pretty good options with my resume and I'll be making a pretty decent living," he said.

ACKNOWLEDGMENTS

When you embark on a nearly two-year-long journey such as this one, you cannot do it alone, and I didn't.

First and foremost, I must give my sincerest thanks to the nine kids who are featured in this book. In no particular order, Ona McConnell and Alex Thomas of Yale, Keith Wright and Melanie Baskind of Harvard, Sheila Dixon of Brown, Andy Iles of Cornell, Greg Zebrack of Penn, Kyra Caldwell of Columbia, and Lucky Mkosana of Dartmouth.

These kids were playing Division I college athletics, and studying at some of this country's finest institutions, yet they managed to find time in their busy schedules and were willing to spend hours upon hours of their precious time on the phone with me in our weekly interviews. They opened to me, and ultimately you the reader, the windows of their lives and they were honest, well-spoken, and passionate about their pursuits, both on the field, court, or ice as well as in the classroom. I doubt I could have picked nine finer men and women for this project.

Next, I would like to thank the sports information departments at the seven schools that cooperated with the publication of the book. Jeremy Hartigan and Brandon Thomas of Cornell, Chris Humm and Lyndsey Maurer of Brown, Kurt Svoboda and Tim Williamson of Harvard, Darlene Camacho of Columbia, Rick Bender of Dartmouth, Steve Conn and Sam Rubin of Yale, and Mike Mahoney and Alex Keil of Penn.

They helped me identify the type of student-athletes I was seeking, those with interesting back stories and intriguing personalities who would be willing to share their lives with readers, and would provide support whenever I needed it.

It bears noting at this point that the administration at Princeton declined to participate in the project. This was obviously disappointing, primarily because there were surely many student-athletes who would have provided a wonderful story had they been allowed. Still, we soldiered on without a Tiger.

Thank you to Harvard graduate Ryan Fitzpatrick, whom I have come to know quite well in my job as the Buffalo Bills beat writer for the *Democrat and Chronicle* in Rochester, New York. Ryan wrote a terrific foreword for the book, and shared with me some of his thoughtful insights regarding his time as an Ivy Leaguer.

Finally, I would like to thank those who worked directly with the manuscript—project manager Jessica Stevens; copyeditor Gary Hamel; and my editor, Steve Hull. Steve believed in this project from the outset and shepherded it through some struggles as we tried to find the right way to structure the manuscript and present the information in a page-turning fashion. I believe we succeeded.

S.M.